The
Reference Shelf®

The Digital Age

The Reference Shelf
Volume 87 • Number 4
H.W. Wilson
A Division of EBSCO Information Services

Published by
GREY HOUSE PUBLISHING
Amenia, New York
2015

The Reference Shelf

The books in this series contain reprints of articles, excerpts from books, addresses on current issues, and studies of social trends in the United States and other countries. There are six separately bound numbers in each volume, all of which are usually published in the same calendar year. Numbers one through five are each devoted to a single subject, providing background information and discussion from various points of view and concluding with an index and comprehensive bibliography that lists books, pamphlets, and articles on the subject. The final number of each volume is a collection of recent speeches. Books in the series may be purchased individually or on subscription.

Publisher's Cataloging-In-Publication Data
(Prepared by The Donohue Group, Inc.)

Publisher's Cataloging-In-Publication Data
(Prepared by The Donohue Group, Inc.)

The Digital Age / [compiled by H. W. Wilson].

    pages : illustrations ; cm. -- (The reference shelf ; volume 87, number 4)

Series previously published by H. W. Wilson, a division of EBSCO Information Services.
Includes bibliographical references and index.
ISBN: 978-1-61925-693-4 (v. 87, no. 4)
ISBN: 978-1-61925-689-7 (volume set)

1. Information society--United States--Sources. 2. Privacy, Right of--United States--Sources. 3. Education--Data processing--Sources. 4. Economics--Data processing--Sources. 5. Computer crimes--United States--Sources. 6. Internet and activism--United States--Sources. I. H.W. Wilson Company. II. Series: Reference shelf ; v. 87, no. 4.

HM851 .D54 2015
303.48/34/0973

Printed in Canada

Contents

3

Education and the Brain

4

Crime and Justice

5

Economy and the Workforce

6

Politics and Globalism

Preface

In the 1948 issue of *Bell Systems Technical Journal*, researcher Claude Shannon published the article, "A Mathematical Theory of Communication." The arguments Shannon made were taken from his own observation of electrical relays, from which he started to develop the idea that all communication was reducible to basic logic, and from there to two basic elements, "yes" and "no," signified mathematically as "one" and "zero."[1] Shannon had no idea that the theory he was proposing would be the spark for a global information revolution, but scientists and engineers immediately saw the potential in his idea, a revolutionary system of encoding data that inspired decades of research and development.

It took half a century for digital technology to become the norm and this involved inventing new methods for encoding data that gave rise to new technological fields including personal computing, cellular communication, and Internet networking. Each of these technological fields was transformative on its own, but each was also a stepping stone in the progression inspired by Shannon's theory: the digitization of all human communication and knowledge. This process has been so encompassing that the entire period from the 1980s to the present, has been called "The Digital Age," bringing a symbolic end to the "Industrial Age" in which industrial manufacturing and consumer machines changed every aspect of society.

The Power of Knowledge

The idiom "knowledge is power," often attributed to Sir Francis Bacon's *Meditationes Sacrae* (1597), became a symbolic expression of the scientific revolution.[2] The essential meaning is that knowledge is the essential fuel for personal, social, and societal development, allowing individuals and groups to understand and address their needs, empowered by a rational understanding of the problems they face. One of the hallmarks of the digital age has been the conversion of human knowledge to digital media, which led to a subsequent decentralization and democratization of both knowledge and power.

Digitization, the conversion of data to digital "ones" and "zeroes," greatly enhanced the capacity for preserving, transmitting, and communicating information. The digital age is also therefore known as the "information age," a term attributed to Richard Leghorn, a 1960s pioneer in aerospace intelligence technology.[3] The ability to digitize information developed alongside "digital storage," from the first floppy disks to later DVDs and drives, that allowed for encoded data to be stored and transported. The first personal computers, introduced to the public in 1975, brought digital technology to the consumer market.

From the very beginning of the digital age, there have been pioneers who envisioned that digital technology would be a powerful force in the democratization of knowledge. One such pioneer was Michael S. Hart, who created Project Gutenberg in 1971, with the goal of creating a digital public library of books in the public domain, available to the public for free. By 2015, Project Gutenberg had digitized more than 49,000 books, and was still guided by Hart's belief that digital technology could "universalize" knowledge because digital books could be cheaply produced, without the need for physical paper and ink, and could be reproduced and shared infinitely from a single copy.[4] Similar efforts to create public libraries of important information followed. For instance, in 1994, the Library of Congress began its Digital Library Program (NDLP), which resulted in the digitization of thousands of books, periodicals, manuscripts, photos, videos, and audio files for public use and research.[5] Digitization would not have been as transformative without the capability to easily transmit digital data. This is the primary innovation behind the Internet, the name now used for the networks of computers linked through utility lines that allow users to transmit information instantly across any distance. Interestingly, the pioneers that developed the first "Internet," known as the World Wide Web, also envisioned this technology as a powerful tool for democratization, sharing the "power" of knowledge with everyone around the world. The World Wide Web Consortium, established by pioneer Tim Berners-Lee, was created with these goals in mind, fostering a new, non-corporate, non-governmental mode of communication for the people that would foster the free, open, exchange of information and ideas.[6]

The democritization of knowledge *has* been a central feature of the digital age. The invention of "electronic mail" enabled individuals to instantly share documents, videos, audio files and to communicate freely across International lines, and the addition of instant online chat and video chat programs effectively eliminated the monopoly of long distance phone providers on International communication. However, as the digital age progressed a new breed of corporate giants emerged, competing to gain a monopoly over the new digital information market.

Management consultant Peter Drucker theorized in his 1960s books and articles that the economies of western nations would become "knowledge economies," in which data would become the most important resource.[7] The Internet corporations of the twenty-first century, like Google and Facebook, have made Drucker's predictions reality, essentially using customer data as currency to be traded with advertisers for revenue. Internet companies provide free services, but in return collect and analyze all data provided by their customers, and also filter the Internet experience, inundating users with a constant flow of directed advertisements based on their history of Internet browsing. Critics of this development, including Internet pioneer Tim Berners-Lee, have spoken out against corporate manipulation of the Internet, calling it a threat to the potential for democratization that the Internet represents.

Corporate manipulation aside, many nations around the world censor or limit Internet communication in an effort to protect traditional institutions of power. The so called "Arab Spring" of 2011, in which a wave of protests, many organized through digital communication, spread from Tunisia into Egypt and throughout the Middle East, has been seen as the prime example of how digital communication is transforming politics.[8] Fearful of this new capacity for social/political organization many nations have enacted laws and policies that prohibit certain Internet sites and services and effectively limit free speech and expression in digital domains.

Even in nations that have attempted to protect free speech and expression on the Internet, digital technology poses a host of new national security issues, including the potential for terrorists to use social media for organization and recruitment and the growing fields of cyberterrorism and cyberwarfare in which digital weapons are used to disrupt or destroy computer systems in enemy nations. In attempting to address these concerns, the United States and many other governments, have engaged in controversial digital surveillance programs, and these programs are part of a growing field of concern regarding "digital rights" and "digital privacy," one of the central legal/human rights issues of the twenty-first century.

As the digital exchange has become more important, there is also increasing concern that access to the latest in digital technology is creating new socio-economic classes around the world. This phenomenon, often called the "digital divide" by social scientists, is a growing problem as access to technology and careers in emerging digital fields is unevenly distributed across gender and socio-economic lines. The problem is especially acute in the field of education, where digital tools and Internet access are increasingly important in preparing students for professional careers. The digital divide is one of the most essential and pressing humanitarian issues of the twenty-first century, drawing together issues in education, public and social policy, and the social sciences.[9]

The Cyber Cipher

In his 1982 story *Burning Chrome,* science fiction author William Gibson invented the term "cyberspace," which he envisioned as a virtual world contained within computer networks where "hackers" could interact with computers linked to financial, governmental, and corporate security systems. Gibson, whose books helped create the "cyberpunk" genre, envisioned a dystopian future in which nation-sized corporations dominated the economic and social landscape and technological rebels fought for political freedom.[10]

Today, "cyberspace" is an often-used slang expression for the virtual "world" of the Internet. While the darkest predictions of cyberpunk have not come to fruition, Internet media and communication *have* created a "virtual level" of existence that has become increasingly essential to modern lives and livelihoods. Commerce, education, and recreation take place through virtual platforms and social networks accessible from any location, and this has rapidly become the new norm of social interaction. The importance of this new digital mode of existence is so prevalent that educational expert Mark Prensky coined the term "digital natives" in 2001, as a way to refer to the first generation of young people who "grow up" as "native speakers" of a new language based on digital communication and technology.[11]

As individuals communicate, shop, play, and conduct business online, they create an "online identity" or "online presence," formed from their browsing history, social media activity, and both intentional and unintentional communication. This online identity is one of the most important tools in the digital age, and some analysts of the digital age have theorized that a person's online persona may one day be more important professionally than traditional professional references. In the 2010s, there has been increasing interest in "personal branding," by controlling one's online identity to present a more positive professional image.

However, online identities have also become targets for exploitation. Cybercriminals, for instance, can use malicious codes and programs to conduct identity theft, using information found online to make purchases or to apply for loans and credit. Likewise, the phenomenon of cyberbullying, in which an individual torments, insults, or harasses another individual through social media and digital channels, is another example of how a person's online identity presents a target for abuse. Sexual predators and violent criminals have used online tracking to locate victims and an increasing study of online misogyny and racism indicates that the freedom of expression offered through digital media has also made the Internet a haven for those who wish to conduct abuse or issue threats of racial or misogynistic violence. As police struggle to address the prevalence of virtual crime, activists and social scientists are faced with a conundrum, making online environments safe for users without censoring or restricting free speech. Psychologists have also found that the gradual acclimation to digital trends and tools is having a profound and potentially lasting affect on the human brain, in both positive and negative ways. Educators note that individuals are more accustomed to writing and literary expression, thanks to social media, but also that "digital natives" have difficulty with long-term concentration and focus. Likewise, as the tools of communication from the previous age become obsolete, social scientists are increasingly considering whether or not humanity is losing important skills and techniques in the process.

It is important to remember that the digital age is in its infancy. Though digitization began in the 1960s, the broader, social transition began far more recently and the social institutions and structures of society are only now beginning to adjust. The digital age offers tremendous benefits, but these benefits come with a cost, in the form of industries, livelihoods, and cultural institutions made obsolete by new norms of communication, commerce, and recreation. Moving forward, global societies have difficult decisions and negotiations that will determine how digital technology shapes evolution, what aspects of the past will be preserved, and how growth and change can be accommodated without sacrificing

Micah L. Issit

Notes

1. Waldrop, "Claude Shannon."
2. Berend, *An Economic History of Nineteenth-Century Europe*, 47.
3. Gleick, "The Information Palace."
4. Tucker, "The Inventor of the Digital Age."
5. "About Digital Collections & Services."
6. Jeffries, "How the Web Lost its Way—And its Founding Principles."
7. Wartzman, "What Peter Drucker Knew About 2020."
8. "The Arab Spring: A Year of Revolution."
9. "Digital Divide."
10. Thill, "March 17, 1948: William Gibson, Father of Cyberspace."
11. Prensky, "Digital Natives, Digital Immigrants."

1
Individual Rights

American flags fly at full mast in front of Penn Station in NYC near a street sign for Father Mychal Judge Way. Father Judge is one of the most famous victims of the World Trade Center attack and known as the beloved New York Fire Department chaplain. New York City's police department is using tens of thousands of closed circuit security cameras set up on the streets as surveillance (like in this photo), part of a Homeland Security and Defense program to track terror suspects and solve crimes. Civil-rights activists worry about the impact of the new cameras and the people's right to privacy.

Toward a Digital Bill of Rights

In many ways, cyberspace is the new frontier of human exploration. Like the colonies founded by oceanic explorers in antiquity, cyberspace offers previously unimagined resources and the ability to explore new domains of thought and expression. However, the digital world is also unregulated, in many ways lawless, and fraught with new and unexpected dangers. With the growing importance of digital technology and Internet connectivity, many around the world now believe that digital access is a basic right that should be afforded to all people. However, protecting and maintaining this utility requires addressing fundamental questions about the rights of digital citizens. Many of these issues, including the protection of free speech and the limits of a person's right to privacy, mirror the revolutionary struggles that gave rise to the United States Constitution and its amendments. These issues and a host of new digital-specific concerns are shaping digital rights in the modern era and into the future.

Digital Privacy

As of 2015, all information transmitted through the Internet or digital data carriers by United States citizens is subject to joint ownership. Facebook's policy on data collection, for instance, states clearly that Facebook claims partial ownership over any data provided on a user's Facebook page, including photos, text, and information in the user's personal profile.[1] Essentially then, whatever information users share on sites like Facebook, YouTube, and Twitter, is also being given to and shared with the company and its advertisers.

Ownership of digital data became controversial in the 2000s, as journalists revealed that digital data providers and web-service companies were sharing personal consumer data with the National Security Agency (NSA) and Federal Bureau of Investigation (FBI). These organizations, under the Bush administration, were collecting data as part of a broader effort to prevent foreign and domestic terrorism. The 1978 Foreign Intelligence Surveillance Act (FISA), requires that government agencies obtain special warrants before they can conduct surveillance on American citizens.[2] However, after 9/11 Congress passed measures that allowed security agencies to collect "digital data" without court orders.

Widespread concern about digital surveillance developed only after former NSA analyst Edward Snowden leaked government documents to the press in 2013 that revealed the scope of ongoing surveillance operations. Among other revelations, the leaked documents indicated that the NSA collected more than 250 million emails and contact lists from Facebook, Gmail, and Yahoo[3] and collected millions of facial images from posted photos and web cams that were used to develop software that would allow government agencies to identify individuals by matching facial features with digital images.[4] In addition, security agencies had been able to obtain access to cell phone records and digital voice data with the cooperation of cell phone carriers like AT&T and Sprint.

There is no explicit right to privacy in the United States Constitution. However, the Fourth Amendment of the Bill of Rights, which guarantees freedom from "unreasonable searches and seizures," has been used to justify protecting the privacy of individuals within their homes and in private communications.[5] In the December 2013 case of *Klayman v. Obama*, Federal District Judge Richard J. Leon ruled that NSA surveillance programs violate Fourth Amendment protections.[6] That same month, however, District Judge William Pauley ruled, in the case of *American Civil Liberties Union v. Clapper*, that the metadata collected by the NSA has already been "shared" with the phone company. Pauley therefore ruled that the consumer has no "expectation of privacy," and that the companies, like Google, Facebook, and Sprint, have the right to share customer data with federal agencies.

A number of important court rulings have extended Fourth Amendment protections to cover digital data and devices. For instance, in 2010, a Federal Appeals Court ruled that government agencies needed a court order to search an individual's email. Similarly, in the 2014 case of *Riley v. California*, the Supreme Court held that government agencies needed a specific warrant to search a cellular phone, even if the owner had already been arrested for a crime.[7] These protections, however, are still subject to interpretation and debate and protecting digital data is complicated by joint corporate/user ownership. Digital rights organizations like the Electronic Frontier Foundation (EFF) are also concerned about corporate invasion of privacy. The EFF has been one of the strongest critics of corporations like Facebook and Google, which collect and analyze communications from users in an effort to create better advertising. The question remains whether regulations should be put into place to clarify the rights of users in terms of *both* government and corporate surveillance.

Corporate Censorship

In 2014 and 2015, the terrorist organization ISIS captured and executed a number of American and European journalists working in the Middle East and distributed videos of the executions (by beheading) to the international media. A number of news agencies worldwide refused to allow videos or photos of the executions to be shared, published, or posted. Social media sites in the United States, like the Google owned site YouTube and the social media giant Twitter, also refused to allow users to post or share ISIS videos claiming justification under "community guidelines" and a corporate designation between "free expression" and "terrorist propaganda."[8] Other media outlets, however, published or allowed users to publish both the full videos and still photos on the basis that the public had a right to uncensored communication and information.

Though most are not as graphic as the infamous ISIS videos, there are a variety of videos and photos published through mainstream media that depict violent events. Military operations and police shootouts with suspects provide examples of when the media have accepted videos or photos of real-life violence as legitimate journalism. Any content that depicts real-life events in which an individual is killed or physically abused might be considered inappropriate or immoral for distribution, especially by the family, friends, or individuals depicted. Given that moral value is a highly subjective issue, it remains unclear whether or not there is a reliable way to determine when it is appropriate to censor content.

Writing in the *Guardian*, journalist James Ball called Twitter's decision to block ISIS videos a form of corporate censorship. Ball argues that Twitter claims to be a "platform" for public expression and not a news organization. While news organizations can decide what constitutes appropriate content based on internal policies on morality and ethics, Twitter's censorship essentially means that the company is claiming responsibility for what is posted on their site, rather than serving as a legitimate open platform for expression.[9]

Should corporations be permitted to determine when content is morally out of bounds for expression or consumption, or should this decision belong Internet users? In past eras, books, television programs, films, and many other types of media have been censored for moral reasons. United States court rulings have determined that government censorship is permissible only when the speech or expression poses an imminent, demonstrable threat to public safety or directly violates the rights of others. In the digital age, the question is one of corporate censorship. Those interested in the rights of expression must now determine whether social media constitute a legitimate forum for free speech or whether they are corporate publishing platforms that can be justifiably policed and controlled by a corporation's own policies on morality and ethics. As of 2015, social media fall into the latter category and remain a forum for free speech only in so far as that speech meets with corporate guidelines.

New Concerns and the Bill of Rights

In the 2014 book *So You've Been Publicly Shamed* author Jon Ronson discusses a new rights issue that has emerged from the sharing and transmission of digital data: the phenomenon of digital public humiliation. The concept is simple: an individual digitally stores or more often shares a photo, video, or text that portrays the original poster in an unfavorable light, and the content inadvertently becomes public. In the many examples shared by Ronson are examples in which inappropriate or distasteful photos or jokes have led to individuals being fired from their jobs, publically insulted through social media, and turned into media pariahs.[10]

Incidents like this raise a new question, should Internet users have a "right to be forgotten," meaning the right to have information about themselves removed from the Internet. The right to be forgotten is an important part of the evolving concept of digital ethics. The European Union has passed laws giving individuals the right to request that information about them be removed from Internet search engines in cases where the information is "abusive, excessive, or inaccurate" for data processing.[11] As of 2015, the United States had not adopted similar legislation, but privacy advocacy groups are currently lobbying for a similar United States law to protect digital privacy.

In his book, Ronson quotes digital privacy expert Michael Fertik as saying, "The biggest lie, is *The Internet is about you*."[12] Ferkit argues that, despite the claims of Internet service companies, the Internet isn't about expression and creativity, but rather it is a landscape generated by companies in the process of selling products and content. Public shaming is good for Internet providers, driving traffic to websites and advertisers. Digital privacy, censorship, and new issues like public shaming are all essentially rooted in the same issue: that the digital sphere of human activity is, as it currently exists, a public space that creates the illusion of a private venue for expression. One might know, logically and rationally, that Twitter posts are potentially transferrable to the Internet at large, but few imagine that their Tweets will reach beyond their select group of followers.

Tim Berners-Lee, often considered the person who most directly "invented" the Internet, has argued in the media for the adoption of a "Digital Bill of Rights" that would explicitly guarantee the rights of users and place limitations on the corporate and governmental rights of organizations that want to manipulate, intercept, and use digital data.[13] Until such a measure is passed and reliably enforced, Internet users in the United States must accept that the Internet belongs to the companies that facilitate it, and to the extent that digital expression belongs to the people, it belongs to all people and therefore to no one in particular.

Micah L. Issit

Notes

1. "Data Policy," *Facebook*, Jan 30, 2015.
2. "About the Foreign Intelligence Surveillance Court."
3. Gellman, "NSA Collects Millions of E-mail Address Books Globally."
4. Risen and Poitras, "N.S.A. Collecting Millions of Faces from Web Images."
5. Linder, "The Right to Privacy."
6. Savage, "Judge Questions Legality of N.S.A. Phone Records."
7. "Riley v. California," 2.
8. Bercovici, "YouTube's Policies Are Clear."
9. Ball, "Twitter: From Free Speech Champion to Selective Censor?"
10. Ronson, *So You've Been Publically Shamed*, 70-74, 206-214.
11. "Factsheet on the 'Right to be Forgotten' Ruling."
12. Ronson, 276.
13. Finley, "Inventor of the Web is Right: We Need an Internet Bill of Rights."

The Internet of Things Has Arrived—And So Have Massive Security Issues

By Andrew Rose
Wired, January 11, 2013

Internet. Things. Add the "Of" and suddenly these three simple words become a magic meme—the theme we've been hearing all week at CES, the oft-heralded prediction that may have finally arrived in 2013.

While not devoid of hype and hyperbole, the Internet of Things (IoT) does represent a revolution happening right now. Companies of all kinds—not just technology and telecommunications firms—are linking "things" as diverse as smartphones, cars, and household appliances to industrialstrength sensors, each other, and the \ Internet. The technical result may be mundane features such as intercommunication and autonomous machine-to-machine (M2M) data transfer, but the potential benefits to lifestyles and businesses are huge.

But ... with great opportunity comes great responsibility. Along with its conveniences, the IoT will unveil unprecedented security challenges: in data privacy, safety, governance, and trust.

It's scary how few people are preparing for it. Most security and risk professionals are so preoccupied with putting last week's vulnerability-malware-hacktivist genie back into the bottle that they're too distracted to notice their R&D colleagues have conjured up even more unpredictable spirits. Spirits in the form of automated systems that can reach beyond the digital plane to influence and adjust the physical world ... all without human interfacing.

The Loopholes

Security loopholes can occur anywhere in the IoT, but let's look at the most basic level: the route data takes to the provider.

Many smart meters, for example, don't push their data to an Internet service gateway directly or immediately. Instead, they send collected information to a local data collation hub—often another smart meter in a neighbor's house—where the data is stored until later uploaded in bulk.

Placing sensitive data in insecure locations is never a good idea, and the loss of physical security has long been considered tantamount to a breach. Yet some early elements of the IoT incorporate this very flaw into their designs. It's often an attempt to compensate for a lack of technological maturity where always-on network connectivity is unavailable or too expensive, or the central infrastructure does not scale to accommodate the vast number of input devices.

As the IoT crawls through its early stages, we can expect to see more such compromises; developers have to accommodate technical constraints—by either limiting functionality or compromising security. In a highly competitive tech marketplace, I think we all know which of these will be the first casualty.

And it's not just security: it's privacy, too. As the objects within the IoT collect seemingly inconsequential fragments of data to fulfill their service, think about what happens when that information is collated, correlated, and reviewed.

Because even tiny items of data in aggregate can identify, define, and label us without our knowledge. Just consider the scenario of the IoT tracking our food purchases. At the innocuous end of the privacy spectrum, the frequency and timing of these purchases can easily reveal we're on a diet; at the other end of the spectrum, the times and dates of those purchases could even reveal our religion (Jewish holidays, Muslim fasts).

Bottom line: As technology becomes more entwined with the physical world, the consequences of security failures escalate. Like a game of chess—where simple rules can lead to almost limitless possibilities—the complexity of IoT interconnections rapidly outstrips our ability to unravel them.

By accident or by design, useful IoT solutions could mash together, introducing or accelerating black swan events: catastrophic failures that are unexpected but obvious in hindsight. The key to addressing these is to plan for and address these scenarios, now.

With great opportunity comes great responsibility. Along with its conveniences, the IoT will unveil unprecedented security challenges.

The Evolutions
The Internet of Things will mature in three main stages.

Stage 1: Personification of Dumb Objects
In the initial stages of the IoT, identity is provided to selected objects through QR codes, for example. Value to users here comes from the interaction of these identities with other intelligent systems, such as smartphones or web services. Think about "smart" car keys that don't have to be taken out of the pocket to allow the car to start. Unfortunately, these devices can and have already been subverted.

Stage 2: Partially Autonomous Sensor Networks
In this intermediary stage, the "things" in the IoT develop the ability to sense their surroundings, including the environment, location, and other devices. Value to users here comes from those things taking action, albeit limited in scope, based on that information. Think about a residential thermostat that can be adjusted via a smartphone and authenticated web service, or that may self-adjust based on its awareness of the homeowner's location (e.g., switching on the heating/cooling as it detects the owner nearing home). While a centralized failure here leaving vast

numbers of people without heating may be tolerable, imagine the scenario where a hacktivist collective or state-sponsored attacker switches off an entire country's electrical supply as an act of punishment.

Stage 3: Autonomous Independent Devices
In this final stage of maturity for the IoT, technology availability, capacity, and standardization will have reached a level that doesn't require another device (such as a smartphone or web service) to function. Not only will the "things" be able to sense context, but they will be able to autonomously interact with other things, sensors, and services. Think about drug dispensers that can issue medication in response to sensing conditions in the human body through a set of apps, sensors, and other monitoring/feedback tools. It requires little imagination to consider the potential disaster scenarios that could originate from system failures or malicious threats in this scenario.

Now, let's take one popular and heatedly discussed example from CES to sum up these stages of maturity: the smart refrigerator. In the personification stage (1), the refrigerator owner scans cartons of milk with his smartphone, which triggers a reminder when the milk expires. In the semi-autonomous sensor network stage (2), the refrigerator detects the milk on its own and issues reminders across a broader range of connected apps. In the autonomous and independent stage (3), the refrigerator orders replacement milk just before it's empty or expires—entirely on its own.

> **With great opportunity comes great responsibility. Along with its conveniences, the IoT will unveil unprecedented security challenges.**

I am hard-pressed to find a catastrophic scenario associated with the refrigerator —other than the refrigerator spending your entire month's pay on milk or becoming self-aware like Skynet—but the fact remains we can't predict how things will look. That makes regulation and legislation difficult.

Even the European Union Commission, with its strong track record on privacy issues, acknowledged that its well-regarded Data Protection Directive law would be unable to cope with the Internet of Things:

The technology will have moved on by leaps and bounds by that stage; the legislation simply cannot keep up with the pace of technology. So it's possible that frameworks around regulating the IoT will parallel the PCI (Payment Card Industry) Data Security Standard, where an industry recognized the need for regulation and introduced its own rather than wait for government intervention.

Either way: Given the wide-reaching impact of the IoT, formal legislation and government involvement is almost certain, especially when we consider the safety risks of automated systems interacting in the physical world—governments won't be able to stand by silently if autonomous decisions endanger lives.

People can somehow take other people doing bad things, but they won't allow their machines to make such mistakes.

How Your Data Are Being Deeply Mined

By Alice E. Marwick
The New York Review of Books, January 9, 2014

The recent revelations regarding the NSA's collection of the personal information and the digital activities of millions of people across the world have attracted immense attention and public concern. But there are equally troubling and equally opaque systems run by advertising, marketing, and data-mining firms that are far less known. Using techniques ranging from supermarket loyalty cards to targeted advertising on Facebook, private companies systematically collect very personal information, from who you are, to what you do, to what you buy. Data about your online and offline behavior are combined, analyzed, and sold to marketers, corporations, governments, and even criminals. The scope of this collection, aggregation, and brokering of information is similar to, if not larger than, that of the NSA, yet it is almost entirely unregulated and many of the activities of data-mining and digital marketing firms are not publicly known at all.

Here I will discuss two things: the involuntary, or passive, collecting of data by private corporations; and the voluntary, or active, collection and aggregation of their own personal data by individuals. While I think it is the former that we should be more concerned with, the latter poses the question of whether it is possible for us to take full advantage of social media without playing into larger corporate interests.

Database Marketing

The industry of collecting, aggregating, and brokering personal data is known as "database marketing." The second-largest company in this field, Acxiom, has 23,000 computer servers that process more than 50 trillion data transactions per year, according to *The New York Times*.[1] It claims to have records on hundreds of millions of Americans, including 1.1 billion browser cookies (small pieces of data sent from a website, used to track the user's activity), 200 million mobile profiles, and an average of 1,500 pieces of data per consumer. These data include information gleaned from publicly available records like home valuation and vehicle ownership, information about online behavior tracked through cookies, browser advertising, and the like, data from customer surveys, and "offline" buying behavior. The CEO, Scott Howe, says, "Our digital reach will soon approach nearly every Internet user in the US."[2]

Visiting virtually any website places a digital cookie, or small text file, on your

---

computer. "First-party" cookies are placed by the site itself, such as Gmail saving your password so that you don't have to log in every time you visit the site. "Third-party cookies" persist across sites, tracking what sites you visit, in what order. For those who have logged in, Google Chrome and Firefox sync this browsing history across devices, combining what you do on your iPad with your iPhone with your laptop. This is used to deliver advertising.

For example, a few nights ago I was browsing LLBean.com for winter boots on my iPhone. A few days later, LLBean.com ads showed up on a news blog I was reading on my iPad. This "behavioral targeting" is falling out of fashion in favor of "predictive targeting," which uses sophisticated data-mining techniques to predict for L.L.Bean whether or not I am likely to purchase something upon seeing an LL-Bean.com ad.

Acxiom provides "premium proprietary behavioral insights" that "number in the thousands and cover consumer interests ranging from brand and channel affinities to product usage and purchase timing." In other words, Acxiom creates profiles, or digital dossiers, about millions of people, based on the 1,500 points of data about them it claims to have. These data might include your education level; how many children you have; the type of car you drive; your stock portfolio; your recent purchases; and your race, age, and education level. These data are combined across sources—for instance, magazine subscriber lists and public records of home ownership—to determine whether you fit into a number of predefined categories such as "McMansions and Minivans" or "adult with wealthy parent."[3] Acxiom is then able to sell these consumer profiles to its customers, who include twelve of the top fifteen credit card issuers, seven of the top ten retail banks, eight of the top ten telecom/media companies, and nine of the top ten property and casualty insurers.

Acxiom may be one of the largest data brokers, but it represents a dramatic shift in the way that personal information is handled online. The movement toward "Big Data," which uses computational techniques to find social insights in very large groupings of data, is rapidly transforming industries from health care to electoral politics. Big Data has many well-known social uses, for example by the police and by managers aiming to increase productivity. But it also poses new challenges to privacy on an unprecedented level and scale. Big Data is made up of "little data," and these little data may be deeply personal.

Alone, the fact that you purchased a bottle of cocoa butter lotion from Target is unremarkable. Target, on the other hand, assigns each customer a single Guest ID number, linked to their credit card number, e-mail address, or name. Every purchase and interaction you have with Target is then linked to your Guest ID, including the cocoa butter.

Now, Target has spent a great deal of time figuring out how to market to people about to have a baby. While most people remain fairly constant in their shopping habits—buying toilet paper here, socks there—the birth of a child is a life change that brings immense upheaval. Since birth records are public, new parents are bombarded with marketing and advertising offers. So Target's goal was to identify parents *before* the baby was born. The chief statistician for Target, Andrew Pole, said,

"We knew that if we could identify [new parents] in their second trimester, there's a good chance we could capture them for years."[4] Pole had been mining immense amounts of data about the shopping habits of pregnant women and new parents. He found that women purchased certain things during their pregnancy, such as cocoa butter, calcium tablets, and large purses that could double as diaper bags.

Target then began sending targeted mail to women during their pregnancy. This backfired. Women found it *creepy*—how did Target know they were pregnant? In one famous case, the father of a teenage girl called Target to complain that it was encouraging teen pregnancy by mailing her coupons for car seats and diapers. A week later, he called back and apologized; she hadn't told her father yet that she was pregnant.[5]

So the Target managers changed their tactics. They mixed in coupons for wine and lawnmowers with those for pacifiers and Baby Wipes. Pregnant women could use the coupons without realizing that Target knew they were pregnant. As Pole told *The New York Times Magazine*, "Even if you're following the law, you can do things where people get queasy."

These same techniques were used to great effect by the Obama campaign before the 2012 election. Famously, the campaign recruited some of the most brilliant young experts in analytics and behavioral science, and put them in a room called "the cave" for sixteen hours a day.[6] The chief data scientist for the campaign was an analyst who had formerly mined Big Data to improve supermarket promotions. This "dream team" was able to deliver microtargeted demographics to Obama— they could predict exactly how much money they would get back from each fundraising e-mail. When the team discovered that East Coast women between thirty and forty were not donating as much as might be expected, they offered a chance to have dinner with Sarah Jessica Parker as an incentive.[7] Every evening, the campaign ran 66,000 simulations to model the state of the election. The Obama analysts were not only using cutting-edge database marketing techniques, they were developing techniques that were far beyond the state of the art.

The Obama campaign's tactics illuminate something that is often missed in our discussions of data-mining and marketing—the fact that governments and politicians are major clients of marketing agencies and data brokers. For instance, the campaign bought data on the television-watching habits of Ohioans from a company called FourthWallMedia. Each household was assigned a number, but the names of those in the household were not revealed. The Obama campaign, however, was able to combine lists of voters with lists of cable subscribers, which it could then coordinate with the supposedly anonymous ID numbers used to track the usage patterns of television set-top boxes.[8] It could then target campaign ads to the exact times that certain voters were watching television. As a result, the campaign bought airtime during unconventional programming, like *Sons of Anarchy, The Walking Dead*, and *Don't Trust the B—in Apt. 23*, rather than during local news programming as conventional wisdom would have advised.

The "cave dwellers" were even able to match voter lists with Facebook information, using "Facebook Connect," Facebook's sign-on technology, which is used for many sign-ups and commenting systems online. Knowing that some of these users were Obama supporters, the campaign could figure out how to get them to persuade their perhaps less motivated friends to vote. Observing lists of Facebook friends and comparing them with tagged photos, the campaign matched these "friends" with lists of persuadable voters and then mobilized Obama supporters to convince their "real-life" friends to vote.

Social Media

In view of these sophisticated data- mining and analyzing techniques, is there any way we can use social media—or the Internet itself—without adding to our profiles collected by companies like Acxiom, Experian, or Epsilon?

Social media allow us to collect and track data about ourselves. For instance, I have been using a website called Last.fm since 2005 to track every piece of digital music I have listened to when using iTunes or Spotify. As a result, I have a fascinating picture of how my musical tastes have changed over time, and Last.fm is able to recommend obscure bands to me based on this extensive listening history.

Using social media allows us to connect with friends; to learn more about ourselves; even to improve our lives. The Quantified Self movement, which builds on techniques used by women for decades, such as counting calories, promotes the use of personal data for self-knowledge. Measuring your sleep cycles over time, for instance, can help you learn to avoid caffeine after 4:00 pm, or realize that, if you want to fall asleep, you can't use the Internet for an hour before bedtime.

But these data are immensely beneficial to data brokers. Imagine how a health insurer might react to viewing your caloric intake on MyFitnessPal, the number of steps you walk per day tracked by Fitbit, how often you check in to your local gym using Foursquare, and what you eat based on the pictures of your meals that you post on Instagram. Each piece of information, by itself, may be inconsequential, but the aggregation of this information creates a larger picture. Data trackers can centrally access such information and add it to their databases. Two large consequences of this collection of data deserve more attention.

The first is data discrimination. Once customers are sliced and diced into segmented demographic categories, they can be sorted. An Acxiom presentation to the Consumer Marketing Organization in 2013 placed customers into "customer value segments" and noted that while the top 30 percent of customers add 500 percent of value, the bottom 20 percent actually cost 400 percent of value. In other words, it behooves companies to shower their top customers with attention, while ignoring the bottom 20 percent, who may spend "too much" time on customer service calls, and may cost companies in returns or coupons, or otherwise cost more than they provide.

These "low-value targets" are known in industry parlance as "waste." Joseph Turow, a University of Pennsylvania professor in communications who studies niche marketing, asks what happens to those people who fall into the categories of "waste," entirely without their knowledge or any notification. Do they suffer price discrimination? Poor service? Do they miss out on the offers given to others? Such discrimination is still more insidious because it is entirely invisible.

Second, we may be more concerned with government surveillance than with marketers or data brokers collecting personal information, but this ignores the fact that the government regularly purchases data from these companies. ChoicePoint, now owned by Elsevier, was an enormous data aggregator that combined personal data extracted from public and private databases, including Social Security numbers, credit reports, and criminal records. It maintained 17 *billion* records on businesses and individuals, which it sold to approximately 100,000 clients, including thirty-five government agencies and seven thousand federal, state, and local law enforcement agencies.[9]

For instance, the State Department purchased records on millions of Latin American citizens, which were then checked against immigration databases. Choicepoint was also investigated for selling 145,000 personal records to an identity theft ring. More recently, Experian, one of the three major credit bureaus, mistakenly sold personal records to a Vietnamese hacker. Scammers refer to these records, which include Social Security numbers and mothers' maiden names, as "fullz," because they contain enough personal information for crooked operators to apply for credit cards or take out loans.

A few years ago, I toured the experimental lab of a large advertising agency. They showed me the cutting edge of consumer-monitoring technologies. Someday, not too far in the future, if you're at Duane Reade, aimlessly staring at a giant shelf of shampoo trying to figure out which to buy, the shelf will track your eye movements and which bottles you pick up and examine in more detail. Using this data, Duane Reade can algorithmically generate a coupon for a particular brand of shampoo, which you can then print from the shelf. I watched an experimental application that tracks the movements of individuals through a mall, based on the unique identifiers, or MAC addresses, of their cell phones, kept in purses or pockets but available to wireless tracking devices. Again, in all of these cases, the individuals are unaware that they are being tracked. A description of such procedures may be hidden at the end of a byzantine privacy policy people may not have noticed when they bought their devices, or written on a notice next to a CCTV camera. Though they may not be technically illegal, they seem ethically dubious.

While the easy answer to these problems is to opt out of loyalty cards, Internet use, or social media, this is hardly realistic. In fact, it is practically impossible to live life, online or offline, without being tracked—unless one takes extreme measures of avoidance. Cities track car movements; radio-frequency identification (RFID) tags are attached to clothing and dry cleaning; CCTV cameras are in most stores.[10] The technology is developing far more rapidly than our consumer protection laws, which in many cases are out of date and difficult to apply to our networked world.

The Federal Trade Commission and the Senate Commerce Committee are currently investigating data brokers and calling for more transparency in the collection and dissemination of personal information. Those of us concerned with privacy must continue to demand that checks and balances be applied to these private corporations. People should be encouraged to investigate the various opt-out tools, ad-blockers, and plug-ins that are available for most platforms. While closer scrutiny of the NSA is necessary and needed, we must apply equal pressure to private corporations to ensure that seemingly harmless targeted mail campaigns and advertisements do not give way to insidious and dangerous violations of personal privacy.

Notes

1. See Natasha Singer, "Acxiom, the Quiet Giant of Consumer Database Marketing," *The New York Times*, June 16, 2012.
2. See Judith Aquino, " Acxiom Prepares New 'Audience Operating System' Amid Wobbly Earnings," *AdExchanger.com*, August 1, 2013.
3. See Natasha Singer, "A Data Broker Offers a Peek Behind the Curtain," *The New York Times*, August 31, 2013.
4. See Charles Duhigg, "How Companies Learn Your Secrets," *The New York Times Magazine*, February 16, 2012.
5. See Kashmir Hill, " How Target Figured Out a Teen Girl Was Pregnant Before Her Father Did," *Forbes*, February 16, 2012.
6. See Jim Rutenberg, " Data You Can Believe In: The Obama Campaign's Digital Masterminds Cash In," *The New York Times Magazine*, June 20, 2013.
7. See Michael Scherer, " Inside the Secret World of the Data Crunchers Who Helped Obama Win," *Time*, November 7, 2012.
8. See Lois Beckett, " Everything We Know (So Far) About Obama's Big Data Tactics," *ProPublica*, November 29, 2012.
9. See " ChoicePoint," at the Electronic Privacy Information Center.
10. See Sarah Kessler, " Think You Can Live Offline Without Being Tracked? Here's What It Takes," *Fast Company*, October 15, 2013.

Constitutional Rights in the Digital Age

By Nancy Leong
The Huffington Post, July 19, 2014

The U.S. Supreme Court's recent decision in *Riley v. California* held that the police must obtain a warrant before searching the cell phone of someone who has been arrested. This decision applied the Fourth Amendment of the U.S. Constitution —which prohibits "unreasonable searches and seizures"—to take account of vast advances in technology since the time the Constitution was written.

What should Riley tell us about how the development of technology affects other constitutional protections? In particular, how does the rise of the Internet affect the First Amendment to the U.S. Constitution, which guarantees the right to free speech?

The Court's decision in *Riley* rested on a simple premise: Cell phones are different from ordinary physical objects. The latter may be searched following a lawful arrest. The former, after *Riley*, may not. That is because, to use the Court's own words, "Modern cell phones, as a category, implicate privacy concerns far beyond those implicated by the search of a cigarette pack, a wallet, or a purse."

So if searches of cell phones are different from searches of ordinary physical objects, then should online speech be analyzed differently from offline speech? The logical answer is yes. Just as cell phones are different from ordinary physical objects, the Internet is dramatically different from earlier speech mediums. And the Court should acknowledge those differences in determining the scope of First Amendment protection for speech.

The differences between offline and online communication closely parallel *Riley's* distinction between ordinary physical objects and cell phones. One such distinction is quantitative. As the Court wrote in *Riley*: "One of the most notable distinguishing features of modern cell phones is their immense storage capacity. Before cell phones, a search of a person was limited by physical realities and tended as a general matter to constitute only a narrow intrusion on privacy." This quantitative distinction extends to online speech. A large distribution of fliers might reach a few thousand people; in contrast, a public posting anywhere on the Internet can be read by billions. For instance, reddit.com—where anyone can post content—reports between 15 and 20 million unique visitors per month.

Riley also noted qualitative differences between ordinary physical objects and cell phones. The Court stated: "The term 'cell phone' is itself misleading shorthand;

many of these devices are in fact minicomputers that also happen to have the capacity to be used as a telephone. They could just as easily be called cameras, video players, rolodexes, calendars, tape recorders, libraries, diaries, albums, televisions, maps, or newspapers." That is, cell phones "collect[] in one place many distinct types of information—an address, a note, a prescription, a bank statement, a video."

The Internet likewise enables qualitatively different speech. Internet speech incorporates linking, which—not unlike the cell phone in *Riley*—aggregates a great quantity of information in a single place and creates a close connection between original and linked material. A much greater quantity of Internet speech is anonymous, and research indicates that anonymity breeds incivility as well as harassment and threats, which research has found disproportionately affect women. As many people have learned the hard way, the combination of the Internet and other electronic forms of communication enable the viral spread of information in a manner vastly different from people passing copies of a news article from hand to hand or calling up their neighbors to spread a juicy bit of gossip. And Internet speech is often both permanent and easily retrieved in a matter of seconds using a search engine, in stark contrast to the effort required to locate a yellowed news clipping stored in a box in the attic.

The First Amendment should take account of these differences between online and offline speech, as the following examples illustrate.

Consider, first, the doctrine of obscenity. The Supreme Court held in *Miller v. California* that speech is obscene only if "the average person, applying contemporary community standards," would believe that the allegedly obscene item appeals to the "prurient interest," or an excessive and unhealthy interest in sexual matters. The Court specified that contemporary community standards should be evaluated locally: that is, what counts as prurient in Topeka might not in San Francisco. Yet while perhaps locally-calibrated evaluation made sense in 1973, when *Miller* was decided, the standard requires updating now that an image posted on the Internet is theoretically viewable by anyone in the world.

Second, the Supreme Court will soon take up the question of whether and how the First Amendment protects arguably threatening speech posted on the Internet. The Court recently granted review in *Elonis v. United States*, a case involving a man who was convicted under a federal law that criminalizes "true threats" after he posted disturbing rap lyrics about his ex-wife on Facebook. The lyrics included such statements as:

> There's one way to love you but a thousand ways to kill you. I'm not going to rest until your body is a mess, soaked in blood and dying from all the little cuts. Hurry up and die, bitch, so I can bust this nut all over your corpse from atop your shallow grave. I used to be a nice guy but then you became a slut.

The defendant's lyrics also involved a number of other violent statements, including a reference to "making a name for himself" with a kindergarten shooting and a fantasy about killing an F.B.I. agent. An issue in the case is whether the statements were "true threats"—in particular, whether the defendant's claim that

> **The Supreme Court's decision in Riley is a timely acknowledgment of the need for Fourth Amendment doctrine to take account of developments in technology.**

he did not intend his statements as serious threats should matter. Here again, the distinct qualities of the Internet make a difference. Because the Internet filters out voice and demeanor cues, online statements provide less information about the seriousness of the statement and are thus more likely to be reasonably interpreted as threats. Likewise, because the Internet is not tied to a particular physical location, disturbing statements are more alarming to a reasonable person: one doesn't know whether the person making the threats is in a different state or in the next room. The Court should take these realities into account next term in fashioning a "true threats" doctrine for the digital age.*

Third, the Internet medium poses novel considerations when it comes to First Amendment doctrine governing hate speech. The Court's past decisions on that issue have been mixed: in *RAV v. City of St. Paul*, the Court unanimously struck down a hate-crime ordinance that had been interpreted to criminalize cross-burning, while in *Virginia v. Black*, it upheld a statute that criminalized cross-burning so long as "intent to intimidate" was proven. Yet there are good reasons for the Court to analyze Internet hate speech differently. First, the Internet facilitates the gathering of like-minded individuals united by their hatred of particular groups. Second, the anonymity of the Internet facilitates easy expression of hateful ideas. And finally, Internet hate speech sometimes leads to serious real-world consequences: consider, for example, the ease with which al-Qaeda's hateful anti-American sentiments facilitate recruitment of new members.

Fourth, the phenomenon of "revenge porn"—the distribution of intimate pictures of another person without that person's consent—is another instance in which First Amendment analysis should take account of the unique characteristics of Internet speech. Some have argued that new state laws criminalizing revenge porn are, in at least some instances, constitutionally sound and good policy; others are more ambivalent. But broadcasting intimate images to the public via the Internet is quantitatively and qualitatively different from, say, distribution of such images by mail. I do not mean to imply that offline non-consensual distribution could not also be prohibited consistent with the U.S. Constitution. But First Amendment analysis of statutes criminalizing Internet revenge porn should not ignore the real-world differences associated with online distribution. The Internet allows easy dissemination of large quantities of revenge porn, facilitates the viral spread of such material, and potentially preserves the material online indefinitely, with devastating consequences for victims.

The Supreme Court's decision in *Riley* is a timely acknowledgment of the need for Fourth Amendment doctrine to take account of developments in technology. It's time for the Court to do the same with other areas of constitutional law, starting with the First Amendment.

Editor's Note
*On June 1, 2015, the Supreme Court reversed the conviction of Elonis in an 8–1 decision.

The Right to Be Forgotten

By Patricia J. Williams
The Nation, September 17, 2014

A debate erupted in the comment section of Dave Zirin's *Nation* blog after he wrote that "showing and reshowing [the elevator video of then-fiancée, now wife, Janay Palmer] just because we can is an act of harm." He argued that "just as we would protect the name of an alleged rape victim, just as we would not show a video of Ray Rice committing a sexual assault, we should not be showing this video like it's another episode of *Rich People Behaving Badly*."

Yet it's not necessarily against the law to publish the identities of rape victims. And there are thousands of online "we's" who post everything from the rape of drunken classmates to the torture of kittens to human beheadings. But Zirin's point is an important one, reminding us of the purpose behind America's best traditions of journalistic integrity. Many millions of people have now seen Janay Palmer knocked to the floor, her limp body sprawled facedown, her dress crumpled above her waist, a portrait of one woman's degradation. For those who believe that "we," "the public," "need" to see this, or even have some kind of "right" to see it—well, let's think carefully about all which that implies.

Hearst and Murdoch notwithstanding, FCC oversight and clear ethical standards have made U.S. journalism generally fairer and more accurate than elsewhere—Britain's Fleet Street, for example. But the digital-age trend toward "it's all out there anyway" punditry trades values of privacy, fairness, and relevance for a standard of pure transparency, no matter who is exposed. *Fox News* has done much to break apart the old conventions. It is, after all, a subsidiary of Fox Entertainment; its only outer limit seems to be child pornography or physical threat. TMZ, too, deserves scrutiny, as publisher not merely of the Ray Rice footage but of much with which we've been obsessed recently: the hundreds of pictures of nude celebrities stolen from their cloud storage systems, as well as the film of Solange Knowles kicking Jay-Z, purchased from a hotel employee for $250,000. TMZ practices what is called "checkbook journalism," encouraging legions of little Big Brothers eager to contribute to a culture of surveillance that has consequences for all of us.

A major tenet of the women's movement over the past thirty years has been that rape trials, for example, frequently retraumatize victims by forcing them to relive the experience through the presentation of evidence in court. Now, with social media, that evidence can be posted anywhere or sold to anyone. As Julia Angwin notes in her book *Dragnet Nation,* the very attempt to shield yourself online, as with encrypted e-mails, is likely to place you "on some kind of red-flag list at the NSA." In the United States, corporate and mar-

But the digital-age trend toward "it's all out there anyway" punditry trades values of privacy, fairness, and relevance for a standard of pure transparency, no matter who is exposed.

keting lobbyists are quick to denounce any and all attempts to protect privacy as "censorship." But there do exist basic legal as well as ethical limits we may wish to propose as starting points for a more robust discussion about our changing world.

A recent ruling by the European Court recognizes a "right to be forgotten." This is derived from a right, originally accorded to criminals who had served their time, to have their records expunged so that they're able to start life over. It is a right premised on the possibility of rehabilitation—not popular in America's highly punitive culture. But in Europe, the right to be forgotten has become a cause that extends beyond criminal history to a more general concern that in cyberspace, we never grow past the moment of our greatest humiliation and that in the long run this record will make us a less mobile society. We risk becoming serfs to our surfing history, as well as pawns to be experimented on by companies, like Facebook, whose business is data. The European Court found that search engines like Google must remove information that is "inadequate, irrelevant or no longer relevant" when a member of the public so requests. The ruling seems broad enough to apply to resolved debts, revenge porn, indeed any information that affects people's honor, dignity, or privacy.

In Europe, Google is currently fighting any such obligation. In the United States, the Supreme Court has ruled that free-speech concerns allow publication even of embarrassing material as long as it was legally obtained. Of course, in the face of near-zero regulation, little can be categorized as illegally obtained. But we could make tougher sanctions against government and private surveillance if we wanted to. We could create higher standards for encryption of our stored information. That would hobble the use of cookies by advertisers and other collectors of data, who make billions of dollars from our purchasing histories and viewing habits. This is a technological quandary to some degree, but the balancing of privacy, surveillance, freedom of information, and censorship is not new or irremediable.

Meanwhile, it's hard to imagine that Ray Rice will ever work again. No matter how much therapy and soul-searching he undertakes, it's going to be hard for him to find a job doing so much as raking leaves. Unless, of course, he sells his story to the perpetual shaming machine known as reality TV. It's not hard to imagine him locked on an island with Dr. Phil and Richie Incognito and Adrian Peterson and Bristol Palin (who, according to reports about a recent melee at her father's birthday party, "has a particularly strong right hook"). *Rehab With Ray Rice,* they'll call it. Poor Janay Palmer Rice will be forced to make ends meet by spending her days in some spin-off of *Mob Wives,* titled something like *Ex-Wives* (one can hope!) *of the NFL.* An entertaining thought, no? Feels not just possible but likely? My commission, please, Fox Channel! Yet this is an outcome that degrades not only the Rices, but all of us as citizens and as vulnerable human beings. If we capitulate to the idea that pornographic reiteration is our only future, all sentences become life sentences.

How One Stupid Tweet Blew Up Justine Sacco's Life

By Jon Ronson
The New York Times, February 12, 2015

As she made the long journey from New York to South Africa, to visit family during the holidays in 2013, Justine Sacco, 30 years old and the senior director of corporate communications at IAC, began tweeting acerbic little jokes about the indignities of travel. There was one about a fellow passenger on the flight from John F. Kennedy International Airport:

"'Weird German Dude: You're in First Class. It's 2014. Get some deodorant.'— Inner monologue as I inhale BO. Thank God for pharmaceuticals."

Then, during her layover at Heathrow:

"Chilly—cucumber sandwiches—bad teeth. Back in London!"

And on Dec. 20, before the final leg of her trip to Cape Town:

"Going to Africa. Hope I don't get AIDS. Just kidding. I'm white!"

Sacco boarded the plane. It was an 11-hour flight, so she slept. When the plane landed in Cape Town and was taxiing on the runway, she turned on her phone. Right away, she got a text from someone she hadn't spoken to since high school: "I'm so sorry to see what's happening." Sacco looked at it, baffled.

Then another text: "You need to call me immediately." It was from her best friend, Hannah. Then her phone exploded with more texts and alerts. And then it rang. It was Hannah. "You're the No. 1 worldwide trend on Twitter right now," she said.

Sacco's Twitter feed had become a horror show. "In light of @Justine-Sacco disgusting racist tweet, I'm donating to @care today" and "How did @JustineSacco get a PR job?! Her level of racist ignorance belongs on Fox News. #AIDS can affect anyone!" and "I'm an IAC employee and I don't want @JustineSacco doing any communications on our behalf ever again. Ever." And then one from her employer, IAC, the corporate owner of *The Daily Beast*, OkCupid and Vimeo: "This is an outrageous, offensive comment. Employee in question currently unreachable on an intl flight." The anger soon turned to excitement: "All I want for Christmas is to see @JustineSacco's face when her plane lands and she checks her inbox/voicemail" and "Oh man, @JustineSacco is going to have the most painful phone-turning-on moment ever when her plane lands" and "We are about to watch this @JustineSacco bitch get fired. In REAL time. Before she even KNOWS she's getting fired."

The furor over Sacco's tweet had become not just an ideological crusade against

Reprinted with permission of A P Watt at United Agents on behalf of Jon Ronson Ltd.

her perceived bigotry but also a form of idle entertainment. Her complete ignorance of her predicament for those 11 hours lent the episode both dramatic irony and a pleasing narrative arc. As Sacco's flight traversed the length of Africa, a hashtag began to trend worldwide: #HasJustineLandedYet. "Seriously. I just want to go home to go to bed, but everyone at the bar is SO into #HasJustineLandedYet. Can't look away. Can't leave" and "Right, is there no one in Cape Town going to the airport to tweet her arrival? Come on, Twitter! I'd like pictures #HasJustineLandedYet."

A Twitter user did indeed go to the airport to tweet her arrival. He took her photograph and posted it online. "Yup," he wrote, "@JustineSacco HAS in fact landed at Cape Town International. She's decided to wear sunnies as a disguise."

By the time Sacco had touched down, tens of thousands of angry tweets had been sent in response to her joke. Hannah, meanwhile, frantically deleted her friend's tweet and her account—Sacco didn't want to look—but it was far too late. "Sorry @JustineSacco," wrote one Twitter user, "your tweet lives on forever."

In the early days of Twitter, I was a keen shamer. When newspaper columnists made racist or homophobic statements, I joined the pile-on. Sometimes I led it. The journalist A. A. Gill once wrote a column about shooting a baboon on safari in Tanzania: "I'm told they can be tricky to shoot. They run up trees, hang on for grim life. They die hard, baboons. But not this one. A soft-nosed .357 blew his lungs out." Gill did the deed because he "wanted to get a sense of what it might be like to kill someone, a stranger."

I was among the first people to alert social media. (This was because Gill always gave my television documentaries bad reviews, so I tended to keep a vigilant eye on things he could be got for.) Within minutes, it was everywhere. Amid the hundreds of congratulatory messages I received, one stuck out: "Were you a bully at school?"

Still, in those early days, the collective fury felt righteous, powerful, and effective. It felt as if hierarchies were being dismantled, as if justice were being democratized. As time passed, though, I watched these shame campaigns multiply, to the point that they targeted not just powerful institutions and public figures but really anyone perceived to have done something offensive. I also began to marvel at the disconnect between the severity of the crime and the gleeful savagery of the punishment. It almost felt as if shamings were now happening for their own sake, as if they were following a script.

Eventually I started to wonder about the recipients of our shamings, the real humans who were the virtual targets of these campaigns. So for the past two years, I've been interviewing individuals like Justine Sacco: everyday people pilloried brutally, most often for posting some poorly considered joke on social media. Whenever possible, I have met them in person, to truly grasp the emotional toll at the other end of our screens. The people I met were mostly unemployed, fired for their transgressions, and they seemed broken somehow—deeply confused and traumatized.

One person I met was Lindsey Stone, a 32-year-old Massachusetts woman who posed for a photograph while mocking a sign at Arlington National Cemetery's Tomb of the Unknowns. Stone had stood next to the sign, which asks for "Silence and Respect," pretending to scream and flip the bird. She and her co-worker

> "Of all the things I could have been in society's collective consciousness, it never struck me that I'd end up a brutal nadir."

Jamie, who posted the picture on Facebook, had a running joke about disobeying signs—smoking in front of No Smoking signs, for example—and documenting it. But shorn of this context, her picture appeared to be a joke not about a sign but about the war dead. Worse, Jamie didn't realize that her mobile uploads were visible to the public.

Four weeks later, Stone and Jamie were out celebrating Jamie's birthday when their phones started vibrating repeatedly. Someone had found the photo and brought it to the attention of hordes of online strangers. Soon there was a wildly popular "Fire Lindsey Stone" Facebook page. The next morning, there were news cameras outside her home; when she showed up to her job, at a program for developmentally disabled adults, she was told to hand over her keys. ("After they fire her, maybe she needs to sign up as a client," read one of the thousands of Facebook messages denouncing her. "Woman needs help.") She barely left home for the year that followed, racked by PTSD, depression, and insomnia. "I didn't want to be seen by anyone," she told me last March at her home in Plymouth, Mass. "I didn't want people looking at me."

Instead, Stone spent her days online, watching others just like her get turned upon. In particular she felt for "that girl at Halloween who dressed as a Boston Marathon victim. I felt so terrible for her." She meant Alicia Ann Lynch, 22, who posted a photo of herself in her Halloween costume on Twitter. Lynch wore a running outfit and had smeared her face, arms, and legs with fake blood. After an actual victim of the Boston Marathon bombing tweeted at her, "You should be ashamed, my mother lost both her legs and I almost died," people unearthed Lynch's personal information and sent her and her friends threatening messages. Lynch was reportedly let go from her job as well.

I met a man who, in early 2013, had been sitting at a conference for tech developers in Santa Clara, Calif., when a stupid joke popped into his head. It was about the attachments for computers and mobile devices that are commonly called dongles. He murmured the joke to his friend sitting next to him, he told me. "It was so bad, I don't remember the exact words," he said. "Something about a fictitious piece of hardware that has a really big dongle, a ridiculous dongle. . . . It wasn't even conversation-level volume."

Moments later, he half-noticed when a woman one row in front of them stood up, turned around, and took a photograph. He thought she was taking a crowd shot, so he looked straight ahead, trying to avoid ruining her picture. It's a little painful to look at the photograph now, knowing what was coming.

The woman had, in fact, overheard the joke. She considered it to be emblematic of the gender imbalance that plagues the tech industry and the toxic, male-dominated corporate culture that arises from it. She tweeted the picture to her 9,209 followers with the caption: "Not cool. Jokes about . . . 'big' dongles right behind me."

Ten minutes later, he and his friend were taken into a quiet room at the conference and asked to explain themselves. A day later, his boss called him into his office, and he was fired.

"I packed up all my stuff in a box," he told me. (Like Stone and Sacco, he had never before talked on the record about what happened to him. He spoke on the condition of anonymity to avoid further damaging his career.) "I went outside to call my wife. I'm not one to shed tears, but"—he paused—"when I got in the car with my wife I just. . . . I've got three kids. Getting fired was terrifying."

The woman who took the photograph, Adria Richards, soon felt the wrath of the crowd herself. The man responsible for the dongle joke had posted about losing his job on *Hacker News*, an online forum popular with developers. This led to a backlash from the other end of the political spectrum. So-called men's rights activists and anonymous trolls bombarded Richards with death threats on Twitter and Facebook. Someone tweeted Richards's home address along with a photograph of a beheaded woman with duct tape over her mouth. Fearing for her life, she left her home, sleeping on friends' couches for the remainder of the year.

Next, her employer's website went down. Someone had launched a DDoS attack, which overwhelms a site's servers with repeated requests. SendGrid, her employer, was told the attacks would stop if Richards was fired. That same day she was publicly let go.

"I cried a lot during this time, journaled and escaped by watching movies," she later said to me in an email. "SendGrid threw me under the bus. I felt betrayed. I felt abandoned. I felt ashamed. I felt rejected. I felt alone."

Late one afternoon last year, I met Justine Sacco in New York, at a restaurant in Chelsea called Cookshop. Dressed in rather chic business attire, Sacco ordered a glass of white wine. Just three weeks had passed since her trip to Africa, and she was still a person of interest to the media. Websites had already ransacked her Twitter feed for more horrors. (For example, "I had a sex dream about an autistic kid last night," from 2012, was unearthed by BuzzFeed in the article "16 Tweets Justine Sacco Regrets.") A *New York Post* photographer had been following her to the gym.

"Only an insane person would think that white people don't get AIDS," she told me. It was about the first thing she said to me when we sat down.

Sacco had been three hours or so into her flight when retweets of her joke began to overwhelm my Twitter feed. I could understand why some people found it offensive. Read literally, she said that white people don't get AIDS, but it seems doubtful many interpreted it that way. More likely it was her apparently gleeful flaunting of her privilege that angered people. But after thinking about her tweet for a few seconds more, I began to suspect that it wasn't racist but a reflexive critique of white privilege—on our tendency to naïvely imagine ourselves immune from life's horrors. Sacco, like Stone, had been yanked violently out of the context of her small social circle. Right?

"To me it was so insane of a comment for anyone to make," she said. "I thought there was no way that anyone could possibly think it was literal." (She would later write me an email to elaborate on this point. "Unfortunately, I am not a character on 'South Park' or a comedian, so I had no business commenting on the epidemic in such a politically incorrect manner on a public platform," she wrote. "To put it simply, I wasn't trying to raise awareness of AIDS or piss off the world or ruin my life. Living in America puts us in a bit of a bubble when it comes to what is going on in the third world. I was making fun of that bubble.")

I would be the only person she spoke to on the record about what happened to her, she said. It was just too harrowing—and "as a publicist," inadvisable—but she felt it was necessary, to show how "crazy" her situation was, how her punishment simply didn't fit the crime.

"I cried out my body weight in the first twenty-four hours," she told me. "It was incredibly traumatic. You don't sleep. You wake up in the middle of the night forgetting where you are." She released an apology statement and cut short her vacation. Workers were threatening to strike at the hotels she had booked if she showed up. She was told no one could guarantee her safety.

Her extended family in South Africa were African National Congress supporters—the party of Nelson Mandela. They were longtime activists for racial equality. When Justine arrived at the family home from the airport, one of the first things her aunt said to her was: "This is not what our family stands for. And now, by association, you've almost tarnished the family."

As she told me this, Sacco started to cry. I sat looking at her for a moment. Then I tried to improve the mood. I told her that "sometimes, things need to reach a brutal nadir before people see sense."

"Wow," she said. She dried her eyes. "Of all the things I could have been in society's collective consciousness, it never struck me that I'd end up a brutal nadir."

She glanced at her watch. It was nearly 6 p.m. The reason she wanted to meet me at this restaurant, and that she was wearing her work clothes, was that it was only a few blocks away from her office. At 6, she was due in there to clean out her desk.

"All of a sudden you don't know what you're supposed to do," she said. "If I don't start making steps to reclaim my identity and remind myself of who I am on a daily basis, then I might lose myself."

The restaurant's manager approached our table. She sat down next to Sacco, fixed her with a look and said something in such a low volume I couldn't hear it, only Sacco's reply: "Oh, you think I'm going to be grateful for this?"

We agreed to meet again, but not for several months. She was determined to prove that she could turn her life around. "I can't just sit at home and watch movies every day and cry and feel sorry for myself," she said. "I'm going to come back."

After she left, Sacco later told me, she got only as far as the lobby of her office building before she broke down crying.

A few days after meeting Sacco, I took a trip up to the Massachusetts Archives in Boston. I wanted to learn about the last era of American history when public shaming was a common form of punishment, so I was seeking out court transcripts from the eighteenth and early nineteenth centuries. I had assumed that the demise of public punishments was caused by the migration from villages to cities. Shame became ineffectual, I thought, because a person in the stocks could just lose himself or herself in the anonymous crowd as soon as the chastisement was over. Modernity had diminished shame's power to shame—or so I assumed.

I took my seat at a microfilm reader and began to scroll slowly through the archives. For the first hundred years, as far as I could tell, all that happened in America was that various people named Nathaniel had purchased land near rivers. I scrolled faster, finally reaching an account of an early Colonial-era shaming.

On July 15, 1742, a woman named Abigail Gilpin, her husband at sea, had been found "naked in bed with one John Russell." They were both to be "whipped at the public whipping post 20 stripes each." Abigail was appealing the ruling, but it wasn't the whipping itself she wished to avoid. She was begging the judge to let her be whipped early, before the town awoke. "If your honor pleases," she wrote, "take some pity on me for my dear children who cannot help their unfortunate mother's failings."

There was no record as to whether the judge consented to her plea, but I found a number of clips that offered clues as to why she might have requested private punishment. In a sermon, the Rev. Nathan Strong, of Hartford, Conn., entreated his flock to be less exuberant at executions. "Go not to that place of horror with elevated spirits and gay hearts, for death is there! Justice and judgment are there!" Some papers published scathing reviews when public punishments were deemed too lenient by the crowd: "Suppressed remarks ... were expressed by large numbers," reported Delaware's *Wilmington Daily Commercial* of a disappointing 1873 whipping. "Many were heard to say that the punishment was a farce. ... Drunken fights and rows followed in rapid succession."

The movement against public shaming had gained momentum in 1787, when Benjamin Rush, a physician in Philadelphia and a signer of the Declaration of Independence, wrote a paper calling for its demise—the stocks, the pillory, the whipping post, the lot. "Ignominy is universally acknowledged to be a worse punishment than death," he wrote. "It would seem strange that ignominy should ever have been adopted as a milder punishment than death, did we not know that the human mind seldom arrives at truth upon any subject till it has first reached the extremity of error."

The pillory and whippings were abolished at the federal level in 1839, although Delaware kept the pillory until 1905 and whippings until 1972. An 1867 editorial in *The Times* excoriated the state for its obstinacy. "If [the convicted person] had previously existing in his bosom a spark of self-respect this exposure to public shame utterly extinguishes it. ... The boy of 18 who is whipped at New Castle for larceny is in nine cases out of 10 ruined. With his self-respect destroyed and the taunt and sneer of public disgrace branded upon his forehead, he feels himself lost and abandoned by his fellows."

At the archives, I found no evidence that punitive shaming fell out of fashion as a result of newfound anonymity. But I did find plenty of people from centuries past bemoaning the outsize cruelty of the practice, warning that well-meaning people, in a crowd, often take punishment too far.

It's possible that Sacco's fate would have been different had an anonymous tip not led a writer named Sam Biddle to the offending tweet. Biddle was then the editor of Valleywag, Gawker Media's tech-industry blog. He retweeted it to his 15,000 followers and eventually posted it on Valleywag, accompanied by the headline, "And Now, a Funny Holiday Joke From IAC's P.R. Boss."

In January 2014, I received an email from Biddle, explaining his reasoning. "The fact that she was a P.R. chief made it delicious," he wrote. "It's satisfying to be able to say, 'O.K., let's make a racist tweet by a senior IAC employee count this time.' And it did. I'd do it again." Biddle said he was surprised to see how quickly her life was upended, however. "I never wake up and hope I [get someone fired] that day— and certainly never hope to ruin anyone's life." Still, he ended his email by saying that he had a feeling she'd be "fine eventually, if not already."

He added: "Everyone's attention span is so short. They'll be mad about something new today."

Four months after we first met, Justine Sacco made good on her promise. We met for lunch at a French bistro downtown. I told her what Biddle had said—about how she was probably fine now. I was sure he wasn't being deliberately glib, but like everyone who participates in mass online destruction, uninterested in learning that it comes with a cost.

"Well, I'm not fine yet," Sacco said to me. "I had a great career, and I loved my job, and it was taken away from me, and there was a lot of glory in that. Everybody else was very happy about that."

Sacco pushed her food around on her plate and let me in on one of the hidden costs of her experience. "I'm single; so it's not like I can date, because we Google everyone we might date," she said. "That's been taken away from me too." She was down, but I did notice one positive change in her. When I first met her, she talked about the shame she had brought on her family. But she no longer felt that way. Instead, she said, she just felt personally humiliated.

Biddle was almost right about one thing: Sacco did get a job offer right away. But it was an odd one, from the owner of a Florida yachting company. "He said: 'I saw what happened to you. I'm fully on your side,'" she told me. Sacco knew nothing about yachts, and she questioned his motives. ("Was he a crazy person who thinks white people can't get AIDS?") Eventually she turned him down.

After that, she left New York, going as far away as she could, to Addis Ababa, Ethiopia. She flew there alone and got a volunteer job doing P.R. for an NGO (nongovernmental organization) working to reduce maternal-mortality rates. "It was fantastic," she said. She was on her own, and she was working. If she was going to be made to suffer for a joke, she figured she should get something out of it. "I never would have lived in Addis Ababa for a month otherwise," she told me. She was struck by how different life was there. Rural areas had only intermittent power and no running water or Internet. Even the capital, she said, had few street names or house addresses.

Addis Ababa was great for a month, but she knew going in that she would not be there long. She was a New York City person. Sacco is nervy and sassy and sort of debonair. And so she returned to work at Hot or Not, which had been a popular site for rating strangers' looks on the pre-social Internet and was reinventing itself as a dating app.

But despite her near invisibility on social media, she was still ridiculed and demonized across the Internet. Biddle wrote a Valleywag post after she returned to the work force: "Sacco, who apparently spent the last month hiding in Ethiopia after infuriating our species with an idiotic AIDS joke, is now a 'marketing and promotion' director at Hot or Not."

"How perfect!" he wrote. "Two lousy has-beens, gunning for a comeback together."

Sacco felt this couldn't go on, so six weeks after our lunch, she invited Biddle out for a dinner and drinks. Afterward, she sent me an email. "I think he has some real guilt about the issue," she wrote. "Not that he's retracted anything." (Months later, Biddle would find himself at the wrong end of the Internet shame machine for tweeting a joke of his own: "Bring Back Bullying." On the one-year anniversary of the Sacco episode, he published a public apology to her on Gawker.)

Recently, I wrote to Sacco to tell her I was putting her story in *The Times,* and I asked her to meet me one final time to update me on her life. Her response was speedy. "No way." She explained that she had a new job in communications, though she wouldn't say where. She said, "Anything that puts the spotlight on me is a negative."

It was a profound reversal for Sacco. When I first met her, she was desperate to tell the tens of thousands of people who tore her apart how they had wronged her and to repair what remained of her public persona. But perhaps she had now come to understand that her shaming wasn't really about her at all. Social media is so perfectly designed to manipulate our desire for approval, and that is what led to her undoing. Her tormentors were instantly congratulated as they took Sacco down, bit by bit, and so they continued to do so. Their motivation was much the same as Sacco's own—a bid for the attention of strangers—as she milled about Heathrow, hoping to amuse people she couldn't see.

After the Silk Road Conviction, Tor Must Be Protected

By Craig A. Newman

The Guardian, February 19, 2015

The first information superhighway was not the Internet, but the Silk Roads. Built during the Han dynasty, the 4,000 mile network of trade routes brought perfume, spices, and unprecedented knowledge of distant cultures to civilizations from China to Persia to Europe. Twenty-five centuries later, it has surprising relevance to a heated debate over digital privacy.

The Silk Road name, of course, was co-opted by the now infamous online bazaar for illegal goods and services. And its mastermind creator, Ross William Ulbricht, was recently convicted in New York federal court of operating the Internet's biggest black market for drugs. Although Silk Road is now viewed as a criminal enterprise, more vexing to some authorities is Tor, the anonymizing software that allowed Ulbricht's customers to visit his site without leaving so much as a digital fingerprint.

Tor, a free application created by a nonprofit group, is used by citizens worldwide to elude government snooping and censorship. Like the original Silk Roads, it provides a pathway to otherwise impossible communication—for activists during the Arab spring, for Turkish citizens after their government blocked Twitter last year, and for Chinese citizens seeking to hurdle the Great Firewall and connect to the wider world. Journalists, too, use Tor to safely contact sources, dissidents, and whistleblowers.

Like many beneficial technologies, Tor was fostered in a government lab—the U.S. Naval Research Laboratory—and the federal government has continued to support it. According to financial statements on Tor's website, it received approximately 90 percent of its grants in 2013 from three federal agencies, including $830,269 from the U.S. Department of Defense.

But as the Silk Road trial showed, Tor is also used by the bad guys who turn its privacy protections into a shield for communications of a darker nature. Thus, at the same time the U.S. was funding Tor, documents revealed by Edward Snowden demonstrate that the United States National Security Agency and allied intelligence services were working to crack it.

Tor is not the only privacy tool that has come under fire of late. Government officials have chastised U.S. technology companies for incorporating encryption technology into products, like Apple's latest iPhone, which put user data out of reach of law enforcement. Google has adopted similar technology for Android devices. Yahoo is reportedly working on an encrypted email project. These products are just the crest of what is likely to be a new wave of advanced privacy technology.

The advanced features of Tor, encrypted phones, and whatever is still to come, satisfy a consumer appetite for digital privacy that increased after Edward Snowden's revelations. That appetite may become ravenous, with recent reports that surveillance software has been embedded in consumer devices such as computer hard drives—let alone the fact that the Internet of things spreads surveillance possibilities beyond laptops and smartphones to cars, home security systems, and countless other personal devices.

Law enforcement is predictably less hungry to see privacy tools implemented. The Times Square bomber, Faisal Shahzad, admitted that he used encryption technology to communicate with his co-conspirators in Pakistan to plan the aborted 2010 attack.

In a time of extreme sensitivity to terrorism, we should be equally wary of intrusions on privacy that enable the creep of government surveillance programs.

Against that background, director of GCHQ—the UK intelligence agency—Roger Hannigan said U.S. tech companies, "have become the command and control networks of choice for terrorists and criminals, who find their services as transformational as the rest of us."

UK prime minister David Cameron, for his part, has demanded that there be, "no safe spaces for terrorists to communicate." If preventing crime were the only thing we valued, that call would have appeal.

Stepping back, however, we can see just how strange it is to debate the prohibition of privacy tools that serve positive ends—including the enhancement of the right, first articulated by U.S. supreme court justice Louis Brandeis, "to be let alone."

Sympathizing with the challenges of law enforcement, after all, has never required us to forgo access to any instrument that can be used by bad actors. Should we have banned pagers, cellphones, or laptop computers in light of their utility to drug lords?

In a time of extreme sensitivity to terrorism, we should be equally wary of intrusions on privacy that enable the creep of government surveillance programs. Citizens of Saudi Arabia and the UAE, threatened with a ban on Blackberry messaging in 2010, would agree. Not to mention motorists in the US, who recently learned of the U.S. Drug Enforcement Administration's license plate tracking program that watches the movement of vehicles in the U.S. in real time.

The Silk Route of 200 BC, like modern privacy tools, came with risks and opportunities for misuse. It carried disease along its trails, and tempted thieves with its valuable cargo. Last year, it was designated a UNESCO World Heritage Site. It's a fearful thing to consider what the world would have lost without it.

The NSA Debate We Should Be Having

By Fred Kaplan
Slate, June 8, 2015

One week after Congress voted to stop the National Security Agency from collecting and storing millions of Americans' phone records, partisans on both sides are exaggerating the significance of this new reform. NSA supporters lament the loss of a key tool for fighting terrorists, while the agency's critics hail the new law as (in Edward Snowden's words) an "historic victory for the rights of every citizen," with some calling its passage a vindication of Snowden himself as an authentic whistleblower who should be let back home as a hero, not a convict.

Both sides are off the mark.

The NSA's bulk collection of telephone metadata was the subject of the first news stories based on the trove of highly classified documents that Snowden leaked, and it stirred the biggest commotion. But in fact the metadata program never comprised more than a tiny percentage of the agency's vast and global surveillance net. The new law's reform measure—to keep the metadata stored with the telecom companies, allowing NSA access only to specified materials, and then only through the Foreign Intelligence Surveillance Court—was first proposed not by some libertarian critic but by Gen. Keith Alexander, then-director of the NSA.

Under the system that has been in effect, as authorized by Section 215 of the Patriot Act (or, rather, by the FISA [Foreign Intelligence Surveillance Act] Court's now-discredited reading of that section), the NSA routinely collected metadata from some of the biggest cellular companies—not the contents of conversations, but the phone numbers, dates, times, and duration of the calls. If someone inside the United States called a number linked to one of three terrorist organizations (including al-Qaida), an NSA alert system would note that fact. The NSA could then ask the FISA Court for permission to search the database for a list of all the other numbers that the American phone had called, as well as all the numbers that *those* numbers had called, going back as far as five years. If this search revealed a suspicious pattern, the NSA would turn the materials over to the FBI, which could seek a warrant to listen to conversations.

Under the new reform law, called the USA Freedom Act, the NSA would no longer possess the database, so it would seek a FISA Court order to get it from the telecom companies—and the FISA Court would now include a privacy advocate who could argue against relinquishing the data. If the court sided with the NSA, what happened next would be exactly the same as before the new law passed.

So, it's not exactly a giant step in the annals of either national-security risk or civil liberties reform—unless one of two things had been true. First, if the NSA had been abusing the process—if analysts or senior officials had been searching metadata for personal, political, or vindictive purposes—the changes in custody and oversight would have a huge impact. But neither Snowden's documents nor any subsequent probes have uncovered any such evidence.

Second, if authoritarians or worse—say, modern-day versions of Richard Nixon and J. Edgar Hoover—were to come to power, they *could* suspend the internal controls at NSA and use the agency's vast databases to track domestic enemies or any target of their choosing. In that case, the Freedom Act would serve as a powerful brake to oppression: Because the government would no longer possess the data, it couldn't exploit the data.

That is the real—and the intended—effect of the reform: not so much to change the way surveillance technology is used today, but rather to limit the *potential* for abuse in the future.

For now, surveillance through telephone metadata is pretty sparse. In 2012, the NSA queried the database for 288 U.S. telephone numbers. As a result of those queries, the agency passed just 12 tips to the FBI. None of those tips led to the capture of a single terrorist or the halting of a terrorist plot. In fact, according to President Obama's independent commission on NSA reform, the telephone metadata program has never had any impact on countering terrorism.

A separate program called PRISM—authorized under Section 702 of the Foreign Intelligence Surveillance Act—lets the NSA track foreign terrorists and adversaries by intercepting their Internet traffic as it zips through U.S.—based servers. (Because of the nature of the technology, about 80 percent of the world's Internet traffic passes through U.S. servers at some point.) PRISM was another highly classified NSA program that Snowden uncovered. The *Washington Post* and *The Guardian* made it the subject of their Day 2 Snowden stories (right after the revelations about telephone metadata). Yet PRISM isn't touched at all by the USA Freedom Act, nor does any serious politician propose overhauling it. This is the case, even though PRISM datamining is a *much* bigger program than telephone metadata ever was, and it's potentially more intrusive, since it's hard to know whether, at first glance, an IP address belongs to an American or a foreigner.

The key difference is that PRISM has been a far more effective intelligence tool. Obama's independent commission—the same body that refuted official claims about telephone metadata's usefulness—concluded that PRISM had played an important role in stopping 53 terrorist plots.

Snowden's documents cited the names of all nine U.S. servers that cooperated (or, in some cases, were compelled to cooperate) with PRISM. His documents also provided details about the interception of Taliban email on the Afghan–Pakistan border, the monitoring of Iran's nuclear program, the line-item budget of the CIA, and the complete 50-page catalog of tools and techniques used by the elite hackers

> **No one should infer that government surveillance and cyberespionage have been dealt a serious setback.**

in the NSA's Office of Tailored Access Operations. (This last document is so sensitive that no U.S. or British publication wrote about it, though Germany's *Der Spiegel* reprinted it.)

This litany of leaks raises *doubts* about Snowden's claims as a whistleblower (the vast majority of his documents have nothing to do with domestic surveillance or malfeasance of any sort), and it highlights the fact that the NSA is involved in a lot more than probing the metadata of a few hundred telephone calls a year.

One valid point that Snowden and his defenders make is that the disclosures have sired a public discussion about the balance between privacy and security that otherwise would not have taken place, because everything about the NSA—including, for many years, its very existence—has been shrouded in such extreme secrecy. (The inside joke used to be that NSA stood for "No Such Agency.")

That said, the public discussion—despite a lot of good, well-informed articles in many publications—has, so far, been alarmingly shallow. Too many of these discussions, in the media and elsewhere, assume that the NSA "monitors" millions of Americans' phone calls. Too many newspaper articles about telephone metadata have been illustrated by a photo of the NSA's new 100,000-square-foot data center in Utah—when, in fact, all of its metadata files could probably fit in a camping trailer. And very little of the coverage draws a distinction—a few know that there is a difference—between Section 215 metadata collection (which has had no effect on stopping terrorism) and Section 702 data-interception (which has been remarkably successful).

A debate is certainly worth having on the latest nugget from Snowden's trove, reported in the June 5 *New York Times*, about an NSA program—secretly approved by the Justice Department in mid-2012—to monitor Internet servers for the presence of foreign hackers. The *Times* cites the concern of some legal scholars that the NSA may be crossing a line between intelligence and law-enforcement. In the wake of the Sept. 11 terrorist attacks, many criticized that the line had become too thick—so much so that the CIA, NSA, and FBI couldn't share intelligence information about the plotters in the lead-up to the attack. Some of the subsequent laws, which are now being reformed or called into question, were answers to those critics: Their sponsors spoke of the need to "break down the walls" and "connect the dots." Did we go too far in that direction, and are we going too far the other way as part of a backlash?

Ironically, right next to the *Times*' front-page scoop about the NSA's effort to track down hackers was a story reporting that China had hacked the personal data—including Social Security numbers—of 4 million U.S. government employees. A debate has been going on for some time—much of it outside public purview—over the extent to which the government should get involved in fighting hackers. One reason for the debate is that the NSA is the only government agency with the talent, technology, and resources to fend off hackers effectively. But letting the NSA loose on their trail discomfits many who contemplate the idea, because stopping hackers means monitoring the networks they're hacking, which means accessing the communications of ordinary Americans. How, and where, to draw the line? This is very much a conversation worth having. No one is having it just now.

One disturbing tidbit in that *Times* story: The NSA asked for the legal authority to monitor malicious cyberactivity even if the agency's analysts didn't know if the cyberattacker was a foreigner. The Justice Department did not grant that authority. But this is a cautionary tale about the need for government oversight—and a reassuring tale, as far as it goes, that oversight, to some meaningful extent, does exist.

The whole point—really, the only point—of the USA Freedom Act, and the overhaul of Section 215 telephone metadata, was to strengthen that oversight, to erect yet another fence that the intelligence agencies have to hurdle to get access to private information.

But no one should infer from this that we've entered into a new era or that government surveillance and cyberespionage have been—for better or worse—dealt a serious setback. The NSA is not in retreat, nor are its counterparts in Russia, China, Israel, France, Iran, North Korea, and other countries. That's not an excuse for complacency or alarm; it's cause for vigilance, oversight—and an understanding of what these programs are about.

2
Culture, Entertainment, and Media

© Bo Zaunders/Corbis

Two women with iPhones and sleeping child in a New York City subway car.

The Digital Stage and Its Players

In 2015, movie theaters, network and cable television, printed books, magazines, and newspapers still exist. However, the future of these now-venerable modes of entertainment and information is uncertain. The technological evolution of the digital age has brought about new cultural paradigms, changing the way that individuals interact with each other and with the broader world of information. Like an ecosystem in the grips of rapid environmental change, the transformation of the cultural landscape has opened up niches for new species of entertainment, connectivity, and information, while other cultural species are in a state of decline and some are heading for inevitable extinction. There are a few features that have become characteristics of the new breed of cultural products, including connectivity and collective participation, personalization, and the democratization of expression.

The End of the Captive Audience

American television began with three networks that created, produced, and distributed content to consumers. In this formative period, television became an American tradition and the networks operated on a fairly simple model, earning revenues from advertisers, as consumers were essentially "captive audiences" forced to sit through advertisements between each segment of a television show. In the 1980s, the model changed with the emergence of cable and satellite television, which led to a vastly increased number of networks and began the subscription service system in which viewers paid for a bundled package of channels. In the music industry, companies and artists once earned revenues through the sale of physical media like cassettes and CDs. Even as digital music became popular in the late 1990s, record companies still had sway, setting prices for consumers without other options. The standard model for television and music began changing in the 2000s with the growth of two new phenomena, "digital delivery" and "shared content."[1]

The shared content model is one in which users create and share their own videos and music, and largely began with the pioneer of the industry, YouTube, which debuted in 2005 and has been owned by Google since 2006.[2] YouTube is a social media platform that offers users a forum to "share" content and to engage in discussions about the content that they or other users post. Millions of videos appear on YouTube each month, most of which have little public appeal. However, amidst this sea, a small number of videos are so innovative, creative, or entertaining that they can attract tens of millions of viewers. YouTube created the concept of the "viral video," and helped to create a new breed of celebrity through YouTube videoblogs and web series. Internationally popular teen-singer Justin Bieber, for instance, was discovered through a video posted on YouTube.[3] A 2014 survey in *Variety*, found that Internet celebrities are more popular with viewers age 13 to 18 than traditional film and television stars.[4] YouTube video series have been a springboard to success for a wide variety of genres including comedy, self-help, fashion, design, cooking, and music.

Cable television networks and music companies have also been faced with a new form of competition from "digital delivery" or "streaming video and music services," like Netflix, Amazon, Hulu, Spotify, Pandora, and LastFM. Streaming radio and television companies offer users the ability to customize content, providing access to libraries of film and music that can be streamed at any time without the need to adhere to broadcast schedules. The model has vast advantages for consumers, providing more flexibility, and streaming services feature fewer advertisements and are funded primarily through subscription. In terms of streaming television, prices can remain low because Netflix, Amazon, and other streaming content providers do not need to pay cable television providers to show their content. By the 2010s, networks like ABC, NBC, HBO, AMC, IFC, and FX, once available only through cable or satellite providers, began offering content directly to the public or through one of the emerging streaming services.[5]

In the 2010s, streaming services like Amazon, Hulu, and Netflix began creating original television content available exclusively to subscribers. Netflix has been especially successful with original series like *Orange is the New Black* becoming among the most popular television series of the decade. Between 2013 and 2015, streaming channels began offering to stream feature films on the same date that they appear in theaters. Netflix took this a step further, with the announcement that the company would begin creating original films for streaming *and* theatrical release, thus creating a new source of competition for the theatrical industry as well. By 2015, every branch of the entertainment industry had been disrupted by the advent of streaming and shared content providers, but these developments were also a boon to consumers, increasing autonomy and variety in industries once limited by broadcast schedules and an outdated model of determining the worth and appeal of artists and expression.

No News is New News

As the entertainment industry struggles to adjust to the digital revolution, a similar transformation is underway in the news industry. Social media, especially Twitter and Facebook feeds, have become an important source of news information, in many cases outpacing traditional television and print news in terms of readership and popularity.[6] Web-only magazines and news sites like the *Huffington Post*, which debuted in 2005, and *BuzzFeed*, which emerged in 2006, have also been a transformative force. In 2008, Pew Research reported that online news surpassed print journalism for the first time in history and, in 2011, online news surpassed television news as well.[7]

Digital and shared content news offer a personalized news environment in which users can search for content without needing to adhere to a specific print or broadcast format. Digital news outlets are also more competitive because they operate at a fraction of the production costs of a traditional news service (including needing far fewer employees) and are able to offer "integrated" content that includes text, video, and audio through a single interface and a social component in which readers or viewers can comment on and discuss news stories.

Digital news services started as "news aggregators," collecting news from other sources, but not producing their own content. As online news dominated in the 2010s, some digital companies like *Vox Media, Huffington Post*, and *BuzzFeed*, began producing their own news stories. Between 2010 and 2015, a number of high profile journalists left traditional outlets to join digital services, including Glenn Greenwald of the *Guardian* and Pulitzer Prize winning journalist Mark Schoofs, of the *Wall Street Journal*. This exodus of major talent accompanied drastic reductions in revenues and audiences for mainstream news. A Pew Research study indicated that the growth of the digital market created 5,500 new media jobs between 2000 and 2013 but also resulted in the loss of more than 50,000 newspaper and broadcast media positions.[8] The impact of digital news sources is further compounded by informal sources like amateur news sites, blogs, and social media.

For all the advantages that digital news provides, the digital shift has had deleterious effects on the quality of coverage. Pew Research studies in 2014 indicate a drastic reduction in international, local, and investigative journalism around the world. This is primarily due to the fact that, while digital news costs less to produce, it is also far less profitable as many news magazines are offered to readers "free." Digital providers therefore have no subscription revenues to supplement advertising and cannot maintain adequate staff to provide in-depth coverage. The shrinking of the industry led to a reduction of interest in journalism studies at colleges and universities, and therefore to a smaller population of trained professionals serving a growing audience. Essentially news has become more participatory, personalized, interactive, and immediate, but with drastically reduced scope, quality, and reliability.

Digital Relationships and the Future of Expression

Digital dating is a multi-billion dollar industry around the world in which websites, like *Match, eHarmony*, and *OkCupid* offer virtual matchmaking services. Online matchmaking is increasingly accepted as a normal way to meet a prospective romantic partner and a 2009 study indicated that 22 percent of the heterosexual couples and more than 60 percent of same-sex couples met through online services.[9] However, some studies indicate that virtual matches, for a variety of reasons, are not as strong as those formed through traditional channels. A Michigan State University study from 2014, for instance, found that online matchmaking produces fewer lasting relationships[10] and a 2012 study found that the "matchmaking algorithms" that dating websites use are not effective indicators of compatibility.

The digital dating trend is only one example of how the digital age is influencing personal and social relationships. Increasingly, humans meet, become friends, and socialize through text, cellular phones, and video/voice chat, and the phenomenon of virtual socialization is a driver of cultural change. With the spread of mobile devices, individuals can remain constantly connected and almost any free moment can be used for socialization. However, some social scientists worry that the increasing reliance on virtual friendships and technology might have deleterious effects on personal relationships, especially for the generation raised to embrace digital social environments. A 2014 study from the Boston University School of Medicine, for instance, found that children introduced to interactive screens suffered from impaired social-emotional development,[11] and a UCLA study on sixth-grade students, found that students that went five days without interacting with a digital screen scored substantially better at reading facial expressions.[12]

Social media enables users to form large groups of "contacts" and can lead to more effective and innovative collaboration, but do social media friends fill the same psychological and social needs as "real" friends? Social scientist Robin Dunbar argues that there is a psychological aspect to traditional friendship, built on physical intimacy and shared experience, which cannot be reproduced in the digital environment. The addition of touch and the ability to see emotions in a person's face and body, provide levels of information that are not available through digital communication.[13] The question, then, is whether social media explosion is enhancing or inhibiting people's social lives.

Media experts report that there has been a recent backlash to the digital social and media trends of the past 20 years. In 2015, for instance, the sale of electronic books plummeted and traditional print books showed signs of making a comeback. The recent resurgence of interest came after years of declines that saw the number of physical bookstores in the world drop by more than 23 percent between 2000 and 2009.[14] Defenders of printed literature argue that there is no substitute for the experience of reading on paper, even if e-books offer benefits of convenience, reduced use of paper products, and other advantages.

Print literature is not the only evidence of a cultural backlash to the digital age. There has been an resurgence of interest in board games and tabletop role playing games since 2010, driven by consumers interested in the social phenomenon of gathering with friends and family to play together.[15] The smart phone revolution has similarly inspired "no cell phone" nights as a trend among young couples and friend groups, and an increasing number of businesses and educational institutions have banned carrying or using smart devices while in the office or the classroom. In general, the digital dominance of the modern world has raised concern over what might be lost as traditional modes of entertainment, information, and culture become obsolete.

For every industry and facet of culture struggling to remain profitable or relevant, the digital age has also introduced exciting new modes of expression and has enhanced connectivity and opportunity for people around the world. Modern consumers are not living in an apocalyptic era of cultural expression, but rather are witnessing the chaotic period that accompanies evolution. Moving forward, societies must attempt to figure out how best to protect expression and creativity in changing markets and for new generations of consumers.

Micah L. Issit

Notes

1. Magid, "Households Abandoning Cable and Satellite for Streaming."
2. Seabrook, "Streaming Dreams."
3. Mitchell, "Usher Introduces Teen Singer Justin Bieber."
4. Ault, "Survey: YouTube Stars More Popular."
5. Woodruff, "Can the Music Industry Survive the Streaming Revolution?"
6. Coyle, "Is Twitter The 21st Century News Source?"
7. Caumont, "12 Trends Shaping Digital News."
8. Jurkowitz, "The Growth in Digital Reporting."
9. Sohn, "Does Online Dating Work? Yes and No."
10. Aditi, "Cyberpsychology, Behavior, and Social Networking."
11. Walters, "Tablets and Smartphones May Affect Social and Emotional Development."
12. Wolpert, "In Our Digital World, Are Young People Losing the Ability to Read Emotions?"
13. Konnikova, "The Limits of Friendship."
14. Wallop, "The Kindle is Dead, The Book is Back. Or is it?"
15. Duffy, "Board Games' Golden Age: Sociable, Brilliant and Driven by the Internet."

Generation Y, Dating, and Technology: Digital Natives Struggle To Connect Offline

By Lauren Lord
Huffington Post Canada, January 14, 2013

As a professional matchmaker, Alison Green has seen all kinds of things get in the way of successful relationships.

But the Millennial Generation, aged 18 to 30, faces a particular problem with technology, she said, recalling one of her female clients who wanted to stop seeing a guy because he didn't text her enough between dates.

"I know people who have broken up or stopped dating because when they've come face-to-face, they can't communicate at all," Green said. "They could only communicate well through typing; but the smile on someone's face and the twinkle in their eye cannot be seen or felt by text message."

Effective communication is essential to the success of any relationship, but experts are divided on whether technology helps or hinders interpersonal connections.

"The bottom line is we're not going to fight technology. That's an impossible thing," said Green. "When it comes to dating, I think it's a matter of being grounded, realistic and understanding what technology's uses are for and what face-to-face is for."

The digitization of Millennials' social and romantic lives has changed everything. Love can be won, nurtured, and lost on social platforms, dating sites, and through text and instant messaging.

But the reliance on technology has made some milliennials wary of face-to-face communication and uncomfortable with the idea of venturing outside their social spheres, experts say.

"I think that, unfortunately, technology has been the demise of the relationship," said Karen Nemet, president of Matchmaking Canada and a professional matchmaker. "I think technology should be put aside when it comes to relationships, but I don't think it will be, because this generation was born with it attached to them."

The U.S-based Pew Research Center found in a 2010 study that 62 percent of Millennials are connected wirelessly to the Internet when they are not at home or work and that 65 percent of Millennials are disconnected just one hour a day or less. These numbers are believed to be higher for Canadians, who spend on average about 45 hours a month on the Internet, more time per capita than the populations of 11 countries, including the U.S. and China, according to a 2012 comScore study.

One in six Canadian Millennials owns a smartphone, and they are the largest users of Facebook and Youtube, says the 2011 broadband report by the Canadian Radio-television and Telecommunications Commission.

Sticking to Social Circles

Breeana Labella, a 20-year-old baking and pastry arts student at Toronto's George Brown College, feels that all this time spent indoors online is a major contributor to Millennials' lack of interpersonal skills.

"We're a lot more socially anxious now," said Labella, who recently met her boyfriend through a friend. "We would rather meet a friend of a friend than someone we have no connection to."

Technology acts as a crutch for many Millennials. Labella knows that it can be used to hide behind when too nervous to say something in person or used to meet people when too uncomfortable to approach people in a public setting.

"Millennials don't have the courage or guts to go up to people," Nemet said. "They don't know how to interact with people or how to approach people to find a spark."

Galena Rhoades, a senior researcher for the Center for Marital and Family Studies at the University of Denver, found that Millennials are much less likely than previous generations to date people they meet outside of their social groups or to go where other singles hang out. She also found that Millennials want to be socially connected to the people they date.

"I agree that there are not as many chance meetings as there used to be," Nemet said.

"As much as technology allows us to reach beyond our social circles, it makes us stay within them because of how we communicate."

Green believes that Millennials want to meet new people but are afraid to.

"They're afraid to try something new on their own. Everybody's insecure and everyone fears being judged," Green said.

"I think technology makes it easier to find someone who is part of your social network, and it's more likely that that person is going to be a good fit for you," Rhoades said.

She believes that Facebook 'stalking', a covert way of getting to know someone through their Facebook profile, is a "pretty darn good idea" because it provides a way for people to weed out those they know won't be a good fit for them.

Meeting Online

Many Millennials also try online dating, especially those who have finished college and are out in the working world, though some feel there's a stigma attached to it.

"You don't want to be the person who needed help to meet someone," said Labella, whose sister made an online dating account for her. "But I do think it will become a primary way to meet people, because people are lazy. We have so much information at our fingertips, so why not have dating the same way?"

> **"How do you create something meaningful if all you're doing is pressing a few buttons while you're sitting in your own space?"**

As Nemet puts it, online dating is like a candy store with thousands of profiles to choose from. She believes that it changes the way we look at people. People have become disposable and replaceable.

"I think (online dating) is a bad thing if people are not authentic and aren't telling the truth," Green said. "You have to be very cautious because these are complete strangers. When you're introduced to a friend or you meet somebody at school or work, you can maybe get a better sense of them. I'm not saying that everyone out there is a bad person, but you have to be careful today."

Balancing Text and Talk

Labella knows all too well that people try to make themselves look as good as they can online, even if it means lying. After a few bad online dating experiences, she has had enough. She met her current boyfriend through a friend and realizes that meeting new people in person is a "very natural and rewarding" experience. But even LaBella admits that Facebook and texting played a crucial role in the growth of her new relationship.

"I think in lots of ways these technologies can be a good thing for relationships," said Rhoades. "Being able to send one another flirty texts is a pretty useful tool in a relationship."

Samantha Joel, a University of Toronto PhD candidate in psychology studying dating and decisions about romantic relationships, agrees that technology is a force for good.

"Technology has made physical distance much less of a barrier than it used to be, which is a major advantage," said Joel.

On the downside, technology can make things worse when communication is misinterpreted.

"How you read something may not have been how it was intended," said Nemet. "There's no human interaction, and fights can happen this way," she said.

"Millennials are basically getting to know one another through their smartphones," said Green. "That creates a lack of motivation and effort. How do you create something meaningful if all you're doing is pressing a few buttons while you're sitting in your own space? Maybe you can create intrigue, but eventually you've got to spend quality time together in person."

Another problem, Green said, is that Millennial men haven't learned how to ask women out or how to woo them, and Millennial women aren't receiving this sort of attention.

Technology also means that partners can be in almost constant contact, when sometimes, as the old expression goes, distance makes the heart grow fonder.

"When you get home you don't have anything to talk about because you already know what happened in their day," Nemet said. "The age of technology seems to make it worse for people to have interaction."

Millennials will always be dependent on technology, but this doesn't mean that traditional methods of communication should be forgotten. Green believes that, when used well, technology can enhance a relationship, but it can't replace the chemistry of exploring each other in person.

"When it comes to love and when it comes to dating, you simply cannot replace face-to-face meetings with texting, typing or any other kind of technology, but you can find the balance," she said. "Technology will always be there, but we were born with a mouth and we have to use it."

The Selfie in the Digital Age: From Social Media to Sexting

By Holly Peek
Psychiatric Times, December 25, 2014

Because of the widespread use of selfies by young people in social media and digital communication, it is important to examine the psychology behind the selfie as well as ways mental health professionals can talk to adolescents and their parents about these issues.

The selfie phenomenon is a pervasive part of our culture: "selfie" was even *Oxford Dictionary's* word of the year in 2013. Because of the widespread use of selfies by young people in social media and digital communication, it is important to examine the psychology behind the selfie as well as ways mental health professionals can talk to adolescents and their parents about these issues.

Close-up of a "selfie"

Selfies are often seen as a representation of the narcissistic stereotype of the Millennial Generation or even as an indicator of low self-esteem, social dependence, or attention-seeking behavior. However, in the context of the digital age, in which young people are immersed in technology and connecting with one another via texting or social media, the selfie is perhaps not always negative. As a way to connect, selfies are often used to share important experiences and to express feelings at a particular time. It is not a new phenomenon for people to use photographs to document experiences or events. However, with smartphone capabilities, it is now possible to capture a moment spontaneously and to express mood without having to wave down a passerby to take a photo. These expressive images can immediately be shared with social circles via social media. A selfie can be more intimate than a staged photograph because it captures a moment in time that is meant to be shared with others. Many adolescents are trying to develop their sense of identity, experimenting with different looks and experiences, and deciding how they feel while sharing with their social circle. Selfies can be an important part of development within the digital age. Social networking itself has the potential to increase self-esteem and well-being in adolescents because they receive positive feedback on their social network profile. It also gives an opportunity for affiliation, self-expression, and control over self-presentation.[1] Since people control how they are portrayed in their social network profile, they are able to increase their self-esteem momentarily while presenting

> **A key point to healthy selfie and social media use is establishing and focusing on the digital interactions and connections made with others, rather than passively browsing others' digital lives.**

a positive self-view to others.[2] Social networking can enhance a person's self-esteem and positively affect his or her well-being, particularly when he or she is focused on strong ties to other people while browsing social network pages.[1]

Not all selfies and social media use are benign and without consequences. In fact, studies have shown that increased social media use can actually decrease life satisfaction. Researchers from the University of Michigan found that the more time spent on Facebook, the worse people felt. Researchers also found that more "direct" contact with other people, such as face-to-face interactions, led people to feel better about themselves over time.[3] Researchers from Humboldt University, Berlin, found that one-third of Facebook users in their study felt worse after visiting the site, which sparked frustration, jealousy, and decreased life satisfaction—particularly when viewing others' vacation and holiday photos. Those most vulnerable to these negative feelings were people who did not post or engage in any interpersonal Facebook interactions themselves, but who used it as an information source by browsing newsfeeds and others' profiles.[4]

Sexting

Perhaps a key point to healthy selfie and social media use is establishing and focusing on the digital interactions and connections made with others, rather than passively browsing others' digital lives. Whether social media use has a positive or negative effect on self-esteem or life satisfaction can be debated. However, a clear danger often comes with the private texting of nude or sexually charged selfies, often referred to as "sexting." When adolescents are caught sending nude selfies to one another, the issue of child pornography along with subsequent legal implications arises.

As a recent article in *The Atlantic*, "Why Kids Sext," demonstrates, sexting is prevalent in high school culture.[5] A 2009 Cox Communications study showed that 20 percent of teens reported having "participated in sexting" and a study by Pew Internet and American Life Project found that 15 percent of teens had received "nude or sexually suggestive" photographs on their cell phones.[6,7]

So why do teens sext? In a study of 617 college freshman, 30 percent reported sending a nude picture at some point during high school and 45 percent reported receiving one. The most common reason for sexting was because a date or a boyfriend or girlfriend wanted the picture: the hope was that sexting would attract that person. However, the most concerning motivation behind sexting was pressure or coercion. When a sext was sent under pressure, it was more likely to have a negative emotional impact on the person than if the sext was sent voluntarily. These pressured students were also more likely to have a history of excessive anxiety or dating violence. Luckily, 79 percent of the sexters reported that the picture itself caused no social or legal problems for them after they sent it.[8]

The cultural phenomenon of the selfie has taken many forms, whether in detailing events of our daily lives by sharing them on social media or sending nude or suggestive selfies through text messages. In our digital age, it is important for mental health professionals to be knowledgeable about the pervasiveness of social media use and sexting and to be able to talk about it with adolescent patients and their families. Exploring how an adolescent uses selfies, social media, and digital communication can be an important part of a mental health assessment and can open the door for discussions about self-esteem, body image, healthy relationships, and digital safety.

References:

1. Wilcox K, Stephen AT. Are close friends the enemy? Online social networks, self-esteem, and self-control. *J Consum Res*. 2013;40. doi:10.1086/668794.
2. Gonzales AL, Hancock JT. Mirror, mirror on my Facebook wall: effects of Facebook exposure on self-esteem. *Cyberpsychol Behav Soc Netw*. 2011;14:79-83.
3. Kross E, Verduyn P, Demiralp E, et al. Facebook use predicts declines in subjective well-being in young adults. *PLoS One*. August 2013. http://www.plosone.org/article/fetchObject.action?uri=infopercent3Adoipercent2F10.13.... Accessed November 12, 2014.
4. Krasnova H, Wenninger H, Widjaja T, Buxmann R. Envy on Facebook: a hidden threat to users' life Page 2 of 3 *The Selfie in the Digital Age: From Social Media to Sexting Published on Psychiatric Times satisfaction?* 2013. http://warhol.wiwi.hu-berlin.de/~hkrasnova/Ongoing_Research_files/WIpercent202... (http://www.psychiatrictimes.com). Accessed November 12, 2014.
5. Rosin H. Why kids sext. *The Atlantic*. October 14, 2014. http://m.theatlantic.com/magazine/archive/2014/11/why-kids-sext/380798/?.... Accessed November 12, 2014.
6. Thomas K. Teen *Online & Wireless Safety Survey: Cyberbullying, Sexting and Parental Controls*. May 2009. http://ksdresources.pbworks.com/f/2009_teen_survey_internet_and_wireless.... Accessed November 12, 2014.
7. Lenhart A. *Teens and Sexting*. Pew Research Center; December 15, 2009. http://www.pewinternet.org/files/old-media//Files/Reports/2009/PIP_Teens....Accessed November 12, 2014.
8. Englander E. Low risk associated with most teenage sexting: a study of 617 18-year-olds. In: *MARC Research Reports*. 2012. http://vc.bridgew.edu/cgi/viewcontent.cgi?article=1003&context=marc_reports. Accessed November 12, 2014.

Smartphones Are Killing Us— and Destroying Public Life

By Henry Grabar
Salon.com, November 2, 2013

The host collects phones at the door of the dinner party. At a law firm, partners maintain a no-device policy at meetings. Each day, a fleet of vans assembles outside New York's high schools, offering, for a small price, to store students' contraband during the day.* In situations where politeness and concentration are expected, backlash is mounting against our smartphones.

In public, of course, it's a free country. It's hard to think of a place beyond the sublime darkness of the movie theater where phone use is shunned, let alone regulated. (Even the cinematic exception is up for debate.) At restaurants, phones occupy that choice tablecloth real estate once reserved for a pack of cigarettes. In truly public space—on sidewalks, in parks, on buses and on trains—we move face down, our phones cradled like amulets.

No observer can fail to notice how deeply this development has changed urban life. A deft user can digitally enhance her experience of the city. She can study a map; discover an out-of-the-way restaurant; identify the trees that line the block and the architect who designed the building at the corner. She can photograph that building, share it with friends, and in doing so contribute her observations to a digital community. On her way to the bus (knowing just when it will arrive) she can report the existence of a pothole and check a local news blog.

It would be unfair to say this person isn't engaged in the city; on the contrary, she may be more finely attuned to neighborhood history and happenings than her companions. But her awareness is secondhand: She misses the quirks and cues of the sidewalk ballet, fails to make eye contact, and limits her perception to a claustrophobic one-fifth of normal. Engrossed in the virtual, she really isn't here with the rest of us.

Consider the case of a recent murder on a San Francisco train. On Sept. 23 [2013], in a crowded car, a man pulls a pistol from his jacket. In [journalist] Vivian Ho's words: "He raises the gun, pointing it across the aisle, before tucking it back against his side. He draws it out several more times, once using the hand holding the gun to wipe his nose. Dozens of passengers stand and sit just feet away—but none reacts. Their eyes, focused on smartphones and tablets, don't lift until the

---

> **Smartphone users in public operate under the illusion that they are in private. They exist... in "portable, private, personal territories."**

gunman fires a bullet into the back of a San Francisco State student getting off the train."

The incident is a powerful example of the sea change that public space has suffered in the age of hand-held computing. There are thousands of similar stories, less tragic, more common, that together sound the alarm for a new understanding of public space—one that accounts for the pervasiveness of glowing rectangles.

The glut of information technology separating us from our surroundings extends well beyond our pocket computers. "Never has distraction had such capacity to become total," writes the urban theorist Malcolm McCullough in *Ambient Commons: Attention in the Age of Embodied Information*. "Enclosed in cars, often in headphones, seldom in places where encounters are left to chance, often opting out of face-to-face meetings, and ever pursuing and being pursued by designed experiences, post-modern post urban city dwellers don't become dulled into retreat from public life; they grow up that way. The challenge is to reconnect."

McCullough sees ambient information, from advertisements to the music in shops to Taxi TV, as an assault on our attention. But he's no Luddite, and he's not oblivious to the powerful ideas that spring from the shared ground of technology and urbanism, like Citizen Science, SeeClickFix, or "Smart Cities." What he's calling for, in *Ambient Commons*, is "information environmentalism," the idea that the proliferation of embedded information deserves attention and study, from planners, architects, politicians, and especially from you and me.

Personal technology may be only a small part of McCullough's interpretation of "peak distraction," but for most people, the computer, tablet, and phone are a focal point. What permanent connectivity does to our minds is the subject of great debate. What it does to public space is less often acknowledged. Essentially, smartphone users in public operate under the illusion that they are in private. They exist, in the words of two Israeli researchers, in "portable, private, personal territories." Their memories of visited places are much worse than those of control subjects.

Our current strategy is to wire everything, everywhere—Wi-Fi in parks and subway tunnels; chargers in the squares bubbling with free electrical current like Roman drinking fountains. McCullough believes this freedom is irreversible. "To restrict information would be unacceptable," he writes. "The communications rights of individuals and communities must be inalienable, insuppressible, and not for sale." The tasks of filtering and decorum, he believes, fall to us as individuals.

Not everyone is so sure. Evgeny Morozov, reviewing McCullough's book in the *New Yorker*, approvingly cites the Dutch writer Christoph Lindner's argument for "slow spots" in cities. Morozov points out that the candy bar Kit Kat ("give me a break!") has set up benches with Wi-Fi blockers in Amsterdam. Would we like to see such a thing occur on a larger scale, in a museum, park, or in a neighborhood?

Of the three interwoven motivations for such regulations—danger, civility, and health—the first has been the most effective. Just as forty one states rapidly banned texting while driving, there are rumblings of "texting while walking" bans in reaction to pedestrian fatalities. Last year, Fort Lee, N.J., made international news when it began issuing jaywalking tickets to errant, phone-in-hand pedestrians who had veered into traffic. Distracted walking bans have been proposed (with little success, so far) in Arkansas, Illinois, Utah, New York, and Nevada. New York City paints "LOOK!" in its crosswalks.

In Japan, more than a dozen people fall off railway platforms while looking at their phones each year. Some pundits there have called for bans on texting while walking modeled after successful "smoking while walking" campaigns. Train station announcements remind commuters to look where they're going, and even mobile phone companies have begun to educate users about the dangers of looking at a phone while walking.

But for all the talk of danger, it's clear that the more frequent problem with "distracted walking" is that it's annoying—and one of several uncivil side effects of smartphone growth. Thus we have the "phone stack" game, where participants compete not to use their phones, and *The Guardian* columnist [Oliver Burkeman] who has pledged to almost bump into smartphone walkers, to teach 'em a lesson. Blind people in Japan say they are being jostled like never before; a man in a Seattle restaurant took a break from his three companions to watch "Homeland" on his iPad. Some restaurants, bars, and coffee shops have banned smartphones and computers for their corrosive social effects.

Anti-technology zoning for cognitive health—to protect us from our own worst instincts—is a more complex challenge. Ought urban parks, designed as restorative environments for a different age, be adapted to insulate visitors from the Internet as from noise, traffic, and commerce? The fact that you can address the connectivity problem yourself—just turn it off—doesn't preclude the possibility of an enforced solution. Airlines turn off the cabin lights despite the existence of blinders; earplugs don't reduce the popularity of Amtrak's Quiet Car. William Powers' idea for digitally free "Walden Zones," for example, has caught on in libraries—though because work, relaxation and distraction look so similar, the rules are hard to design. (A ready counter-argument: We are all so addicted to our media that withdrawal could be more stressful than blissful, buzzing distraction.)

Broadly speaking, any such regulations would require agreement that public computing has negative externalities—that your hand-held device is my problem.

McCullough is eager to situate these concerns in history and refers to movements against invasive advertising, light pollution, and smog. Morozov is particularly interested in the history and success of the anti-noise campaigners who reshaped the sound of the city.

But while it is obvious that light, noise, and smoke corrupt darkness, silence, and clean air, the consequences of smartphone use are far more opaque. What, exactly, does the man texting at the bar disrupt? Is the situation different if he is watching a violent movie or playing a visually arresting game? What does it mean to fellow patrons if his face is bathed in the steady glow of an e-book?

In the past, it has taken decades to pinpoint the external costs of other people's activities. Though smoking was often considered a bother in the nineteenth century, it wasn't until the 1920s that the aggravated parties coined the expression "second-hand smoke." (All this far before any awareness of its health risks.)

It seems clear that there is such a thing as secondhand glow. It impedes our movement on busy sidewalks, breaks our concentration in movie theaters and libraries, and makes our public places as dull and private as phone booths. The question is what to do about it.

Editor's Note

*In March 2015, the Department of Education lifted the ban on cell phones in New York City public schools.

What's Next for Art in the Digital Age: A Conversation To Be Continued

By Lori Kozlowski
Forbes, June 18, 2014

As the Internet, and technology in general, becomes more pervasive and enters into almost every sector of business—from education to the art world,—new markets naturally emerge and new questions get raised about our collective culture.

Specifically, fine art and technology—where these two disciplines touch—is a fascinating arena, as it opens up a plethora of ideas about what art is, how we exchange it, who makes money from it, and how we experience it.

In Los Angeles, a panel series on art and technology created by Saatchi Art, the world's leading online art gallery, started this spring and has continued throughout 2014.

Their most recent talk entitled "What's Next For Art In the Digital Age?" (which I moderated)—spurred artists, collectors, casual observers of art to ask several different questions about how we go forward, whether or not art is meant to be experienced in person, and how online outlets have helped artists to have better career paths.

While some believe art can only be experienced in person (in a gallery), others said that online platforms have aided their ability to make a living as working artists (something that has become increasingly harder to do).

As Los Angeles has become a less expensive alternative to other global hubs (like New York and London)—an artist community has grown. Alongside it, a burgeoning techeconomy has emerged in the last three years.

So it's become natural that we'd communally discuss what these mergers mean, how we can benefit from the disciplines colliding, and how art might be changing all together.

It's raised questions like: *Is it really the same thing to own a piece of original art, as it is to take an Instagram photo of it? Should you view art in person or can you get the same experience from viewing it online? What is the gallery experience like now?*

Other themes in these talks have included:

Art Exposure: Who Sees, Views, and Buys Art?

Saatchi Art's Chief Curator Rebecca Wilson, said, "We are very much at the heart of a very exciting moment where technology is beginning to change the way artists show their work and the way they are discovered by people who love art. We want to continue to be part of this conversation and are excited to hear a range of opinions on this and related topics."

> **"The world of technology itself has its roots in craftsmanship and art, so I think it makes perfect sense for artists to directly create, confront, and utilize technology."**

"From the events we have done so far here—and from the event I did in New York with Artspace, Artsy, and Artsicle—it seems evident that artists are looking for new ways to show their work and are no longer sitting back and waiting for the 'gallery moment' when someone from a gallery finally comes to their studio and agrees to represent them," she said.

"I think artists are open to exploring new paths to showing their work and finding people who might buy it."

"There is a recognition that the art world is intimidating and unwelcoming to many people. The Internet cuts across all this and, in contrast, provides an accessible, transparent, non-intimidating way to discover art."

Technology as an Artist's Medium

Part of the merger of art and tech also involves using technology as a medium. Much as one would use a paintbrush.

Los Angeles-based digital artist Sterling Crispin, said "Technology is an extension of humanity, and an embodiment of the human spirit. We are by our very nature, tool users. The world of technology itself has its roots in craftsmanship and art, so I think it makes perfect sense for artists to directly create, confront, and utilize technology."

"Personally, I try to engage technology in a poetic, humanist sense, by looking for truths closer to the nature of being, and expressing them through high technology. For instance, there is a visceral spark, when two people look into each other's eyes. That sort of warmth of the human experience is something I think technology can enhance and extend."

Maritza Lerman Yoes, Social Media Manager at the Los Angeles County Museum of Art, mentioned the museum's Art + Tech Lab—an experimental lab meant for selected artists to use technology provided by giant tech companies (like Google and SpaceX).

"The Art + Tech Lab at LACMA is so exciting because it's giving artists direct access to incredible technology that is usually hidden behind closed doors," she said.

"Presumably, the companies that chose to work with the lab are also interested to see how artists will use their technology. Maybe these artists will discover new uses for the technology. Maybe the companies and their technologies will be affected by the artists' work. That seems like a grand idea, but I think the conversation needs to expand: Are artists transforming technology? How are artists forecasting culture?" said Yoes.

What Art Is Really Worth

Who decides what art is worth was another theme that's emerged out of these talks and who the gatekeepers are determining an artwork's value.

"As more people gain access to art and are starting to buy it, I think the ecosystem of the art world will shift, expand, change in ways we don't quite know yet. I can imagine new markets being created by people buying and selling art online," said Wilson.

Whatever the micro-theme, the larger conversation has been incredibly popular and is becoming even wider.

Yoes said, "The topic of art and tech is very hot in L.A. right now. In the past three months, I've been invited to maybe six or seven talks."

"I have been thinking about new ways for these dialogues to happen for some time now. A format that helps to foster more creative collaborations between artists, technologists, and other creatives. I want to attend these talks to learn something new. To start asking new questions. So much more is possible."

Saatchi Art's series of panels and talks will continue in Los Angeles throughout the year (likely to be held monthly).

They also have plans to expand the conversation and their panel series to other cities in the U.S., including New York City.

In Los Angeles, a growing number of groups have started to examine the art and tech worlds.

Another organization doing so is the group ArtsTech LA, which has begun holding monthly gatherings hosted by Culture Brain, a think tank, studio, and academy, which examines culture, trends, and creativity.

What's most striking is that these continued conversations are happening more and more frequently and that whatever your relationship to art—artist, collector, curator, dealer, broker, lover, friend—there's great passion from all sides in thinking about how art appreciation, art education, and the careers of artists can be better served or amplified by the Internet.

There's also a strong recognition of what we can gain from the online experience and what we just have to see in person.

Further, there's an overall knowledge that the world we live in now demands both the digital and the tangible. The virtual and the reality.

Her Story: The Computer Game Where *True Detective* Meets Google

By Keith Stuart

The Guardian, February 27, 2015

In a cramped police interrogation room a woman is being questioned about her missing husband. Is he dead? Has she killed him? There are seven separate interviews, chopped up into short, teasing fragments, but the answers aren't immediately obvious. It's up the player to trawl through the video records and piece the mystery together.

This is the bare bones setup to *Her Story*, a fascinating police procedural game written by veteran developer Sam Barlow. Until a year ago, Barlow was working for mainstream studio Climax, where he designed the horror game, *Silent Hill: Shattered Memories*. Although it was part of a long-running series, the title was an oddity, hugely informed by Barlow's interest in the "interactive fiction" genre of highly narrative-based adventure games. Now he has set up on his own and is experimenting with new ways to build compelling interactive mysteries.

In *Her Story*, your job is to sit at a police terminal, accessing the video segments via a database search interface and then inputting relevant words to bring up more footage. The skill is in working out how the segments may have been tagged in this fictitious police system and then studying any newly discovered clips for clues and pointers. *Her Story* is effectively a crime thriller told through the conventions of an Internet search engine. It is *True Detective* crossed with Google.

The game simulates a 1990s PC desktop, placing the player directly into the fictional police mainframe.

"It is very of-the-moment, because we're all now typing words into text prompts more than we ever have before," says Barlow. "We intuitively get the process—the 'game mechanic'—of using the correct search terms, of narrowing a search, etc. I wanted to run with the idea that what you're doing is essentially Googling.

"There is the magic of thinking up the word that unlocks something hidden, the ability to imagine a concept, put into words, type it and the game puts flesh to that idea—it *is* magical, in my opinion."

The game also comments on another facet of modern digital society—the way in which social media and video sharing sites like YouTube have given rise to a culture of armchair detection. In high profile cases like Jodi Arias, Amanda Knox, and the

Boston bombing, the public became both juror and investigator, scouring news clips and search engines for clues, meaning that the justice process could be said to have become weirdly game-like. Jane's Addiction once sang: "The news is just another show." Now, it's just another interactive social media experience.

But *Her Story* also borrows from the ancient history of game design, specifically the late-1980s genre of desktop thrillers. Constrained by the graphical capabilities of machines like the Spectrum and Commodore 64, developers found a way to explore complex stories by using the computer interface itself as a framing mechanism. In titles like *Vera Cruz* and the espionage thriller based on the Forsyth novel, *The Fourth Protocol,* players would take on the role of a coder or researcher using a database or hacking a mainframe to unpick the narrative. In this way the hardware (and its intrinsic limitations) became the medium *and* the experience.

> **In high profile cases like Jodi Arias, Amanda Knox, and the Boston bombing, the public became both juror and investigator, scouring news clips and search engines for clues, meaning that the justice process could be said to have become weirdly game-like.**

In a similar way to *Her Story*, the classic Infogrames adventure *Vera Cruz* gives access to messages, statements, and photos from which the player must solve a crime.

When gaming visuals advanced during the 90s, the genre fell out of favor, but now independent developers are rediscovering its highly immersive appeal. Lucas Pope's award-winning title *Papers, Please* brilliantly explores the politics of immigration by putting the player behind the desk of a single border officer in an unstable Eastern European state. Now, *Her Story* presents its murder mystery though video clips that the players need to discover and retrieve in order to advance.

"The conceit of making the computer itself a prop in the game was so neat," says Barlow. "You weren't being transported to an alien world, the world of the game was being transported to your desk-bound reality. It brings about a different approach to the player-protagonist relationship, that has stuck with me. A lot of the built-in assumptions about modern games are tied so strongly to the conventions of having an avatar, navigating a 3D space … these conventions impose a lot of restrictions.

"3D space also makes things easy for developers," he adds. "Especially in say the horror genre. It's quite straightforward to stick a player inside a dimly lit 3D world, hand them a flashlight and get a certain level of engagement out the gate. I wanted to see what happened if I gave up the prop of immersion in a 3D world. I have a love for police procedural thrillers, so when I started thinking along these lines, my mind naturally pulled up a lot of influence from the 8-bit desktop games."

"The ability to imagine a concept, put into words, type it and the game put flesh to that idea—it is magical."

Sam Barlow

For Barlow, the aim wasn't just accessibility, it was about creating a game process that was familiar, that relied more on real-world skills than a knowledge of game conventions. "The loop of listening to the woman, coming up with search terms, interrogating her story, navigating it via her own words … it feels organic, like a real dialogue," he says. "It has this sense of making connections, of digging for truth that is more like 'being a detective' than many games that let you control a detective avatar. Even when there's frustration—trying hard to hit on the right search words, etc —it ends up feeling very much like the detective work that we see on our screens."

Even *LA Noire*, Rockstar's fifities-based detective drama relied as much on the player's driving and shooting skills as it did on interrogating suspects. Barlow wanted to remove all that video game stuff. "The key skills here are listening and thinking," he says. "I've had a lot of testers tell me that they were compelled to play with a notebook to hand, like a real police detective, which is not something they've done for a long time.

The game contains around two hours of footage, split into dozens of smaller sections.

"I'm very drawn to games where a large proportion of the experience takes place away from the screen. Strangely, I think it can be more involving than games where the attention is entirely focused on the game. I guess it moves the story out into the same sphere as other thought, which means the experience is not so easily compartmentalised."

Indeed, *Her Story* is part of a whole movement in game design that's getting away from familiar twitch-based mechanics and away from using story as merely a setting for the action. Partly this is about the rise of indies, but it's also about the arrival of new platforms. Barlow talks about the rise of the tablet, with its intuitive touch controls, and its sleek form factor that lets players curl in a chair and play – like reading a book. It's personal and intimate. He's been inspired by titles like *Blackbar*, Inkle's *80 days* and Emily Short's *Blood & Laurels*. All deal with themes of mystery and detection in intriguing ways.

Games haven't generally tended toward subtlety—this is something else Barlow wants to tackle. It is important if the medium is to mature and diversify. "One of the things that drew me to the police interview as a setting was a desire to make a game where subtext mattered," he says.

"In most games, because the story is communicating your challenges, it's a usability thing. Everything has to be on the surface: 'Go here, kill this, do that'. This mechanic of searching the woman's words kind of forces you to engage on a deeper level—it highlights those layers of meaning. The heart of any human story is subtext."

Beyond Cute Cats: How BuzzFeed Is Reinventing Itself

By Jennifer Saba
Reuters, February 23, 2014

BuzzFeed has come a long way from cat lists. This month one of its journalists was on the ground in Kiev reporting on the crisis in Ukraine, and last December it published an in-depth article on a Chinese dissident living in Harlem, New York.

The kittens haven't disappeared, but these days there is serious journalism as well.

When Facebook, Inc. tweaked its News Feed filters in December to weed out low-quality stories and other content, many were waiting to see if it would hurt publishers including BuzzFeed, the leading purveyor of "sponsored content" on the Web.

But that didn't happen to BuzzFeed, which continues to log impressive increases in readership. Founder and C.E.O. Jonah Peretti attributes that to the company's investment in building a news operation to complement its staple of entertainment and advertising-sponsored articles.

"There used to be this view that online publishing was about blogs that were very low-cost," said Peretti, 40, who helped start the popular *The Huffington Post*, now a unit of AOL Inc.

"You couldn't do things like investigations or have reporters. You could just do a smart take or snark on things. If you wanted to actually say, 'I'm going to sit down and talk to people and spend more than three hours on a story,' then you go work in old media. I think that is changing."

Founded in 2006, BuzzFeed is now among the top 10 most-visited news and information sites in the United States, joining the ranks of established media outlets like CNN and *The New York Times*.

Over the past year, BuzzFeed's traffic has soared fourfold, with more than 160 million unique visitors, according to online measurement and advertising firm Quantcast.

The social news and entertainment company is famous for producing advertising-sponsored "listicles" that go viral, such as lists of golden retrievers (sponsored by a pet food brand) or popular quizzes like "Which billionaire tycoon are you?" (News Corp's Rupert Murdoch took the quiz and got himself.)

Less known outside media circles is BuzzFeed's foray into serious journalism, which began two years ago when it hired Ben Smith, a former *Politico* reporter, as its editor-in-chief.

Headquartered in New York, BuzzFeed now has more than 150 journalists, an investigative reporting unit, bureaus in Australia and the United Kingdom, and foreign correspondents in far-flung places like Nairobi and the Middle East.

Its expansion comes amid a wave of investor interest in new media companies that are trying to capitalize on a decade-long wave of job cuts at newspapers and new technology that has upended how news and advertising are produced and distributed.

"As these social technology spaces like Google, Facebook, and Twitter compete with each other, they want to be the place you come and live in digital land," said Amy Mitchell, director of journalism research at the Pew Research Center. "A part of what people look for is news."

BuzzFeed, which has about 400 employees, raised $46 million in venture capital from the likes of Lerer Ventures, Hearst, RRE, and Japan's SoftBank.

"On the journalistic side, their new level of ambition makes a difference to me as an advertiser if it grows their audience," said Andrew Essex, vice chairman at advertising agency Droga5.

Supplier to Social Media Pipes

BuzzFeed and other media companies, ranging from upstarts like Vox Media and Upworthy to established media outlets such as *The Washington Post*, depend on social media to fuel readership. BuzzFeed gets about 75 percent of traffic referrals from social media, and the majority of that is from Facebook.

Last August, Facebook made a change to News Feed, which is prominently featured on a user's home page, pushing more stories through the stream. Many media sites saw their referral traffic soar. From September 2012 to September 2013, BuzzFeed's traffic jumped 855 percent, Facebook said in a blog post.

But in December, Facebook made another adjustment to News Feed's filters to improve the "quality" of the content.

BuzzFeed appears to have benefited—the number of people who visited the site rose 20 percent from December to mid-February, according to Quantcast. But other sites have suffered a drop in traffic since Facebook's tweaks.

An oft-cited rival of BuzzFeed is Upworthy, which aggregates material across the Web to help its content go viral. It experienced a dip in traffic during the same period. Upworthy, which grew at an even faster clip than BuzzFeed last year, experienced a 22 percent decrease in unique users from December to mid-February, according to Quantcast.

To be sure, there are many reasons why the number of people visiting a site can fluctuate from month to month, including seasonal factors and news items. An Upworthy spokeswoman pointed to the site's sharp rise in unique users from October to November, and said the number of people visiting Upworthy is still up significantly since October.

Facebook's dominance in social media is similar to Google's leading position in Web search. When the Internet giant made several changes to the formula that determines search query results to ensure more "quality" information, that hurt some media companies that relied on high search results, including Demand Media and Rap Genius.

> **"We don't question news organizations that create entertainment content anymore."**

Peretti said he is not worried that Facebook could harm BuzzFeed's prospects because the company distributes its content through other social media platforms, such as Twitter and LinkedIn. As long as there is benefit for the consumer, he said, any traffic fluctuations should work out in the long run.

BuzzFeed expects revenue to double to $120 million this year, according to a person familiar with the company. BuzzFeed declined to give financial figures. Peretti would only say that the company is profitable.

A Mash-Up

BuzzFeed's investors say they are focused on the company's growth, including news, and decline to discuss exit strategies such as an initial public offering or sale to another company.

"BuzzFeed must be in the real news business," said Kenneth Lerer, chairman of BuzzFeed and an investor in the company through New York-based Lerer Ventures.

"You have to deliver the whole package. There are not a lot of companies serving that demo with hard news," he said, referring to readers between the ages of 18 and 34.

BuzzFeed says it plans to hire more journalists and is keen to expand its foreign news coverage. Still, some media experts say balancing a mix of serious stories with sponsored content can be difficult.

For instance, BuzzFeed published a list of "alleged" secret menu items at McDonald's Corp, such as the Monster Mac, McCrepe, and Pie McFlurry. The list looked like an ad sponsored by the hamburger chain, but it was actually a tongue-in-cheek article produced by a BuzzFeed staff writer.

"The one question for BuzzFeed as they move further to produce their own journalism is whether they will be able to successfully straddle that line of content on their site that is purely for commercial gain and content that is meant to inform people about issues or events they care about," said the Pew Research Center's Mitchell.

No one expects sponsored content to go away, especially as advertisers are expected to earmark more dollars toward the ad form. Several major news organizations, including *The New York Times*, *The Guardian*, Time Inc, and Hearst, are publishing sponsored content. It offers more lucrative advertising rates at an average cost-per-thousand-users of around $10, compared with a banner ad that typically offers only 50 cents to $1 on the ad exchanges.

"We don't question news organizations that create entertainment content anymore," said Kyle Acquistapace, partner and director of media at the advertising firm Deutsch LA, about BuzzFeed's news expansion.

"What causes the question mark in BuzzFeed is if it can credibly make news when the top thing on its home screen is '28 things that people with big boobs can simply never do.' Can that door swing both ways? I think it can. It's a great mash-up."

BuzzFeed is confident that chasing hard news is good for business. Its in-depth report about the Chinese dissident in Harlem, Dr. Gao Yaojie, had more than 700,000 views. A 6,000-word story about buying a house in Detroit for $500 got 1.5 million views. For comparison, *The New York Times'* popular "Snow Fall" interactive feature got about 3.5 million views.

"There are things now that we can try and do that may have been out of our reach before," said Smith, BuzzFeed's editor-in-chief. "We can step back and swing for the fences. We can send reporters down rabbit holes, which I'm really excited about."

Content and Its Discontents

By James Surowiecki
The New Yorker, October 20, 2014

Adam Sandler, whatever his virtues, hardly seems like the kind of guy who might hold the fate of Hollywood in his hands. But when, recently, Netflix announced that it had signed a deal for Sandler to make four movies for its streaming service, and said that it would also be financing and streaming a sequel to *Crouching Tiger, Hidden Dragon,* journalists foretold an apocalypse for traditional moviegoing. The Sandler deal endangered "the underpinnings of the movie business." It promised to "doom theaters" and "destroy the box office." Who knew "You Don't Mess with the Zohan" mattered so much?

Netflix has always provoked hyperbole, with boosters saying that it will change everything and skeptics prophesying its imminent downfall. It has gone from Wall Street darling to Wall Street disaster and back again. Twice, the stock price has fallen more than 60 percent in a matter of months—in 2011 and 2012—but, since the start of 2013, it has risen more than three 300 percent. At the moment, Netflix can do no wrong. Practically everything the company does is being treated as radical and, of course, "hugely disruptive."

The hype is misleading. True, in its seventeen-year history Netflix has created two markets practically from scratch—online DVD rental, then video streaming. In the process, it has reinvented itself three times: it began as a traditional pay-per-rental company, turned itself into a subscription rental service, went into streaming, and then moved into original content. Yet, in the past couple of years, Netflix has actually become a rather familiar kind of business. Jeffrey Ulin, the former head of distribution at Lucasfilm and the author of *The Business of Media Distribution*, told me, "If you really look at Netflix, it's a pay-TV company." He went on, "People still think of Netflix as a video store, because that's their history. But the way a pay-TV service works is that people subscribe and pay a monthly fee for a service that aggregates content and offers original content of its own. That's exactly what Netflix does."

Netflix obviously has a much bigger catalogue of licensed content and less original content than pay-TV services like HBO and Showtime do. But the differences are diminishing: streaming matters more to pay-TV networks now, while Netflix is adding more original shows and movies. Toss in Amazon's streaming service—which has been licensing lots of TV shows and films and has also begun producing its own shows—and you're looking at a crowded marketplace.

"Content and Its Discontents" by James Surowiecki. Originally published by The New Yorker, October 20, 2013.

> **The situation is an unusually stark example of competitive capitalism in action: someone invents a new market and thrives, but the success shows competitors just how lucrative the market can be.**

This is a fundamental shift from streaming's early days. What set Netflix apart then was that it had far more—and far better—content than anyone else. It was able to build up a sizable catalogue of movies cheaply, because the streaming market was still small and Hollywood was happy to get the extra revenue. For instance, Netflix managed to license hundreds of movies from the Starz pay channel for a mere twenty-five million dollars a year.

So what changed? Netflix became a victim of its own success. Once content providers saw how popular streaming was becoming, they jacked up the price of their content. Netflix's success also attracted new competitors to the market (like Amazon) and encouraged existing competitors (like HBO) to invest more in streaming. "The calculus here is simple," Ulin told me. "There's lots more competition for viewers. That means it's harder to get content. And the content you do get costs more." In the past few years, Netflix has lost thousands of movies as licensing deals expired, and this year it will pay at least three billion dollars for content (much of it on children's programming and television shows). Though Netflix still streams plenty of great films, no one really thinks of it as a dream video store in the sky anymore. "Netflix used to really emphasize the breadth and depth of its catalogue," Dan Rayburn, a principal analyst at Frost & Sullivan, told me. "Now it puts a lot more emphasis on its original content."

As recently as 2011, Reed Hastings, Netflix's C.E.O., told investors, "We're better off letting other people take creative risks," rather than investing in original shows and movies. But the rising cost of content and the added competition meant that this approach would no longer fly. Thus *House of Cards* and *Orange Is the New Black* and the Sandler deal. "The carrot for any pay-TV service is really original content," Ulin said. That's the one thing you can guarantee people won't be able to find anywhere else. Of course, everyone is investing in original content, so Netflix just has to do what others are doing and hope that it can do it better.

Netflix has real advantages—the sophistication of its streaming technology, the trove of data it's amassed on viewing habits—but competition will make it hard to boost profits. HBO is making noises about a stand-alone streaming service, and Amazon's service comes free with Prime, so it's unlikely that Netflix will risk raising prices anytime soon. Content costs, meanwhile, will keep going up. The situation is an unusually stark example of competitive capitalism in action: someone invents a new market and thrives, but the success shows competitors just how lucrative the market can be. This may be hard on companies, but it's great for consumers, since they're getting more new shows and movies without having to spend another dime. We can sit on our couches, while Netflix runs as fast as it can just to keep its place.

YouTube at 10: How an Online Video Site Ate the Pop Culture Machine

By Caitlin Dewey
The Washington Post, February 15, 2015

It's a fact easily forgotten, in light of all the fame and the folly that's followed. But before Justin Bieber was a tabloid fixture, a Calvin Klein model and a teen cult leader, he was a tiny, backlit figure swaying in front of a cinderblock wall, singing Ne-Yo's "So Sick" in a pre-pubescent tenor.

It was a clip shot at a local singing competition in Stratford, Ontario, where Bieber—then twelve—placed third. When his mother uploaded it to YouTube in January 2007 to share with family members outside of Stratford, she likely didn't imagine that, eight years later, the fuzzy, handheld video would have 7.3 million views. Or that it would catch the attention of Bieber's now-manager, Scooter Braun. Or that, in the future, Bieber's meticulously orchestrated YouTube videos would be shot by teams of highly paid professionals.

In many ways, the narrative of Justin Bieber—arguably one of YouTube's original mainstream stars—is also the story of YouTube, itself. The massive video-sharing site turned 10 years old Saturday, which almost passes for old age on the Internet. And yet, for much of its history, YouTube was the upstart, the disruptor, the 12-year-old kid just revving to conquer the pop culture machine.

"That's what we're all about," co-founder Chad Hurley said in 2005. "We're the ultimate reality TV."

Of course, at the time, Hurley meant "reality TV" in its most literal sense: actual people, filming dispatches from their actual lives.

When Hurley and his cofounders registered the YouTube.com domain name above a pizza shop in California in February 2005, such a concept was actually, well, pretty much unheard of. The Internet video landscape, pre-YouTube, was like a dank, primordial plasma, virtually inaccessible to the average Web-user. Sure, there were a handful of other small-time video start-ups, most of them long gone today. And there was a class of savvy users who owned the servers and the bandwidth required to host video on their personal Web sites, a technically difficult—and potentially expensive—endeavor.

In fact, pressed to name one viral video that appeared before the dawn of YouTube, I suspect most people could only manage "Numa Numa"—the gloriously simple, unscripted webcam clip of a guy named Gary dancing to a Romanian pop song, which appeared online in December 2004. (Said clip has since, naturally, migrated to YouTube, where it's been watched 56 million times.)

Tech-heads had an inkling that online video could be big, of course. The early aughts had already seen the online migration of audio production (this was, after all, podcasting's pre-"Serial" heyday) and photography (YouTube, in its early days, was often called "Flickr for video.") Blogs were booming. Social networks like Myspace and Facebook, now a year old, were gaining steady steam.

Google was, accordingly, working on its own video product, a thing aptly called Google Video, that promised to bring all the polish of TV to your computer screen. Google Video courted major Hollywood producers and inked a content deal with the National Academy of Motion Picture Arts and Sciences—the same group of olds that brings you the Academy Awards. And Google Video would let plebeians upload content, too, provided they download Google's proprietary file-transfer software, submit a form's worth of content about the video, and wait for moderators to approve it.

YouTube had a way better idea: a video site that anyone and everyone could use. Appropriately, the first video ever uploaded to the site, on April 23, 2005, was an 19-second clip of baby-faced YouTube co-founder Jawed Karim standing in front of the elephant enclosure at the San Diego Zoo.

"Alright, here we are, in front of the elephants," he says. "The cool thing about these guys is that they have really, really, really long trunks. And that's cool. And that's pretty much all there is to say."

There it was: The ultimate reality TV. Life in all its unscripted, pedestrian honesty.

By November of that year, YouTube's users were uploading the equivalent of "one Blockbuster of videos every day," as YouTube's founders liked to tout in marketing materials. Few of the clips were actual blockbusters, of course—just pirated TV clips, or home videos from old concerts dubbed off VHS, or scenes captured from daily life on the new wave of consumer devices that shot digital video.

By December, the site was moving two Blockbusters per day. By January, they had dropped the Blockbuster metaphor all together. YouTube, media theorists and tech analysts argued, was fundamentally different from any genre of video that came before it: It represented the democratization of a medium that had once belonged solely to Hollywood studios and media conglomerates. It was the exaltation of the low and middle-brow. It was video largely for and by the people, with all the messiness and humanity and occasional stupidity that entailed.

Accordingly, many of YouTube's classic viral videos are simple productions, shot in cars or kitchens or suburban bedrooms: stuff like 2007's "Charlie Bit My Finger," in which a chubby-cheeked baby bites his not-much-older brother, or "Leave Britney Alone," in which a sobbing fan defends Britney Spears, or "Double Rainbow Guy"—remember Double Rainbow Guy?—who dissolves into tears when a rare double rainbow appears in Yosemite.

Even Bieber's early videos—the ones that caught the attention of Braun and ultimately launched his career—were amateur affairs, the captions written by his

> **It was video largely for and by the people, with all the messiness and humanity and occasional stupidity that entailed.**

mother, with apologies for the bad lighting. Which makes sense, frankly, because when Paris Hilton and the artist then known as Diddy began to use the platform in a professional capacity in 2006, YouTubers got mad.

There was something distinctly anti-professional, something recognizably ordinary, about those early viral videos. Critics like the Internet writer Paul Ford have gone so far as to argue their banal settings express something integral about "the American room" and the American psyche.

When, exactly, did that change?

As early as October 2006, when Google bought YouTube, users had already begun the usual choral wailing about advertising, corporate involvement, and the end of "the Wild West." (The Wild West couldn't live long, anyway: YouTube was already getting sued for copyright infringement.) That backlash began anew when, in 2007, Google introduced advertising on the platform, a critical pivot that made YouTube less a hobbyist hub for home videos, and more an opportunity to earn actual money.

By its fifth anniversary, in 2010, YouTubers were uploading twenty-four hours of video every minute, and some of them were making enough cash to quit their day jobs. Felix Kjellberg, the unlikely star behind YouTube's most popular channel, PewDiePie, dropped out of school to focus on his "YouTube career"—a phrase that hadn't even existed two years prior. Zoe Sugg, now the author of a record-breaking best-seller inspired in part by her YouTube experience, had transformed a shopping habit into a "lifestyle brand."

That same year, Hank and John Green—YouTube grandfathers, at that point, having vlogged since 2007—organized the first inaugural conference for video creators, called VidCon, at which some 1,400 people showed up. The latest iteration of VidCon drew 20,000 people and was attended by the likes of Fullscreen C.E.O. George Strompolos and Dreamworks C.E.O. Jeffrey Katzenberg.

"My company's budget is not very big. I have, like, 20 employees, and we're trying to make it work," Hank Green told Katzenberg during one on-stage interview. "… Should I be terrified of you?"

Today, you'll rarely come across a viral video that isn't rights-managed by a company like Jukin Media. And of the thirty most popular YouTube networks—basically, bundles of popular YouTube channels—a fifth are owned by media conglomerates, like Comcast, Disney, and AT&T. (Dreamworks, notably, bought the early YouTube network Awesomeness TV in May 2013.)

Now, when you watch a video by a YouTube "star," you're less likely to see beige bedroom walls than you are a slick, green-screened studio. Maybe even one of YouTube's very own studios, which the company launched for the use of its upper echelon in 2012.

This is all, of course, very good for YouTube, and even better for its stars, some of whom have parlayed their bizarre Internet stunts into actual careers and bona fide celebrity. There's no longer any use, in fact, in denying that YouTube's celebrities rank equal to their traditional, in terms of cultural import and influence: Green wrote a scathing essay to that effect on *Medium* shortly after interviewing President Obama in January.

That said, there's a reason videos like "the cutest gangsta I know" still, occasionally, go viral. And there's a reason that so many young, self-made video stars have moved on to Vine, and from Vine to Snapchat. There's something to be said for classic, innocent, garbage YouTube, the "ultimate reality TV."

Incidentally, archaeologists who study ancient cultures often learn about how people actually lived by studying not their temples or their monuments—but by their trash, by the thoughtless, ordinary, unpolished leftovers of daily life. YouTube was like that, once: A screen to show us how we really lived.

It's since moved on to better things. Less honest, maybe, but more profitable—and a whole lot more attractive.

When You "Literally Can't Even" Understand Your Teenager

By Amanda Hess
The New York Times, June 9, 2015

A little paradox of Internet celebrity is that a YouTube personality can amass millions upon millions of young fans by making it seem as if he's chatting with each of them one to one. Tyler Oakley, a 26-year-old man who identifies as a "professional fangirl," is a master of the genre. He has nerd glasses, pinchable cheeks, a quiff he dyes in shades of blue and green and more YouTube subscribers than Shakira. Some of his teenage admirers have told him that he is the very first gay person that they have ever seen. He models slumber party outfits and gushes over boy bands, giving the kids who watch him from their bedrooms a peek into a wider world.

In March 2012, Oakley faced the camera, balanced a laptop in his sightline and paged through a photo set of the curly-haired actor Darren Criss, whose turn as a hunky gay singer in *Glee* made him a fixture of teenage dreams. In these new pictures, which had just been leaked online, Criss was lounging on a beach wearing only a pair of low-rise jeans and a layer of perspiration. Oakley's videotaped reaction was exultant. "I literally cannot even," he informed his fans. "I can't even. I am unable to even. I have lost my ability to even. I am so unable to even. Oh, my God. Oh, my God!"

Soon, Oakley's groupies had immortalized his soliloquy in GIF form: "Can't" upon "can't," looping forever. Now they could conjure the GIF whenever they felt so overcome by emotion that they couldn't even complete a thought. Oakley was not the first to recast the sentence fragment "I can't even" as a stand-alone expression. He just helped shepherd it out of the insular realm of Tumblr fandom and into the wide-open Internet. That June, John Green, a writer of fiction for young adults who was awed by the praise for his breakaway novel, *The Fault in Our Stars*, pledged to "endeavor to regain my ability to even." When Kacey Musgraves, then 25, won Best Country Album at the 2014 Grammy Awards, besting Taylor Swift, she began her acceptance speech with two "I can't evens." And this season, *Saturday Night Live* aired a sketch in which a trio of nasal-toned interns "literally couldn't even" deal with their office's frigid temperature. The punch line lands when they screech at a fourth intern to close her window, and the audience sees her sitting helplessly at her desk, both arms suspended in plaster casts. "I can't," she whimpers. "I literally cannot."

In the all-seeing, all-hearing Internet age...teenage slang curdles from ingenious to embarrassing in record time, snapped up by brands for the purposes of selling their products.

For those who grew up when teenagers didn't "can't," the phrase might register as a whimper, as if Millennials have spun their inability to climb the staircase out of the parental basement into a mantra. At least the Valley Girls of the 1980s and '90s, who turned every statement into a question, and the vocal-fried pop tarts of the early 2000s, who growled almost inaudibly, had the decency to finish their sentences. Kids today, it seems, are so mindless that they can't even complete their verb phrases.

But if you really believe that teenage girls (and boys) don't know what they're talking about, it's more likely that they just don't want *you* to know what they're talking about. Teenagers may not be able to drive or vote or stay out past curfew or use the bathroom during school hours without permission, but they can talk. Their speech is the site of rebellion, and their slang provides shelter from adult scrutiny.

Guarding the secret code has become tricky, though. Teenagers used to listen for the telltale click of a parent eavesdropping on the telephone line. Now somebody (or something) is monitoring every keystroke. If an adult picks up a scrap of inscrutable teenager-speak via text or Twitter or a whisper wafting up from the back seat, she can access its definition on *Urban Dictionary* or *Genius* (which explains that "'I can't even' is a state of speechlessness too deep to even express in any other words"). In 1980, the linguist David Maurer, author of *The Big Con*, a book about underworld slang, wrote that "the migration of words from subculture to dominant culture is sparked by the amount of interaction between these groups," as well as by the dominant group's "interest in the behavior patterns" of the other. Parents are perennially nosy about what their teenagers are saying, and nowadays they can just Google it.

Adolescent slang has evolved a clever defense mechanism against the threat of the search engine. Teenagers have always used words to obscure their most sensitive subjects: He's a *total babe*, but he *sweats* this *ditz* who gets *blazed* every day after school. Now the most creative linguistic innovations elide the discussion topic entirely. "I can't even" is a confession interrupted. A close relative of "I can't even" is the keysmash, a string of actual gibberish—*asdf;lkl,* maybe—meant to signal that the typist has become so excited that she has lost control of her fingers. Or consider "Your fave could never," a gleeful taunt meaning roughly "Your favorite [actor] could never [pull off the beach ensemble modeled by my favorite actor, Darren Criss, over which I am literally dying right now]." A reader can only decipher its meaning if she has been briefed on the speaker's celebrity allegiances and is plugged into the web's breakneck gossip cycle. The modern revelation doubles as a warning: Reveal less.

This game offers only ephemeral rewards, and that's part of the point. If teenage slang stayed cool indefinitely, teenagers would never be able to outpace their parents. Maurer identified a few forking paths along which slang might travel. The word can stay slang, recirculating in the counterculture even when new speakers replace the old. It can be "elevated to respectability," integrated into the discourse of the middle-aged and middle class. Or it can just disappear, a casualty of a cultural shift that renders it moot.

In the all-seeing, all-hearing Internet age, there's a fourth path: Teenage slang curdles from ingenious to embarrassing in record time, snapped up by brands for the purposes of selling their products. "I can't even" has already embarked upon its promotional tour. On Twitter, Cap'n Crunch cereal "just can't even with this right now." Taco Bell "literally can't." When a public relations firm listed Charmin among its favorite Twitter brands last year, the toilet paper company tweeted: "We. Can't. Even." Applebee's favorited it. In turn, the young have found a way to monetize this process of linguistic appropriation. Corporations hire recent undergraduates to tune their Twitter feeds to appeal to their younger siblings. Tyler Oakley himself ran social media for companies before he graduated to what he calls "partnering with brands": Pepsi, MTV, Taco Bell. In exchange, this corporate sponsorship "allows me to stay a kid," Oakley told PBS's *Frontline* last year. "Very Peter Pan."

One old piece of slang that has not survived is "selling out." For the same report, *Frontline* asked a group of teenagers what the phrase meant to them. Nothing, they replied. Yesterday's sellouts, mocked for their contracts, are today's brand ambassadors, admired for their hustle. It's simultaneously depressing and impressive that the youth of America have worked out how to trade their slim cultural advantage for a shot at YouTube stardom or, more likely, a gig tweeting for toilet paper. Then again, when they find some way to talk themselves out of it, we'll be the last to know.

3
Education and the Brain

© Sandy Huffaker/Corbis

Sixth grade students use laptop computers during an algebra math class at Pershing Middle School in San Diego, CA. School districts around the country are racing to equip their classrooms with new technologies such as laptop computers and online networks as older methods of teaching become obsolete.

The E-volution of Education and Thought

In 2001, educational consultant Marc Prensky coined the term "digital natives" to refer to the students of the twenty-first century who grow up in a world suffused by digital technology, and argued that this generation represents the first "native speakers" of an emerging technological language. The "digital immigrants," in Prensky's metaphor, are those who, during their lifetimes, learn to use digital technology and the Internet, which he compares to the process of gaining fluency in a new language.[1]

For both natives and immigrants, digital technology has profoundly transformed the teaching and learning process, and innovative new technologies and trends emerge with each passing year. The evolution of education includes not only formal teaching and learning but also an overall expansion in the availability of knowledge to the population as a whole. As this new era has developed, however, there is increasing concern about how the transition to digital technology and modes of learning are changing the capabilities and habits of the mind.

Advantages of Digital Learning

The integration of digital technology into education began with the first "smart classrooms" in the late 1990s and 2000s in which computers, digital whiteboards, and projectors were integrated into classrooms, allowing teachers to supplement their lessons with digital tools and multimedia presentations. During this same period, a number of educational institutions began using web interfaces to allow students and teachers to communicate online and to allow students to obtain learning materials and turn in assignments digitally.

Education can also be enhanced by providing students with digital tools like laptops, tablets, and other smart devices. Traditionally, the availability of digital technology was limited by household budgets, but increasingly US schools are able to provide students with access to digital technology. A 2014 study found that 33 percent of high school students, and a similar percentage of middle school and elementary school students in the United States had access to school-issued mobile devices to enhance their education. The study found that 75 percent of high school students used computers to access class information through online portals and 52 percent took tests online.[2] Online education was the next major innovation of the digital age, allowing students to participate in classes entirely through the web without needing to visit a classroom. The first online classes were offered in the late 1990s and gained popularity in the 2000s. A 2014 report from the Babson Research Group indicated that 7.1 million higher education students (33.5 percent) took at least one online class per year.[3] The advent of online classes opened educational opportunities to individuals who had been previously unable to take classes due to work and family commitments. Online classes tend to be more flexible and, as they cost less to produce, can also be more affordable for students. The study found that more than 66 percent of higher education administrators considered online education an essential part of modern education and believed that online education quality was similar to traditional education. However, online education has disadvantages as well and learning specialists argue that online classes are best for self-motivated, independent learners and should be avoided by students that benefit more from direct teacher interaction and a more rigid lecture schedule.[4] Another innovation, blending online and traditional models, is the "flipped classroom" in which lectures are presented through online videos, but students still come to classrooms to engage in tutoring and collaborative work. The flipped model has become popular in the 2010s, with supporters arguing that the system allows teachers to provide individual attention to students in helping them to understand the material presented through video lectures.[5]

One of the hallmarks of the digital age has been the democratization of knowledge. This includes the emergence of shared information platforms like Wikipedia, where users collectively create and edit encyclopedia entries. The drawback to Wiki sites is the lack of expert editorial review, making them inappropriate for most types of scholarly research. However, a number of websites have emerged since the late 1990s in which scholars and experts collaborate to create and review databases that are considered appropriate research. One example is the Stanford Encyclopedia of Philosophy, an online collaborative reference that provides articles on scholarly philosophy written and reviewed by experts in the field. Another supplement to education has come in the form of unaccredited online teaching platforms like Lynda.com in which students pay for access to expert tutorials but do not earn credit towards a degree. Lynda.com, which is now owned by the professional networking site LinkedIn, offers education in design, animation, web development, photography, and a variety of other fields.[6]

A new and controversial trend emerged from online learning in the 2010s, known as "Massive Open Online Courses," or "MOOCs," in which scholars allowed open online enrollment to unaccredited classes. Stanford University was a pioneer in the field, offering a 2011 class in Artificial Intelligence that attracted 160,000 students.[7] Some educational analysts believe that the open education model could one day challenge higher education institutions while others believe that the MOOC innovation is little more than a passing trend. In any case, the MOOC is an evolution of the "knowledge for everyone" spirit that has informed and inspired new trends in education in the digital age. Whatever the success of MOOCs, and unaccredited teaching sites like Lynda, the underlying idea, expanding professional level training and instruction to those who are unable to engage in a full degree program, indicates a fundamental shift in the way that humanity is approaching education.

Access and Equality

In a 1996 article in the *New York Times*, "A New Gulf in American Education, the

Digital Divide," journalist Gary Poole called attention to the growing disparity in educational opportunities based on access to digital technology.[8] The term "digital divide" became the accepted term for this technology disparity and further research showed that digital access is becoming one of the most significant determinants of educational and professional attainment.

According to Pew Research studies in 2013, 70 percent of US citizens with web access were using high speed Internet and 56 percent of Americans used smartphones capable of accessing the Internet services through Wi-Fi or cellular networks.[9] The US government's E-Rate program, started in 1998, has been instrumental in bringing the Internet to US k-12 schools, of which 99 percent have had some degree of Internet access since 2006. However, access to the Internet is only one step in bridging the divide as increasingly high speed Internet is required for effective use of websites and services and training in the latest digital technology is also essential as rapid technological evolution makes older generations of devices obsolete.[10] Essentially then, the digital divide isn't only about access, but also about the quality of access. Outside of the developed nations, billions of people are without Internet access of any kind. In the African nation of Chad, for instance, only 2 out of every 100 people have Internet access according to World Bank studies.[11]

Access to digital technology isn't only about providing a portal to the information and connectivity of the web, but also about learning how to use modern, current technology as digital devices become more and more important in the professional environment. This is especially important for young students, as the world's commerce and professional environments will continue to become further ingrained with technology and those who begin training at earlier ages can better attain fluency in the language and techniques needed to work in virtual settings.[12]

Digital Costs and Benefits

One of the most notable technological shifts of the twenty-first century has been the digitization of written knowledge and the subsequent transition from print to digital in book and periodicals. Digital books and periodicals have substantial benefits including giving students and readers the ability to carry thousands of periodicals and books stored in a single device and drastically reducing the cost and ecological demand of the print industry. In addition, digital text is searchable, both through databases and within a document, and this has revolutionized scholarly research.[13] However, as this trend has proceeded, experts have learned that digital reading may have some significant disadvantages. A 2013 article in *Scientific American*, for instance, showed that that reading on paper creates a physical experience that enhances recall, decreases reading speed, and leads to deeper levels of comprehension.[14] Studies focusing on the costs and benefits of literary digitization are part of an increasing body of research studying the psychological and social effects of society's increasing reliance on digital technology. Another example can be found in studies of digital communication and literacy among American students. Whatever the relative literary value of a text message or Facebook post, educators have noted that the importance of writing in Internet communication has led to an overall increase in interest and familiarity among students. In a 2013 article in *The Atlantic*, educator Andrew Simmons argued that social media has improved the quality of student writing and, as an added benefit, has increased the tendency for young students to express themselves emotionally in their communications.[15] Alternatively, some teachers argue that the social media teaches students to write using jargon and that the knowledge of "formal writing" has suffered.[16]

There has also been concern among psychologists that the rapid pace of information and distraction through mobile devices can have lasting effects on attention span. A 2014 study published in the journal *Social Psychology* indicated that even the presence of a cell phone reduced cognitive interaction and conversational ability, whether or not a person was using the device.[17] Studies have also shown that reliance on digital devices has negative effects on memory and may negatively effect the ability to focus during face-to-face interactions.[18] Studies like these indicate that the benefit of constant connectivity may come at significant cost to the individual and society as a whole. The problem may be more pronounced among young learners, whose early adoption of smart devices has a greater impact on cognitive habits and tendencies. It remains to be seen, however, how humanity will adjust as digital natives pass on what they have learned to the next generation. It is possible that future generations will develop the ability to filter and focus through the potential distractions posed by digital tools and toys, essentially learning how to thrive in an increasingly competitive informational environment.

Micah L. Issit

Notes

1. Prensky, "Digital Natives, Digital Immigrants."
2. Nagel, "One Third of U.S. Students Use School-Issues Mobile Devices."
3. Allen and Seaman, "Grade Change."
4. Snyder, "The Benefits of Online Learning."
5. Fitzpatrick, "Classroom Lectures Go Digital."
6. Morgan, "What LinkedIn's Acquisition of Lynda Means for Talent Management."
7 Lewin, "Instruction for Masses Knocks Down Campus Walls."
8. Poole, "A New Gulf in American Education, the Digital Divide."
9. Rainie, "The State of Digital Divides."
10. Ross, "When Students Can't Go Online."
11. "Internet Users (per 100 people)."
12. Gupta, "Addressing the Digital Divide."
13. Novack, "Should College Students Be Forced To Buy E-Books?"
14. Jabr, "The Reading Brain in the Digital Age: The Science of Paper Versus Screens."
15. Simmons, Andrew. "Facebook Has Transformed My Students' Writing—For the Better."
16. Purcell, Buchanan, Friedrich, "The Impact of Digital Tools on Student Writing and How Writing is Taught in Schools."
17. Thornton, et al, "The Mere Presence of a Cell Phone May be Distracting."
18. Lin, "How Your Cell Phone Hurts Your Relationships."

Can the iPad Rescue a Struggling American Education System?

By Christina Bonnington
Wired, March 6, 2013

Matthew Stoltzfus could never get his students to see chemistry like he sees chemistry until he added a digital component to his lesson plan.

Stoltzfus, a chemistry lecturer at Ohio State University, struggled for years to bring complex chemical equations to life on the blackboard, but always saw students' eyes glaze over. Then he added animations and interactive media to his general chemistry curriculum. Suddenly, he saw students' faces light up in understanding.

"When I see a chemical reaction on a piece of paper, I don't see coefficients and symbols, I see a bucket of molecules reacting," Stoltzfus said. "But I don't think our students see that big bucket of molecules. We can give students a better idea of what's happening at a molecular level with animations and interactive elements."

And many such students are getting this multifaceted education on tablets. Tablets are reinventing how students access and interact with educational material and how teachers assess and monitor students' performance at a time when many schools are understaffed and many classrooms overcrowded. Millions of grade school and university students worldwide are using iPads to visualize difficult concepts, revisit lectures on their own time, and augment lessons with videos, interactive widgets, and animations.

"In the shift to digital, it's not just about replacing textbooks but inventing new ways of learning," Forrester analyst Sarah Rotman Epps said. "Some of the education apps being developed for iPad are approaching learning in an entirely new way, and that's exciting."

Sallie Severns, founder and C.E.O. of iOS app Answer Underground, told *Wired* that tablets' simplicity, ease of use, and the massive range of academically minded applications available are drawing teachers and educational technologists to the platform in droves.

Tablet-based learning is no longer the niche it was a year or two ago when we saw a handful of early adopters jump on board with iPad pilot studies in selected grades and classrooms. Schools and teachers are embracing the technology in a big way. A Pew study of 2,462 Advanced Placement and National Writing Project teachers nationwide found that 43 percent have students complete assignments using

Millions of grade school and university students worldwide are using iPads to visualize difficult concepts, revisit lectures on their own time, and augment lessons with videos, interactive widgets, and animations.

tablets in the classroom. A PBS LearningMedia study found 35 percent of K-12 teachers surveyed nationwide have a tablet or e-reader in their classroom, up from 20 percent a year ago.

The iPad is the most popular tablet option among educators. Apple sold 4.5 million of them to schools and other educational institutions nationwide last year (it sold 8 million internationally), up from 1.5 million in 2011.

Tablets have proven especially popular in elementary education, and they've been a "revolution" for kids younger than eight because they're fun and intuitive, said Sara DeWitt, Vice President at PBS KIDS Digital. The taps and swipes are easy to learn, so kids spend more time learning their lessons, not their hardware.

"The iPad has given us an opportunity to make technology transparent," she said. "The touchscreen interface is so much more natural than a mouse and keyboard, kids can jump right in."

That said, there's more to using a tablet in the classroom than handing them out at the door.

Teachers and school district administrators must decide how to best integrate them into the curriculum, considering things like the number of tablets per classroom, which grades receive them first, what content is accessed, and when.

"How tablets are integrated into classrooms is key to success," Severns said. "Planning, preparation, implementation and evaluating apps are key to using this new technology." While adoption is broad, the ways educators are using them varies from class to class, school to district.

Apple's iTunes U is one tool making iPad-based course integration easier by helping teachers create and curate a wholly digital curriculum. Teachers can pack iBooks textbooks (including titles from major publishers like McGraw-Hill, Pearson Education, and Houghton Mifflin Harcourt), audio and video, documents, and even iOS apps into a single package that students navigate as they progress through the course.

When it launched in 2007, iTunes U was a source for audio and video lectures students could use on their iPods, but Apple introduced a new app in January 2012 that leveraged the capabilities of the iPhone and iPad, adding in iOS apps, iBooks, and video to the mix. Downloads have topped 1 billion, and iTunes U is used by more than 1,200 colleges and universities and more than 1,200 K-12 schools and districts.

Severns said iTunes U is "paving the way for how educators teach and students learn" because it allows for unprecedented ease in distributing and accessing academic content. Simply log on and it's there.

Still, it can be easier or more beneficial, particularly in K-12 classrooms, for teachers to just round up a collection of dedicated apps (there are more than 75,000 education related apps in the App Store) for students to use. There, tablets are often supplementary rather than being used for the bulk of coursework, so a full blown iPad-based course (like with iTunes U) isn't necessary. Tablet time is often a reward, where students will get to play a game that isn't just fun, it's building on skills and concepts they're focusing on in class. iOS has built-in controls that can let teachers lock an iPad into a single app and place restrictions on functions like browser access to ensure kids are learning and not goofing off.

Third party apps also can take advantage of the social networking opportunity inherent to mobile devices. Students can ask questions of each other and the teacher, something Severns said is absolutely necessary to ensure everyone understands the information.

Stoltzfus, the chemistry lecturer in Ohio, said the social networking aspect allows him to poll students mid-lecture to determine how well they're understanding the topic. He can adjust his lesson on the fly, which he said is "where tablets can really, really help us in terms of progressing in pedagogy."

We are approaching the day when tablets won't be an option, but a requirement. Arkansas State University, for example, requires all incoming freshman to have their own iPad.

But as tablet adoption proliferates amongst those students and schools with the money to buy the devices, low-income students and cash-strapped schools may be left behind. That could deepen the divide between those with access to the latest learning tools and those with traditional technology and limited Internet access.

We're seeing this kind of segregation already, but some of it is self-imposed. Many college freshmen, for example, are using iPads in class while many upperclassmen prefer their laptops or even pen and paper for coursework.

"Five years from now when young students come into college, the expectation is going to be a lot different than it is now. They'll be used to using tablets in middle and high school," Stoltzfus said. "We have to be the ones that are pushing the limits."

Inside the Flipped Classroom

By Katherine Mangan
The Chronicle of Higher Education, October 4, 2013

Sara Infante listens intently and scribbles notes as her chemistry professor describes how to identify the masses and atomic numbers of two isotopes of carbon. When it's time to fill in a table showing that she understands the lecture so far, she clicks her mouse, and the lecture, which is being delivered online, freezes on the computer screen.

The questions that Ms. Infante and her classmates at Southwestern University ask their professor, Maha Zewail-Foote, will help shape the next day's session in the classroom. There, moving on to more-complex topics, she'll help them tackle the kinds of problems that used to be given as homework.

It's Ms. Infante's first experience with the flipped classroom, where traditional classwork is done at home and homework is done in class.

"I like this because when you're listening to the lecture at home and you don't get something, you can rewind and replay it as many times as you need to," says Ms. Infante, 19, a sophomore majoring in animal behavior who hopes to become a marine-mammal trainer.

"And when you're working through problems," she adds, "you aren't sitting in your room pulling your hair out because you didn't retain the information from the lecture."

The video for the semester's first flipped class, with its accompanying tables and diagrams, lasted just under 10 minutes. They're usually five to seven minutes, which Ms. Zewail-Foote describes as the attention span of most students. But in her opinion, a well-crafted, concise, 10-minute video that students can pause and replay as many times as they want packs more teaching in than a 20-minute lecture.

The course Web site include outlines that students fill in while they're listening to her recorded lessons, each of which ends with a short quiz.

"Between the lecture outline and video, they should come to class ready," Ms. Zewail-Foote says. "They understand how to calculate average atomic mass, so we can jump right in."

At colleges nationwide, more and more professors are inverting homework and classwork this way, using technology to give students a head start on classroom sessions where they can be active participants and not just listeners.

The flipped classroom is not for everyone. Many students feel lost without a traditional lecture to get them started, and some instructors are reluctant to give up the podium for a role on the sidelines, says Carol A. Twigg, president of the National Center for Academic Transformation.

Since 1999 the center has helped redesign about 300 courses on 159 campuses, often in a flipped format, using technology to cut costs and improve learning. (Southwestern did not work with the center on the revamped chemistry course, but it did consult with other proponents of the technique, as part of a project, supported by the Howard Hughes Medical Institute, aimed at making Southwestern's science curriculum more hands-on.)

Many of the national center's course redesigns have been in remedial math, financed by $2.2 million from the Bill & Melinda Gates Foundation. The center has also helped flip courses in subjects as diverse as Spanish, psychology, nutrition, and anatomy.

> **The problem-solving and personalized interaction that take place face-to-face sets these classes apart from massive open online courses, or MOOCs, which too often consist mainly of recorded talks.**

"The traditional classroom typically consists of a lecture of some kind where students are listening or watching the professor," Ms. Twigg says. "Then they do the hard work, solving problems, on their own. The notion is, flip that experience so the professor can help students when they need the help."

Switching from the role of "sage on the stage" to "guide on the side" requires a professional and cultural shift that many faculty members resist, she says. "It's easier to stand up and give the same lecture you've been giving for 20 years than it is to rethink your course, come up with new activities, and really engage your students."

The problem-solving and personalized interaction that take place face-to-face sets these classes apart from massive open online courses, or MOOCs, which too often consist mainly of recorded talks, she says, explaining that flipping the classroom requires more than simply moving lectures online.

Teaching to the masses is tempting, but it's not the same as offering a flipped course, she says. "Let's say I am the most brilliant lecturer of intelligent design, and now I'll have an audience of 200,000 instead of 200.

"The problem is, the success rates are awful," she adds, in a not-so-subtle jab at Sebastian Thrun, the former Stanford University professor who co-founded the MOOC platform Udacity last year, after his online "Introduction to Artificial Intelligence" course attracted more than 160,000 students worldwide. About 23,000 of those students completed the course.

While MOOCs can be effective at delivering content, flipped classrooms make students active participants in their education, says Southwestern's new president, Edward B. Burger. The former mathematics professor at Williams College has created more than 3,000 instructional CD-ROMS and videos in math that are used in classrooms from kindergarten through college. Instead of having students struggle to figure out problems in their dorm rooms at 2 a.m., he says, "I want to be there when students hit those roadblocks."

Although he didn't call it a flipped classroom at the time, Mr. Burger cultivated the technique of "inverting the roles of homework and classwork," an approach that contributed to his winning a national teaching award in 2010.

Back in the common room of her dormitory suite at Southwestern, Ms. Infante has finished listening to the online lecture and asks her roommate, who's curled up in an armchair across the room, for a scientific calculator so she can take the quiz.

Her roommate's own chemistry professor, Emily Niemeyer, offers the format once a week, on what she calls "flipped Fridays."

Ms. Infante aces the quiz and doesn't have any questions for her professor. Other students were stumped by a few questions, Ms. Zewail-Foote notes the following morning as she prepares for class. One student asked: "Will there ever be a time when an atom is not neutral and the number of protons and electrons don't balance each other out?"

The explanation would normally come up in Chapter 4, but Ms. Zewail-Foote decides to work the answer into today's classroom problem-solving session. Reviewing the quiz results, she can tell that students generally understand the material, so she is comfortable accelerating the pace a bit.

There's little danger that students are going to nod off in her class, because she peppers it with questions that they must answer using their hand-held clickers. If twenty-nine students have clicked their answers, she pauses before moving on until all thirty have weighed in.

Shortly after the class begins, students cluster their desks into groups of three or four to work on problems as she walks around, occasionally crouching next to those who seem stuck.

When the semester's first flipped-classroom session is over, at least one student isn't yet sold. "I'm going to fail this class," says Alex Petrucci, a 20-year-old sophomore. The pre-class video didn't adequately prepare her for the problems she was asked to solve in class, she complains, and even with a cluster of classmates to confer with, she felt lost.

That kind of reaction isn't uncommon when classes are flipped.

An aeronautics-engineering professor at Mississippi State University who taught a course in statics, in a flipped format, encountered similar resistance from some students who couldn't get used to online lectures.

Masoud Rais-Rohani, who worked with the National Center for Academic Transformation to revamp the statics course, says having students watch videos, take quizzes, and reflect on what they learned before each class session made it possible to spend class time doing hands-on projects that the course had never before had room for, like working with physical models of bridges and calculating the loads they can carry.

Nevertheless, the flipped format was put on hold for the statics course this year, after tests revealed that learning outcomes were about the same in the flipped class-es, which cost the same, or slightly more, because of the extra tutors and teaching assistants required. In addition, students were grumbling.

"Some complained that the instructors were good, but they were wasted if they weren't standing in front of the class lecturing," says Pasquale Cinnella, head of the aerospace-engineering department.

If engineering enrollment continues to increase, and the classes become more cost-effective, Mr. Cinnella says, he may reinstate the flipped format.

Eventually, Mr. Rais-Rohani hopes to win over skeptics like the student who responded to his survey by saying: "If I am paying for a class and a professor to teach me, then I do not want to teach myself for homework and have homework for class."

In time, the professor hopes, more students will come around to agreeing with the student who found that the flipped format forced him to improve his study skills and take a more active role in his learning. "Now," that student wrote, "I'm respon-sible for my grade."

Educational Technology Isn't Leveling the Playing Field

By Annie Murphy Paul
Slate, July 25, 2014

The local name for the Philadelphia neighborhood of Kensington is "the Badlands," and with good reason. Pockmarked with empty lots and burned-out row houses, the area has an unemployment rate of 29 percent and a poverty rate of 90 percent. Just a few miles to the northwest, the genteel neighborhood of Chestnut Hill seems to belong to a different universe. Here, educated professionals shop the boutiques along Germantown Avenue and return home to gracious stone and brick houses, the average price of which hovers above $400,000.

Within these very different communities, however, are two places remarkably similar in the resources they provide: the local public libraries. Each has been re-tooled with banks of new computers, the latest software, and speedy Internet access. Susan B. Neuman, a professor of early childhood and literacy education at NYU, and Donna C. Celano, an assistant professor of communication at LaSalle University in Philadelphia, spent hundreds of hours in the Chestnut Hill and Badlands libraries, watching how patrons used the books and computers on offer.

The two were especially interested in how the introduction of computers might "level the playing field" for the neighborhoods' young people, children of "concentrated affluence" and "concentrated poverty." They undertook their observations in a hopeful frame of mind: "Given the wizardry of these machines and their ability to support children's self-teaching," they wondered, "might we begin to see a closing of the opportunity gap?"

Many hours of observation and analysis later, Neuman and Celanano were forced to acknowledge a radically different outcome: "The very tool designed to level the playing field is, in fact, un-leveling it," they wrote in a 2012 book based on their Philadelphia library study. With the spread of educational technology, they predicted, "the not-so-small disparities in skills for children of affluence and children of poverty are about to get even larger."

Neuman and Celano are not the only researchers to reach this surprising and distressing conclusion. While technology has often been hailed as the great equalizer of educational opportunity, a growing body of evidence indicates that in many cases, tech is actually having the opposite effect: It is increasing the gap between rich and poor, between whites and minorities, and between the school-ready and the less-prepared.

This is not a story of the familiar "digital divide"—a lack of access to technology for poor and minority children. This has to do, rather, with a phenomenon Neuman and Celano observed again and again in the two libraries: Granted access to technology, affluent kids and poor kids use tech *differently*. They select different programs and features, engage in different types of mental activity, and come away with different kinds of knowledge and experience.

The unleveling impact of technology also has to do with a phenomenon known as the "Matthew Effect": the tendency for early advantages to multiply over time. Sociologist Robert Merton coined the term in 1968, making reference to a line in the gospel of Matthew ("for whosoever hath, to him shall be given, and he shall have more abundance: but whosoever hath not, from him shall be taken away even that he hath").

In a paper published in 1986, psychologist Keith Stanovich applied the Matthew Effect to reading. He showed that children who get off to a strong early start with reading acquire more vocabulary words and more background knowledge, which in turn makes reading easier and more enjoyable, leading them to read still more: a virtuous cycle of achievement. Children who struggle early on with reading fail to acquire vocabulary and knowledge, find reading even more difficult as a result, and consequently do it less: a dispiriting downward spiral.

Now researchers are beginning to document a *digital* Matthew Effect, in which the already advantaged gain more from technology than do the less fortunate. As with books and reading, the most-knowledgeable, most-experienced, and most-supported students are those in the best position to use computers to leap further ahead. For example: In the Technology Immersion Pilot, a $20 million project carried out in Texas public schools beginning in 2003, laptops were randomly assigned to middle school students. The benefit of owning one of these computers, researchers later determined, was significantly greater for those students whose test scores were high to begin with.

Some studies of the introduction of technology have found an overall *negative* effect on academic achievement—and in these cases, poor students' performance suffers more than that of their richer peers. In an article to be published next month in the journal *Economic Inquiry*, for example, Duke University economist Jacob Vigdor and co-authors Helen Ladd and Erika Martinez report their analysis of what happened when high-speed Internet service was rolled out across North Carolina: Math and reading test scores of the state's public school students went down in each region as broadband was introduced, and this negative impact was greatest among economically disadvantaged students. Dousing the hope that spreading technology will engender growing equality, the authors write: "Reliable evidence points to the conclusion that broadening student access to home computers or home Internet service would widen, not narrow, achievement gaps."

Why would improved access to the Internet harm the academic performance of poor students in particular? Vigdor and his colleagues speculate that "this may

occur because student computer use is more effectively monitored and channeled toward
productive ends in more affluent homes." This is, in fact, exactly the dynamic Susan Neuman and Donna Celano saw
playing out in the libraries they

> **As with books and reading, the most-knowledgeable, most-experienced, and most-supported students are those in the best position to use computers to leap further ahead.**

monitored. At the Chestnut Hill library, they found, young visitors to the computer area were almost always accompanied by a parent or grandparent. Adults positioned themselves close to the children and close to the screen, offering a stream of questions and suggestions. Kids were steered away from games and toward educational programs emphasizing letters, numbers, and shapes. When the children became confused or frustrated, the grown-ups guided them to a solution.

The Badlands library boasted computers and software identical to Chestnut Hill's, but here, children manipulated the computers on their own, while accompanying adults watched silently or remained in other areas of the library altogether. Lacking the "scaffolding" provided by the Chestnut Hill parents, the Badlands kids clicked around frenetically, rarely staying with one program for long. Older children figured out how to use the programs as games; younger children became discouraged and banged on the keyboard or wandered away.

These different patterns of use had quantifiable effects on the children's educational experiences, Neuman and Celano showed. Chestnut Hill preschoolers encountered twice as many written words on computer screens as did Badlands children; the more affluent toddlers received 17 times as much adult attention while using the library's computers as did their less privileged counterparts. The researchers documented differences among older kids as well: Chestnut Hill "tweens," or ten- to thirteen-year-olds, spent five times as long reading informational text on computers as did Badlands tweens, who tended to gravitate toward online games and entertainment. When Badlands tweens did seek out information on the Web, it was related to their homework only 9 percent of the time, while 39 percent of the Chestnut Hill tweens' information searches were homework-related.

Research is finding other differences in how economically disadvantaged children use technology. Some evidence suggests, for example, that schools in low-income neighborhoods are more apt to employ computers for drill and practice sessions than for creative or innovative projects. Poor children also bring less knowledge to their encounters with computers. Crucially, the comparatively rich background knowledge possessed by high-income students is not only about technology itself, but about everything in the wide world beyond one's neighborhood. Not only are affluent kids more likely to know how to Google; they're more likely to know what to Google *for*.

Slogans like "one laptop per child" and "one-to-one computing" evoke an appealingly egalitarian vision: If every child has a computer, every child is starting off on equal footing. But though the sameness of the hardware may feel satisfyingly fair, it is superficial. A computer in the hands of a disadvantaged child is in an important sense *not the same thing* as a computer in the hands of a child of privilege.

The focus of educators, politicians, and philanthropists on differences in access to technology has obscured another problem: what some call "the second digital divide," or differences in the use of technology. Access to adequate equipment and reliable high-speed connections remains a concern, of course. But improving the way that technology is employed in learning is an even bigger and more important issue. Addressing it would require a focus on people: training teachers, librarians, parents and children themselves to use computers effectively. It would require a focus on practices: what one researcher has called the dynamic "social envelope" that surrounds the hunks of plastic and silicon on our desks. And it would require a focus on knowledge: background knowledge that is both broad and deep. (The Common Core standards, with their focus on building broad background knowledge, may be education's most significant contribution to true computer literacy.)

It would take all this to begin to "level the playing field" for America's students— far more than a bank of computers in a library, or even one laptop per child.

Will MOOCs Be Flukes?

By Maria Konnikova
The New Yorker, November 7, 2014

On July 23rd, 1969, Geoffrey Crowther addressed the inaugural meeting of the Open University, a British institution that had just been created to provide an alternative to traditional higher education. Courses would be conducted by mail and live radio. The basic mission, Crowther declared, was a simple one: to be open to people from all walks of life. "The first, and most urgent task before us is to cater for the many thousands of people, fully capable of a higher education, who, for one reason or another, do not get it, or do not get as much of it as they can turn to advantage, or as they discover, sometimes too late, that they need," he told his audience. "Men and women drop out through failures in the system," he continued, "through disadvantages of their environment, through mistakes of their own judgment, through sheer bad luck. These are our primary material." He then invoked the message emblazoned on the Statue of Liberty: Open University wanted the tired, the poor, the huddled masses. To them, most of all, it opened its doors.

The mission Crowther described is the same one that has driven the proliferation of massive open online courses, or MOOCs, during the past few years. (Open University has often served as a sort of inspirational model for such ventures, which Nathan Heller wrote about last year in the magazine.) The premise of the MOOC movement is as commendable as it is democratic: quality education should not be a luxury good. MOOCs are flexible, and they can be free; if people want an education, MOOCs can give it to them.

MOOCs started with a bang of optimism. In 2011, Sebastian Thrun, a star professor at Stanford, made his introductory course on artificial intelligence available via an online broadcast. Within three months, he garnered over a hundred and sixty thousand viewers. Soon after, he started Udacity, one of the largest MOOC platforms. Other platforms that have sprung up in recent years include edX, which was developed through a collaboration between Harvard and the Massachusetts Institute of Technology; Coursera, which was co-founded by two of Thrun's colleagues at Stanford; and Khan Academy, the brainchild of the former hedge-fund analyst Salman Khan. Overseas, there are ventures like iversity and FutureLearn. And the number of available classes has been growing at an impressive pace. This month, there are four hundred and ninety-five MOOCs listed as in-progress on the MOOC aggregator Class Central, five times as many as there were a year ago.

And yet, despite the steady spread of the MOOC movement and the growing acceptance among university administrators that quality online education doesn't have to be an oxymoron, enthusiasm for MOOCs has waned in the past year. Last winter, Thrun himself expressed some doubts. "We were on the front pages of newspapers and magazines, and at the same time, I was realizing, we don't educate people as others wished, or as I wished," he told *Fast Company* in an interview. "We have a lousy product." (He later told the *Times* that his enthusiasm had not actually declined as much as he might have indicated.)

On one hand, MOOCs have achieved some worthy goals: they make top educational resources available, for free or for very low prices, to people who wouldn't have access to them otherwise, including older populations, people with unpredictable schedules, and international audiences. And the quality of the education they offer can be quite high: the Open University, for instance, which began to offer online courses in the nineties, has consistently ranked among the top universities in the U.K. in measures of student satisfaction.

MOOCs are a technology with potentially revolutionary implications for education, but without a precise plan for realizing that potential.

On the other hand, there are the numbers that gave Thrun pause. MOOC enrollment has soared, but completion rates are abysmal. According to a 2013 study, an average of only 5 percent of the students in seventeen Coursera classes offered through the University of Pennsylvania actually finished their classes. Other estimated completion rates hover below thirteen per cent. And not all of the students who completed their courses necessarily passed.

The problem with MOOCs begins with the fact that, as their name says, they're massive and open, which means that it can be easy to get lost in them. There are tens or even hundreds of thousands of students in some classes. Often, the students receive no personal acknowledgment or contact to hold them to account. And they can generally drop out the second they're unhappy, frustrated, or overwhelmed. The data suggest, in fact, that the students who succeed in the MOOC environment are those who don't particularly need MOOCs in the first place: they are the self-motivated, self-directed, and independent individuals who would push to succeed anywhere.

Last year, a team from the University of Pennsylvania, led by Gayle Christensen, found that the majority of the people enrolled in thirty-two of the courses offered through Penn's Coursera platform were young, already well educated, from developed countries, and, for the most part, employed—precisely the traditional students that Crowther held in contrast to the Open University's target demographic. And most of the students weren't taking classes in order to gain an essential education that they wouldn't receive otherwise; predominantly, they said they had enrolled to satisfy curiosity or advance in a current job—both of which are worthy pursuits, to be sure, but they are not the main needs that MOOCs were created to meet.

Earlier this year, an M.I.T. post-doctoral researcher named Jennifer DeBoer analyzed student data from an M.I.T. class offered through the edX platform to see if there were any factors that predicted success in the class. When she and her colleagues looked at over seven thousand responses to an exit survey, they found that the students who did the best were the ones who came in with prior education, had the highest intellectual starting points, and collaborated outside of class. In other words, those who succeeded in the MOOC were those who had already succeeded academically.

A 2013 analysis of an ambitious project launched by San Jose State University in collaboration with Udacity showed similar patterns. The program was the first step of a planned push to incorporate online learning into the California's public-university system. It was open to would-be college students as well as those who were already enrolled. The analysis found students who had already matriculated performed notably better than those who hadn't. While overall pass rates were quite low—an average of 33 percent across the three courses in the sample—those who performed the worst were the students who were not already enrolled at the university. In a remedial algebra course, for instance, only a quarter of the students passed, and less than one fifth of the non-matriculated students were among them. To put it in absolute terms, out of eighty-one students in the course, only twenty passed and only six of those were non-matriculated students. As the authors of the report acknowledged, the rates were disappointingly low. The project was suspended for reassessment. Even students who succeed in traditional classrooms can get lost in the MOOC shuffle. In a five-year-long study of over fifty thousand students taking both online and face-to-face courses, researchers at Troy University found that online classes had higher failure rates than traditional classroom courses. When Di Xu, an economist at Columbia University's Teachers College, analyzed data from more than forty thousand students who had enrolled in online courses at thirty-four colleges throughout Washington state, she found that, relative to face-to-face courses, online students earned lower grades and were less persistent. But not all students fared equally: she found that some subsets struggled more than others. Those subsets were male students, younger students, black students, and students who had lower G.P.A.s. What Xu found, in other words, was that MOOCs were the least effective at serving the students who needed educational resources the most.

So what's the solution? How can MOOCs live up to their promise? One possibility is to go back in order to go forward. The MOOC movement started off in a tech whirlwind; the people who pushed it forward were so caught up in its technological possibilities that they scarcely considered decades of research into educational psychology. They might, for instance, have looked at the work of the researchers Patrick Suppes and Richard Atkinson, who in 1962 were charged with designing a course that would use the latest computer technology to teach mathematics and reading to children in kindergarten through third grade. Suppes, a Stanford psychologist and philosopher who had been trained in mathematics, decided to use something called "control theory" as the basis for his approach. Students in his computer-based class wouldn't all receive the same instruction. Instead, their materials and the order in which those materials were presented would shift according to their past performance and other learning metrics—much like the G.R.E.'s adjusted sections, which become harder or easier depending on how you're doing. Some students might get stopped every fifteen minutes for a reassessment and summary of materials; others might go for an hour before they reach a stopping point. The approach combined leveling (in which the same material is presented at different learning and reading levels, depending on the student) with dynamic learning (which involves playing around with the manner and order in which information is presented, so that students don't get bored or frustrated).

The Suppes-Atkinson courses proved so successful that they were soon expanded to include multiple subjects for many age levels. A company called the Computer Curriculum Corporation (which is now a part of Pearson) started distributing them globally. In 1966, the psychologist William Estes, a pioneer of mathematical learning theory, including control theory, presented a paper at the International Congress of Psychology, held that year in Moscow. He spoke Russian. He'd learned it from a Suppes-Atkinson course.

Why don't MOOCs structure their materials in a similar fashion? The technology to do so has only improved, as have the metrics to measure success. Some MOOCs, like mathematics or economics courses, lend themselves to this approach, but even lecture-reliant classes could incorporate the method by, for example, incorporating pauses for reviews and summaries of material, tailored to each student's comprehension level. As it is, individualized methodology has largely gotten lost in the excitement over technological capabilities and large-group approaches. According to numerous interviews I conducted and studies I read, very few MOOCs are using anything like control theory as part of their approach to teaching.

The other major problem is that MOOCs tend to be set up in a way that minimizes frustration for students (who might drop out at any moment). There often aren't pop quizzes or the kinds of challenges that can alienate students in traditional settings. The problem here is that easy learning does not make good learning. In fact, the very tools that we believe make for better education may also make students more likely to quit. More frequent testing, for instance, can improve memory, learning, and retention. And, sometimes, the best test of all is the test that you fail: recent work from the cognitive psychologist Elizabeth Ligon Bjork has shown that pre-testing on never-before-seen materials helps students perform better in a subsequent course covering that material. In general, Bjork has found, speed bumps in learning are good—desirable difficulties, she calls them. MOOCs would likely be more effective if they didn't shy away from challenging students, rather than presenting a fluid experience which gives the false impression of the learning and retention.

In 2012, Stanford president John Hennessy pronounced that the MOOC was going to be "transformative to education." But, he added, "We don't really understand how yet." Two years later, the landscape remains much the same: MOOCs are a technology with potentially revolutionary implications for education, but without a precise plan for realizing that potential. One way of getting there could be for the leaders of the MOOC movement to look more closely at old methods, from when education was less massive, less open, and entirely offline.

What's Lost as Handwriting Fades?

By Maria Konnikova
The New York Times, June 2, 2014

Does handwriting matter?

Not very much, according to many educators. The Common Core standards, which have been adopted in most states, call for teaching legible writing, but only in kindergarten and first grade. After that, the emphasis quickly shifts to proficiency on the keyboard.

But psychologists and neuroscientists say it is far too soon to declare handwriting a relic of the past. New evidence suggests that the links between handwriting and broader educational development run deep.

Children not only learn to read more quickly when they first learn to write by hand, but they also remain better able to generate ideas and retain information. In other words, it's not just what we write that matters—but how.

"When we write, a unique neural circuit is automatically activated," said Stanislas Dehaene, a psychologist at the Collège de France in Paris. "There is a core recognition of the gesture in the written word, a sort of recognition by mental simulation in your brain.

"And it seems that this circuit is contributing in unique ways we didn't realize," he continued. "Learning is made easier."

A 2012 study led by Karin James, a psychologist at Indiana University, lent support to that view. Children who had not yet learned to read and write were presented with a letter or a shape on an index card and asked to reproduce it in one of three ways: trace the image on a page with a dotted outline, draw it on a blank white sheet, or type it on a computer. They were then placed in a brain scanner and shown the image again.

The researchers found that the initial duplication process mattered a great deal. When children had drawn a letter freehand, they exhibited increased activity in three areas of the brain that are activated in adults when they read and write: the left fusiform gyrus, the inferior frontal gyrus, and the posterior parietal cortex.

By contrast, children who typed or traced the letter or shape showed no such effect. The activation was significantly weaker.

Dr. James attributes the differences to the messiness inherent in free-form handwriting: Not only must we first plan and execute the action in a way that is not required when we have a traceable outline, but we are also likely to produce a result that is highly variable.

That variability may itself be a learning tool. "When a kid produces a messy letter," Dr. James said, "that might help him learn it."

Our brain must understand that each possible iteration of, say, an "a" is the same, no matter how we see it written. Being able to decipher the messiness of each "a" may be more helpful in establishing that eventual representation than seeing the same result repeatedly.

"This is one of the first demonstrations of the brain being changed because of that practice," Dr. James said.

In another study, Dr. James is comparing children who physically form letters with those who only watch others doing it. Her observations suggest that it is only the actual effort that engages the brain's motor pathways and delivers the learning benefits of handwriting.

The effect goes well beyond letter recognition. In a study that followed children in grades two through five, Virginia Berninger, a psychologist at the University of Washington, demonstrated that printing, cursive writing, and typing on a keyboard are all associated with distinct and separate brain patterns—and each results in a distinct end product.

> **When the children composed text by hand, they not only consistently produced more words more quickly than they did on a keyboard, but expressed more ideas.**

When the children composed text by hand, they not only consistently produced more words more quickly than they did on a keyboard, but expressed more ideas. And brain imaging in the oldest subjects suggested that the connection between writing and idea generation went even further. When these children were asked to come up with ideas for a composition, the ones with better handwriting exhibited greater neural activation in areas associated with working memory—and increased overall activation in the reading and writing networks.

It now appears that there may even be a difference between printing and cursive writing—a distinction of particular importance as the teaching of cursive disappears in curriculum after curriculum. In dysgraphia, a condition where the ability to write is impaired, sometimes after brain injury, the deficit can take on a curious form: In some people, cursive writing remains relatively unimpaired, while in others, printing does.

In alexia, or impaired reading ability, some individuals who are unable to process print can still read cursive, and vice versa—suggesting that the two writing modes activate separate brain networks and engage more cognitive resources than would be the case with a single approach.

Dr. Berninger goes so far as to suggest that cursive writing may train self-control ability in a way that other modes of writing do not, and some researchers argue that it may even be a path to treating dyslexia. A 2012 review suggests that cursive may be particularly effective for individuals with developmental dysgraphia—motor-control difficulties in forming letters—and that it may aid in preventing the reversal and inversion of letters.

Cursive or not, the benefits of writing by hand extend beyond childhood. For adults, typing may be a fast and efficient alternative to longhand, but that very efficiency may diminish our ability to process new information. Not only do we learn letters better when we commit them to memory through writing, memory and learning ability in general may benefit.

Two psychologists, Pam A. Mueller of Princeton and Daniel M. Oppenheimer of the University of California, Los Angeles, have reported that in both laboratory settings and real-world classrooms, students learn better when they take notes by hand than when they type on a keyboard. Contrary to earlier studies attributing the difference to the distracting effects of computers, the new research suggests that writing by hand allows the student to process a lecture's contents and reframe it—a process of reflection and manipulation that can lead to better understanding and memory encoding.

Not every expert is persuaded that the long-term benefits of handwriting are as significant as all that. Still, one such skeptic, the Yale psychologist Paul Bloom, says the new research is, at the very least, thought-provoking.

"With handwriting, the very act of putting it down forces you to focus on what's important," he said. He added, after pausing to consider, "Maybe it helps you think better."

Why Digital Natives Prefer Reading in Print
Yes, You Read That Right

By Michael S. Rosenwald
The Washington Post, February 22, 2015

Frank Schembari loves books—printed books. He loves how they smell. He loves scribbling in the margins, underlining interesting sentences, folding a page corner to mark his place.

Schembari is not a retiree who sips tea at Politics and Prose or some other bookstore. He is twenty, a junior at American University, and paging through a thick history of Israel between classes, he is evidence of a peculiar irony of the Internet age: Digital natives prefer reading in print.

"I like the feeling of it," Schembari said, reading under natural light in a campus atrium, his smartphone next to him. "I like holding it. It's not going off. It's not making sounds."

Textbook makers, bookstore owners, and college student surveys all say Millennials still strongly prefer print for pleasure and learning, a bias that surprises reading experts given the same group's proclivity to consume most other content digitally. A University of Washington pilot study of digital textbooks found that a quarter of students still bought print versions of e-textbooks that they were given for free.

"These are people who aren't supposed to remember what it's like to even smell books," said Naomi S. Baron, an American University linguist who studies digital communication. "It's quite astounding."

Earlier this month, Baron published "Words Onscreen: The Fate of Reading in a Digital World," a book (hardcover and electronic) that examines university students' preferences for print and explains the science of why dead-tree versions are often superior to digital. Readers tend to skim on screens, distraction is inevitable, and comprehension suffers.

In years of surveys, Baron asked students what they liked least about reading in print. Her favorite response: "It takes me longer because I read more carefully."

The preference for print over digital can be found at independent bookstores such as the Curious Iguana in downtown Frederick, MD, where owner Marlene England said Millennials regularly tell her they prefer print because it's "easier to follow stories." Pew studies show the highest print readership rates are among those ages eighteen to twenty-nine, and the same age group is still using public libraries in large numbers.

It can be seen in the struggle of college textbook makers to shift their businesses to more

> **The time we devote to reading online is usually spent scanning and skimming, with few places (or little time) for mental markers.**

profitable e-versions. Don Kilburn, North American president for Pearson, the largest publisher in the world and the dominant player in education, said the move to digital "doesn't look like a revolution right now. It looks like an evolution, and it's lumpy at best."

And it can be seen most prominently on college campuses, where students still lug backpacks stuffed with books, even as they increasingly take notes (or check Facebook) on laptops during class. At American, Cooper Nordquist, a junior studying political science, is even willing to schlep around Alexis de Tocqueville's 900-plus-page "Democracy in America."

"I can't imagine reading Tocqueville or understanding him electronically," Nordquist said in between classes while checking his e-mail. "That would just be awful."

Without having read Baron's book, he offered reasons for his print preference that squared with her findings.

The most important one to him is "building a physical map in my mind of where things are." Researchers say readers remember the location of information simply by page and text layout—that, say, the key piece of dialogue was on that page early in the book with that one long paragraph and a smudge on the corner. Researchers think this plays a key role in comprehension.

But that is more difficult on screens, primarily because the time we devote to reading online is usually spent scanning and skimming, with few places (or little time) for mental markers. Baron cites research showing readers spend a little more than one minute on Web pages, and only 16 percent of people read word-by-word. That behavior can bleed into reading patterns when trying to tackle even lengthier texts on-screen.

"I don't absorb as much," one student told Baron. Another said, "It's harder to keep your place online."

Another significant problem, especially for college students, is distraction. The lives of Millennials are increasingly lived on screens. In her surveys, Baron writes that she found "jaw-dropping" results to the question of whether students were more likely to multitask in hard copy (1 percent) vs. reading on-screen (90 percent).

Earlier this month, while speaking to sophomores about digital behavior, Baron brought up the problem of paying close attention while studying on-screen.

"You just get so distracted," one student said. "It's like if I finish a paragraph, I'll go on Tumblr, and then three hours later you're still not done with reading."

There are quirky, possibly lazy reasons many college students prefer print, too: They like renting textbooks that are already highlighted and have notes in the margins. While Nordquist called this a crapshoot, Wallis Neff, a sophomore study-ing journalism, said she was delighted to get a psychology textbook last year that had been "run through the mill a few times."

"It had a bunch of notes and things, explaining what this versus that was," she said. "It was very useful."

When do students say they prefer digital?

For science and math classes, whose electronic textbooks often include access to online portals that help walk them through study problems and monitor their learning. Textbook makers are pushing these "digital learning environments" to make screen learning more attractive.

They prefer them for classes in which locating information quickly is key—there is no control-F in a printed book to quickly find key words.

And they prefer them for cost—particularly when the price is free. The Book Industry Study Group recently found that about a quarter of 1,600 students polled either downloaded or knew someone who downloaded pirated textbooks. Students, it turns out, are not as noble in their reading habits when they need beer money. They become knowledge thieves.

But stealing texts probably is more a reflection on the spiraling cost of higher education—and the price of textbooks, up 82 percent from 2002 to 2012—than some secret desire of students to read digitally. If price weren't a factor, Baron's re-search shows that students overwhelmingly prefer print. Other studies show similar results.

The problem, Baron writes, is that there has been "pedagogical reboot" where faculty and textbook makers are increasingly pushing their students to digital to help defray costs "with little thought for educational consequences."

"We need to think more carefully about students' mounting rejection of long-form reading," Baron writes.

And that thinking shouldn't be limited to Millennials, Baron said. Around the country, school systems are buying millions of tablets and laptops for classroom use, promising easier textbook updates, lower costs, less back strain from heavy book bags, and more interactivity. But the potential downsides aren't being considered, she said.

"What's happening in American education today?" she said. "That's what I'm concerned about. What's happening to the American mind?"

When Baron started researching her book on reading, some of her colleagues responded with pity.

"Did I fail to understand that technology marches on?" she writes. "That cars supplanted horses and buggies? That printing replaced handwritten manuscripts, computers replaced typewriters and digital screens were replacing books? Hadn't I read the statistics on how many eReaders and tablets were being sold? Didn't I see all those people reading eBooks on their mobile devices? Was I simply unable to adapt?"

But after learning what Millennials truly think about print, Baron concluded, "I was roundly vindicated."

Think Fast: Smartwatch Slices Thought Into Eight-Second Bursts

By Kevin Maney
Newsweek, May 1, 2015

The Apple Watch's constant notifications are to concentration what a Cinnabon is to fitness. As popular reviewer Joanna Stern found out while field-testing an Apple Watch, the thing can leave you more distracted than a beagle in a squirrel sanctuary.

Early buyers are just beginning to strap on Apple's newest gadget, but ultimately this gizmo and its descendants will have an impact on society that goes far beyond our wrists: The Apple Watch will shrink attention spans like nothing before.

Holding people's attention in a busy media landscape is an old problem—Al Ries and Jack Trout called it out in their famous book *Positioning* in 1976. TV seemed hyper compared with print; the Internet felt like chaos to the TV generation; and now some of our big thinkers mince their brainy theses down to tweetstorms for cellphone screens. Some research shows that our average attention span has dropped from twelve seconds in 2000 to eight seconds today. While the intensity of bombardment is already crazy, smartwatches are going to take this to the next level of demand for our attention, since they will be on your body, all the time.

The chief trait of this new tool is that it shrinks your digital activities down into short bursts. Apple's watch puts these notifications in front of you either by flashing something on its face or vibrating on your skin. Interactions with the watch are expected to take no more than eight seconds—quick glances at calendar items or yes/no answers to texted questions. Depending on what you opt into, the watch could relentlessly interrupt whatever else is going on inside your head or in your life.

Such short attention spurts are not intrinsically bad, unless you're a grandfather who wants to grump that when you were a kid a night's entertainment consisted of reading the entirety of *Atlas Shrugged* by flashlight. And anyway, the trend is not going away. Complain as you may, but the bottom line is: Get used to it.

For the next year or so, the pricey and still-clunky Apple Watch will be conspicuously worn by the same types who a couple of years ago got labeled "Glassholes" for peering through their Google Glass lenses. But in time, as the technology evolves and prices drop, some version of a smartwatch will become a significant new tool that infiltrates our lives.

Evernote C.E.O. Phil Libin argues that spasmodic interactions with the Apple Watch will actually be more in tune with how our brains work naturally. "Our ancestors weren't working on a document for six hours," he tells me. Instead, ancient humans' attention constantly flitted between finding something to eat and checking to see if something was about to eat them. Libin believes we'll be more productive if we can handle simple tasks in seconds on a watch. And he may be on to something: Studies show that people with attention deficit hyperactivity disorder (ADHD) are more creative. Other research, even going back to some Buddhist writings, says five to eight seconds is about the amount of time your brain can hold on to one particular thought.

Of course, somebody at some point has to concentrate long enough to design a skyscraper or write complex code—though even there, the trend is toward dividing big tasks into smaller ones and throwing them to Agile development teams. Fading are the days of attacking a major project like a great white shark hitting a seal. Now the approach has more in common with a school of piranha.

In both business and everyday life, we're about to see the most intensive demand ever on a limited supply of human attention.

> **Our average attention span has dropped from twelve seconds in 2000 to eight seconds today.**

The supply of attention can't keep up. Every human has only twenty-four hours of possible attention, give or take sleep, and YouTube uploads 300 hours of video every minute. As demand for our eyeballs spikes, the value of the supply goes through the roof. If you could buy stock in attention right now, it would be the best investment since Berkshire Hathaway in 1965.

Anything that's really good at getting and holding our attention will become far more sought after—and far more valuable. Take, for instance, the Coachella music festival, which just sold around $80 million worth of tickets for two weekend performance sets in April. It is a veritable magnet for the mind, holding the attention of 100,000 attendees for three days at a time. The amount of attention Coachella controls is so valuable, nearly every band and brand is dying to be a part of it. "It almost matters too much," Flying Lotus, a producer and DJ, told *The New York Times*. "This is one of those festivals where the whole world is watching."

In the age of the smartwatch, Coachella's rare ability to attract attention will become even more remarkable—and more valuable to any entity that wants to make a deep impression. The same will apply to similar events, such as Bonaroo, and major sports events, both live and on television. Or how about Costco? No one can escape a Costco in less than an hour. Its ability to capture so much sustained suburban attention becomes a mega-asset in an age when so many digital retailers have to compete to get you to buy in eight seconds or less.

In a similar way, the value of face-to-face meetings will rocket upwards. It won't matter how good Skype and Google Hangouts get for video conversations. Meeting live is a serious investment of time and focus, and it will make more of an impression in this new age than it did in the old.

An interesting question, though: What will a hyperactive smartwatch do to the live meeting? Laptops can stay in bags and phones can stay in pockets, but watches will be right out there on wrists. As early reviewers have found, glancing at a smartwatch is not a deft and unnoticed gesture. In fact, looking at a watch, even just to tell the time, sends a signal of boredom or agita. George W. Bush took a quick look at his watch during the 1992 presidential debate against Bill Clinton, and some say it cost him the election. It might become a sign of deep respect to show up to a lunch date with nothing on your wrist.

Digital Natives, Yet Strangers to the Web

By Alia Wong
The Atlantic, April 21, 2015

When Reuben Loewy took up his first teaching gig in 2012, he had a major revelation: The digital revolution has dramatically transformed the way that kids perceive reality.

Perhaps that makes the fifty-five-year-old teacher sound like a dinosaur. What he discovered is, after all, one of the most obvious realities shaping education policy and parenting guides today. But, as Loewy will clarify, his revelation wasn't simply that technology is overhauling America's classrooms and redefining childhood and adolescence. Rather, he was hit with the epiphany that efforts in schools to embrace these shifts are, by and large, focusing on the wrong objectives: equipping kids with fancy gadgets and then making sure the students use those gadgets appropriately and effectively. Loewy half-jokingly compares the state of digital learning in America's schools to that of sex ed, which, as one NYU education professor describes it, entails "a smattering of information about their reproductive organs and a set of stern warnings about putting them to use."

Indeed, although many of today's teens are immersed in social media, that doesn't mean "that they inherently have the knowledge or skills to make the most of their online experiences," writes Danah Boyd in her 2014 book *It's Complicated: The Secret Lives of Networked Teens*. Boyd, who works as a principal researcher at Microsoft Research, argues that "the rhetoric of 'digital natives'" is dangerous because it distorts the realities of kids' virtual lives, the result being that they don't learn what they need to know about online living. In other words, it falsely assumes that today's students intrinsically understand the nuanced ways in which technologies shape the human experience—how they influence an individual's identity, for example, or how they advance and stymie social progress—as well as the means by which information spreads thanks to phenomena such as algorithms and advertising. Loewy decided that this void could be eliminated with an honest, interdisciplinary high-school curriculum for the digital age—a program that would fundamentally shift how schools address kids' virtual experiences.

Educational institutions across the board are certainly embracing (or at least acknowledging) the digital revolution, adopting cutting-edge classroom technology and raising awareness about the perils and possibilities of the Internet. On the one end are the movement's champions—the schools where every child has an iPad or the education departments with bureaucrats who go by fancy titles like "Director of

Innovative Learning." In some school districts, virtual courses are a prerequisite for graduation, and it's become almost cliché for teachers to incorporate Minecraft into their instruction. Meanwhile, schools are phasing out physical textbooks, sometimes replacing them with artificially intelligent software. It's hardly surprising that one-third of the country's students in grades six through twelve use school-provided mobile devices to support coursework, according to a 2014 report by the nonprofit Project Tomorrow.

On the other end are the skeptics, among them the adults who fear that kids are being thrusted into a world of cyberbullies and pedophiles. A 2012 Pew Research survey of roughly 800 U.S. parents and their teenage children found that eight in 10 parents are concerned about their kids' Internet privacy, while seven in ten said they worried about their kids interacting with strangers online. As Hanna Rosin explained in a cover story for *The Atlantic* last November about teenage sexting, adults often respond to such scandals with fearmongering and massive information campaigns. The National Association of School Psychologists has helped to develop a curriculum devoted exclusively to raising cyberbullying awareness, while myriad apps have been developed that allow parents to track their children's digital footprints. According to the Pew report, half of the parents surveyed said they had used parental controls or other means of blocking, filtering, or monitoring their teens' online activities.

And then there are the educators who worry—arguably for good reason—that the digitalization of classrooms is severely undermining their pedagogy. At the higher-ed level, some professors have even published manifestos on why they're banning laptops from their lecture courses, while many K-12 campuses to this day maintain no-device policies (though it appears such policies are becoming obsolete).

According to Loewy, this dichotomy amounts to a major missed opportunity. Kids not only need to be proficient in how to use digital technology, becoming savvy coders and prolific eBook readers, he explains—they also need to deeply, holistically, and realistically understand how the digital world works behind the scenes. And that doesn't only mean realizing that sexting is a victimizing and punishable offense with long-term repercussions. Or that social media can be addictive and full of predators. While it's undoubtedly important to keep kids safe when they're online, these focuses give kids "a distorted view of the digital world," Loewy writes. "It is a view that reflects the fears of adults rather than the aspirations of youth."

* * *

Loewy was teaching a summer journalism class for middle-schoolers in Princeton, New Jersey, when he had his epiphany. "This generation has grown up with a completely different type of relationship to the media," he said. "They have not seen a newspaper other than their parents reading one. They don't even watch television—everything is Internet-based." And while such a statement might conjure images of a curmudgeonly cynic convinced that technology is an assault on human intellect, Loewy sees that transformation as positive—or, at least, inevitable. It's just that today's kids need much more guidance on how to live within this world, he argues. "They are consuming and seeing so many things online that they don't know how to put it into context or how to evaluate it," he said.

At the same time, "even schools that have called themselves very technologically advanced haven't even begun to explore how they actually teach [about that technology]," he said. They may hand out iPads or laptops to students, but such education often stops at the hardware. "Curriculum is the microcosm of what's going on in society; I think that curriculum needs to catch up with the reality."

Boyd, it's worth noting, draws similar conclusions:

> Teens will not become critical contributors to this [Internet] ecosystem simply because they were born in an age when these technologies were pervasive.

> Neither teens nor adults are monolithic, and there is no magical relation between skills and age. Whether in school or in informal settings, youth need opportunities to develop the skills and knowledge to engage with temporary technology effectively and meaningfully. Becoming literate in a networked age requires hard work, regardless of age.

After his revelation, Loewy, who spent most of his career as a foreign correspondent writing for major British and Canadian newspapers, started developing what he's now calling "an interdisciplinary curriculum for the digital age," a.k.a. "Living Online." The curriculum, which is designed primarily for high-school students (though he says it can be adapted for younger kids, too), includes a dozen teaching modules that would be integrated into various classes—from "Privacy" and "A is for Algorithm" to "Digital Activism" and "Cyberpsychology." Other units under development include "Remix Culture," "Gaming in Education," and "Reality—Virtual/Actual." In some ways, it could be described as the liberal arts of virtual living.

The curriculum's first unit—"Identity"—aims to give students insight "into how their identities may be unconsciously shaped by digital media and online socialization." The module highlights opposing perspectives on the topic, from that entertained by people like Facebook founder Mark Zuckerberg, who insists users should only have one authentic identity, to the view that individuals are multifaceted and prismatic. "We will examine how individuals craft and express their identities across multiple online and offline contexts," the summary says, "and discuss the implications of having different identities, avatars, and facets of ourselves across different networks." The idea is to get past the emphasis that adults often make on the perils of Internet identity, to show kids that they're in a process of discovery and can play with and explore different personas—even if that means an adolescent boy posing online as a thirty-five-year-old woman. And this, to Loewy, is a good thing: "It's a part of experimenting, exploring who you are, and getting the opportunity to interact with people you normally wouldn't interact with."

Meanwhile, in the unit titled "Economy of the Internet," kids would learn about the role of advertising in the World Wide Web: how websites generate money by attracting visitors and then sell those visitors' personal data. The unit called "Diversity of Thought: Breaking Out of the Bubble" aims to have teens analyze debates about whether digital technology makes users more open-minded or more enclosed in their world views, while that on "Digital Disruption" would use case studies such as Netflix and Uber to explore how these forces destruct and create.

* * *

The idea behind Living Online is by no means new. The University of Pennsylvania English professor Kenneth Goldsmith launched a course this school year called "Wasting Time on the Internet," which requires students to watch YouTube videos, tweet, and even plagiarize. Explaining the course's objective to *The Atlantic* last December, Goldsmith said, "it's [about] understanding that digital existence … You know, we've become so good at using tools, but we've rarely stepped back to consider how and why we're using those tools."

Two years ago, one well-known Florida teacher reasoned in a blog post that the country needs "a coherent plan to teach digital citizenship in schools"—not as an add-on but as a complement to what's already being taught in the classroom. Such citizenship, she said, "is not about the technology itself but rather the effects that arise from its usage." And just a few days ago, the Harvard Internet-law professor Jonathan Zittrain posted a video message on YouTube that coincidentally sounded a lot like Loewy's elevator pitch for the unit titled "Wikipedia and Open-Source Knowledge." Highlighting the success of the site and lamenting the ineffectiveness of American public education, Zittrain—who authored the 2008 book *The Future of the Internet and How to Stop It*—suggested that schools integrate Wikipedia into their curricula, asking kids to edit articles and make the case for their edits. He continued:

> To me, if I think of an advanced civics class, it's great to learn that there are three branches of government and X vote overrides a veto. But having the civics of a collective hallucination like Wikipedia also a part of the curriculum, I think, would be valuable.

But for various reasons, schools have yet to catch on. Data on how much, if at all, schools in the U.S. are teaching these things doesn't exist, but it's worth noting that even the much more obvious subject—computer science—is still largely considered a peripheral course. A 2013 survey of 1,250 educators nationwide found that more than a fourth of them worked on campuses that didn't even offer computer science. Meanwhile, national initiatives to modernize schools—through projects such as The Center for Digital Education's "Curriculum of the Future"—rarely touch on the liberal arts of virtual living, focusing strictly on topics like new technologies and workforce preparation. According to a 2012 report from Common Sense Media based on survey of nearly 700 K-12 U.S. teachers, more than half of them ranked their students' digital-citizenship skills as fair or poor; only a fourth of them said those skills were taught at their schools.

Adults' resistance to new trends, too, is surely part of the reason why schools haven't addressed these needs. For one, Loewy suggests that many educators don't feel digitally literate. A shrinking but still relatively significant percentage of educators—especially those who are fifty-five and older—don't feel confident with these new technologies, according to a 2013 Pew Research survey among roughly 2,500 A.P. and writing teachers. Meanwhile, many teachers simply feel overburdened by the new technology: Three-fourths of the educators surveyed for the same Pew report say the Internet and other digital tools "have added major demands to their lives," largely by "increasing the range of content and skills about which they must be knowledgeable."

Indeed, experienced and accomplished teachers continue to raise questions about schools' embrace of digital technology, which could mean that Loewy's effort is moot. Nancie Atwell, a veteran language-arts teacher who last month won the inaugural Global Teacher Prize, is one of many educators across the country who are deeply concerned about the growing role digital devices are playing in classrooms, primarily because of their arguably negative impact on cognition and learning. "Although the world may be digital, it also remains human," she said. "The emphasis on any device as a panacea—give one to every kid and see what happens—completely ignores everything we know about what motivates people to learn."

> **Kids are learning a distorted view of the digital world "that reflects the fears of adults rather than the aspirations of youth."**

"These are devices—they're a means to an end," she continued. "I'm appalled that we talk about technology as if it's a discipline or a school subject or a content area. It's a way of developing or displaying knowledge. It's a little bit like worshipping a pencil."

Perceptions like these, according to Loewy, are a large reason why rolling out the curriculum is so tricky. It's a chicken-or-the-egg problem: Living Online—and the teacher training that would come with it—could help bring everyone, from the skeptics to the overzealous techies, on the same page and alleviate some of the concerns and misconceptions about the technology. But it's hard to get people on board if they have preconceived notions, many of which are well-founded, about those devices and apps to begin with.

And for now, Living Online is little more than an idea—and one, critics might argue, that's neither feasible nor credible. After all, Loewy is a Baby Boomer with very limited experience as a classroom teacher.

But that hasn't fazed the former journalist, who admitted that he's been developing the program using his own money. (Loewy doesn't want public schools to pay for the curriculum out of their operating budgets—he hopes private foundations will foot the bill—but has yet to secure a grant.) Loewy says he's devoted the bulk of his time over the last few years to creating this program, which he's been putting together with the help of feedback from teachers and professional curriculum developers via education conferences and the range of support and sharing sites available online. He's currently in the process of registering Living Online, which was launched in 2013, as a nonprofit, and as of now the organization only has three board members—none of whom are teachers (and all of whom are men). They include Martin Schneiderman, an IT advisor who works with philanthropic organizations; Peter Lammer, who co-founded the IT-security company Sophos; and David

Loevner, the manager and founder of a global investment firm. Loewy says he hopes to bring on a group of advisors, including teachers, with diverse backgrounds.

The curriculum faces a range of other logistical obstacles, too, including the number of existing requirements that schools are already grappling to juggle. Loewy sees the curriculum as being incorporated into other classes, not as a standalone supplement but as an ingredient built into larger coursework. Still, public-school teachers today say they are already overburdened by a slew of expectations—from the Common Core math and reading standards to additional state and local stipulations. Educators across the country have long complained about their inability to teach subjects as essential as social studies. In that sense, it's hard to imagine this program becoming a reality outside of the private-school sector; in fact, Loewy's only been able to pilot the modules with private-school students.

And even if teachers could find a way to incorporate the curriculum into their classes, they'd have to find a way to keep up with material and technologies that are constantly changing. "The ... problem is that it's evolving every single day—it's not like teaching ancient Rome, it's not static," Loewy acknowledged. "This is what I think holds back the progress: Every single day there is a new app, and teachers [can] become sort of blinded by" its merits and limitations. But without understanding the intricacies and dynamics of the Internet, he continued, "you're not taking advantage of everything digital technology offers. Without the knowledge, you're not able to take advantage of the web and navigate it properly. You can't be an informed, responsible, and critical member of society if you don't have the education."

4
Crime and Justice

Friends, family, neighbors, and concerned citizens leave candles at a sidewalk memorial for Eric Garner on the Staten Island sidewalk where he died. Garner was confronted by police for selling loose cigarettes and had a heart attack while being placed in an illegal chokehold and wrestled to the ground by several police officers. The episode was captured with a video on a bystander's cell phone and went viral online, causing nationwide protests and charges of police brutality.

Digital Delinquency and Its Repercussions

In the twenty-first century, crime and justice are increasingly focused on cyber-space. From the birth of hacking and cybercrime to the increasing levels of global surveillance for both citizens and police, the advances of digital technology have come with new challenges, dangers, and judicial issues that are changing legal and law enforcement techniques and policies around the world. As this evolution proceeds, citizens are reevaluating the systems in place to preserve the law while law enforcement agencies struggle to maintain an edge in an environment where anonymity and virtual landscapes have made traditional investigative methods obsolete.

Hacking the System

The term "hacker," now typically defined as person who uses a computer to gain unauthorized access to data, entered the popular vocabulary in the 1980s, but the concept emerged far earlier. According to *Time* magazine, one of the first groups of hackers were the "phone phreaks" who manipulated early telephone computer systems to gain free long distance phone calls. The most famous, John Draper, became known as Captain Crunch as he used a children's plastic whistle to imitate a tone that tricked the phone system into giving him access.[1]

Hacking began as an experimental type of "play" among the first generation with access to personal computers. Before global networking, hackers learned by creative experimentation to expand computing capability, manipulate digital security systems, and create innovative code and programs.[2] From this creative landscape however, two darker trends emerged. As financial systems increasingly became digital, hackers were able to infiltrate and subvert computer security, creating a new class of crime based on virtual theft. A new variety of virtual civil disobedience also came out of this milieu, with individuals competing to break through the most complex security systems available. These darker strains of hacker culture, sometimes called "black hat hacking," essentially gave birth to what is now known as "cybercrime."[3]

The spread of personal computing and Internet networks in the 1990s led to an explosion in cybercrime. Hackers began to manipulate computer systems using programs known as "malware" and infectious codes called "viruses" which were typically transmitted through email or other Internet activities, such as downloading programs from unknown vendors. Many other forms of hacking attacks have been invented and used in cybercrime, including "code injection," in which codes allow hackers to steal data from online data forms, and "distributed denial-of-service (DDoS)" attacks in which a hacker disables a computer system by flooding the system with data from connected computers.[4]

The e-commerce revolution provided new opportunities for cybercrime, including the emergence of digital identity theft in which cybercriminals steal a person's identity and use it to apply for credit or to make online purchases. In 2007, hacker Albert Gonzalez stole 94 million credit cards, marking one of the first cases to demonstrate the enormous potential for profit from cybercrime.[5] For cybercriminals focused on cyber-vandalism and self-aggrandizement, viruses and malware can also be used to destroy or wreak havoc on systems of virtual networks. The infamous "Love Bug," or "I Love You" virus of 2000, allegedly invented by a Filipino computer engineer, motivated primarily by a desire to demonstrate his own intelligence, caused an estimated $10 billion in damage as it spread around the world.[6]

Cybercrime led to a digital arms war between criminals, security experts, and law enforcement. Governmental agencies have used some of the same malware and viruses to fight back against cybercrime.[7] Ironically, a computer security system developed by the US Naval Research Laboratories (NRL) called "onion routing," or "Tor," which hides a computer user's location by shifting signals through a variety of points, has also facilitated new vistas of cybercrime. The digital rights group Electronic Frontier Foundation (EFF) used Tor to create a free browser highly resistant to tracking, in an effort to protect digital privacy rights for those concerned with government or corporate data security.[8]

However, the anonymity of the Tor system allowed criminals to create the "Dark Net," a collection of hidden websites and networks used to sell drugs, weapons, child pornography, and illegal data. In 2012, the FBI launched "Operation Torpedo," a program that used malware to locate and arrest several prominent operators of Dark Net sites. While few argued with the arrest of the Dark Net criminals, digital rights organizations criticized the FBI over the Torpedo Program because the operation involved invading personal computers owned by hundreds of innocent users before the FBI located the appropriate suspects.[9] The controversial Torpedo program therefore also provides an example of the delicate balance between personal privacy and the efforts to address cybercrime.

In some cases, hackers envision themselves as "anti-heroes," hacking into systems as a form of digital protest sometimes called "hacktivism." The activities of rogue individuals and groups now known as hacktivists, like *Anonymous* and *Lulzsec*, have become a major security concern for governmental and corporate information engineers and a source of fascination and, at times, admiration among the public. Hactivists working under the moniker *Anonymous* have hacked into the databases of large corporations, shutting down networks, and retrieving and distributing classified financial information. Hacktivists have also gone after corporations, government corruption, and even the church of Scientology, promising to disrupt the church's financial system in response to the church's alleged, but well documented, exploitation of members for financial gain.[10]

Who Watches the Watchers?

Police are increasingly using high tech digital techniques and tools to combat crime. Digital forensics, for instance, is a field that investigates computer systems to find evidence, and has greatly enhanced police investigative capabilities in an age where personal and financial data is often digital. Using these new tools, police have captured hundreds of criminals involved in crimes ranging from traffic light violations to murder; however, some critics believe that many modern surveillance tools violate the Fourth Amendment, which says that government agencies may not search an individual's property, possessions, or correspondence, without first proving sufficient and reasonable cause.[11]

A recent controversy involves the use of "stingray" devices that trick cellphones into connecting with false cell tower signals, then intercept cell phone data, thus allowing the police to track a suspect through his or her phone. Critics argue that stingrays also violate privacy rights as they represent a "broad" surveillance program indiscriminately intercepting signals from any passing cellular phone. Cellular phones, especially smart devices, have a special significance in modern society, serving not only as a means of communication, but also as an interface to many aspects of a person's life. In the 2014 Supreme Court case of *Riley v California*, the court held that cell phones were afforded special protection and that police need a warrant to search a suspect's cell phone, even if the suspect has already been arrested for a crime. Some digital rights advocates claim that the case provides precedent for the argument that stingray devices violate constitutional protections.[12]

Another controversy involves the police use of high definition cameras in police surveillance. Persistent Surveillance Systems, a private company, has developed a camera capable of recording all activity across a town or small city over a period of several hours. Police can then review data, zooming in close enough to see crimes occurring on the streets.[13] Mass aerial surveillance, automated cameras that film drivers at traffic lights, and facial recognition systems in use by the FBI to identify individuals from photos, are part of a broader controversy involving surveillance and privacy. Critics argue that government agencies should not be allowed to photograph, record, or otherwise spy on individuals without sufficient cause, and the judicial system is only beginning to address these issues.

The digital age has also led to a new phenomenon of "reverse surveillance," in which members of the public have increasingly been able to capture the actions of police officers in photos and videos, which can then gain "viral" attention through social media. One example includes videos of the death of Eric Garner, a street vendor who was killed in a controversial "chokehold" encounter with police in Long Island, New York. The video of Garner's death helped inspire protests in New York and other cities, partially organized by digital activist groups like *BlackLivesMatter*.[14] Media outlets also publish civilian videos, thus essentially extending the reach of the press to include any and every citizen with a camera or video-enabled smart phone.

In the digital age, therefore, police *and* the public are increasingly being watched, in an environment where news and media can rapidly reach global audiences. These intersecting phenomena are already reshaping law enforcement and may lead to a refinement of the relationship between public opinion and public policy. After the recent police abuse cases, for instance, the federal government announced a new program that will expand the use of "body cameras" among police, filming their interactions with suspects for later review in an effort to prevent the abuse of power and the use of unnecessary force.[15]

The Digital Assault: Bullying and Abuse

The term "cyberbullying" has been traced to Canadian educator Bill Beasley, who coined the term in a 2001 article to refer to the use of digital technology to harass, insult, or socially abuse an individual. There have been attempts to pass anti-bullying legislation, but cyberbullying remains difficult for police to address, especially when it occurs among juveniles.[16] The problem is also severe, with the National Crime Victimization Survey estimating that at least 2.2 million students were the victims of cyberbullying in 2011.[17] While a particular concern for young individuals, cyberabuse and bullying affect individuals of any age. In particular, there has been increasing concern over the way in which women and minorities have been targeted by cyberabusers using social media as a forum for racism and misogyny.[18]

In her 2014 article, "Why Women Aren't Welcome on the Internet," journalist Amanda Hess, who has garnered negative press for her articles on sex, discusses her discovery of a Twitter account, "Headlessfemalepig," that had been set up as a forum for individuals to insult and abuse her. Participators posted death and rape threats, with one user even claiming that he lived in her same state and would be the one to kill her.[19] In her book, *Hate Crimes in Cyberspace*, author Danielle Keats argues that the anonymity and ease of social media has increased the freedom with which individuals espouse violent speech towards women and other minority groups. There are many other examples of cyber-misogyny, including the theft and posting of nude photos and videos, and an overall objectification of women that has become popular on many Internet sites.[20] The prevalence of racist posts and groups on Twitter even led to the origin of a new term, "Twacists," to describe the phenomenon.

Controlling cyberabuse is complicated because the forums by abusers are also forums for free expression and speech. The prevalence of digital abuse is not a technological issue as much as it reveals disturbing currents within society. Addressing these issues through censorship may prohibit the means of distribution but does little to change underlying cultural stereotypes and biases. It is therefore, perhaps, appropriate that social media allow these phenomenon to come to the surface, providing the public, legislators, and victims with a forum to discuss and examine broader cultural issues.

Micah L. Issit

Notes

1. James, "A Brief History of Cybercrime."
2. Schell and Martin, "Cybercrime: A Reference Handbook," 1-10.
3. Pagliery, "The Evolution of Hacking."
4. James, "A Brief History of Cybercrime."
5. Verini, "The Great Cyberheist."

6.   Landler, "A Filipino Linked to 'Love Bug' Talks About His License to Hack."

7.   Michaels, "NSA Data Mining Can Help Stop Cybercrime."

8.   Zetter, "Tor Torches Online Tracking."

9.   Poulsen, "Visit the Wrong Website, And the FBI Could End Up In Your Computer."

10.   Casserly, "What is Hacktivism?"

11.   MacDougall, "The Fourth Amendment Goes Digital."

12.   "*Riley v. California.*"

13.   Timberg, "New Surveillance Technology Can Track Everyone in an Area for Several Hours at a Time."

14.   Goodman, "N.Y. Officer Won't Be Indicted for Fatal Choking."

15.   Berman, "Justice Dept. Will Spend $20 Million on Police Body Cameras Nationwide"; Balko, "Model Legislation for Police Body Cameras."

16.   Gray, Esmail, and Eargle, "Cyberbullying from Schoolyard to Cyberspace: An Evolution," 190-195.

17.   "Student Reports of Bullying and Cyberbullying."

18.   Johnson, "Misogyny is Not Human Nature."

19.   Hess, "Why Women Aren't Welcome on the Internet."

20.   Citron, *Hate Crimes in Cyberspace*, 1-25.

Online Piracy Grows, Reflecting Consumer Trends

By Tom Risen

U.S. News & World Report, September 18, 2013

A new study found that illegal file-sharing websites have grown more popular since 2011, and entertainment industry officials say online piracy is so widespread that they use it to track consumer trends.

According to the new study released on Tuesday by British brand protection firm NetNames, approximately 432 million unique Internet users worldwide "explicitly sought" copyright-infringing content during January 2013. In the regions of Europe, North America, and Asia-Pacific, the study found that approximately one quarter of Internet users in those regions sought infringing content during January, which increased by 10 percent since November 2011. The study was funded by NBC Universal.

"While legitimate services have come along like Netflix, the piracy world hasn't stood still," said David Price, director of piracy analysis at NetNames. "People are infringing all kinds of content, including films, television, music and games. Over 300 million people infringed copyright at least once. That's an enormous number of people. It just shows how embedded this particular activity has become in people's lives."

Sen. Orrin Hatch, R-Utah, said this growth of online piracy damages the ability of artists and creators to profit from their content including movies, television, and music, which in turn damages reinvestment in new, job-creating projects. Hatch spoke on Tuesday during an event unveiling the study hosted by the Information Technology and Innovation Foundation.

"The problem of online piracy is real, and it's weakening our economy," said Hatch, a co-chairman of the International Anti-Piracy Caucus.

Sen. Sheldon Whitehouse, D-RI, also said during the event that online piracy will grow and "become more complicated" as mobile devices get more successful at delivering content.

"More needs to be done," Whitehouse said. "While the financial toll may be unclear we can safely bet that it is significant."

The seizure of file-sharing website MegaUpload in 2012 stunted online piracy use, the NetNames report found. BitTorrent is now the most popular website used to download pirated content in Europe and North America, while in the Asia-Pacific region direct download websites are the preferred option to access copyright-infringing content.

Because online piracy is so popular, legitimate video-streaming websites are studying their illegal file-sharing adversaries to compete with them. When Netflix debuted its video streaming service in the Netherlands, the

Because online piracy is so popular, legitimate video-streaming websites are studying their illegal file-sharing adversaries to compete with them.

company's Vice President of Content Acquisition Kelly Merryman told Dutch website Tweakers that it monitors file-sharing platforms to help determine what TV-series the company buys, according to a report by the *New York Times*. Netflix C.E.O. Reed Hastings told *Tweakers* in a previous interview that some illegal file sharing "just creates the demand" for content that is available on legal download platforms, according to *The New York Times*.

"Netflix is so much easier than Torrenting," Hastings said.

Sandra Aistars, executive director of the Copyright Alliance, said that while piracy damages the ability of creators to profit from their projects, members of her organization watch online piracy platforms to track what content is popular with consumers and what file-sharing distribution models are successful.

"There has perhaps been some learning in that regard, useful intelligence," Aistars said during the event on Tuesday.

The Obama Administration has supported voluntary agreements between companies including Google, Microsoft, and AOL to halt funds that reach piracy Web services. This private sector solution is a departure from the broader Stop Online Piracy Act (SOPA) anti-piracy legislation that was defeated in Congress in 2012 following outcry from Internet users and technology companies including Google. The legislation would have targeted strict penalties at websites for being linked with copyright-infringing material, which critics including Google claimed would curtail free speech.

"People who are involved in creating TV and movies have learned that they need to be able to work more closely with the tech community," says Howard Gantman, vice president of communications for the Motion Picture Association of America.

With that in mind, the entertainment industry wants to combat piracy with more options for legal TV watching websites, Gantman says. Legal TV and movie download sites have grown in the past three years with the increase in broadband speeds, and can be found on the MPAA's Where To Watch website. Part of that boom is also a learning response to widespread online piracy, Gantman says. The music industry lagged behind pirate websites after Napster rose to offer downloads in 1999 and led a piracy boom while digital music was in its infancy. It took until 2003 with the launch of the Apple iTunes Store for steady options to become available for legal digital music downloads.

"If you look at what the movie and TV industries have done in the last three years in terms of making content available online, it's an incredible story," Gantman says. "Yes the piracy has happened and yes there are lessons that can be learned from that, but it has been mainly the growth of technology."

When Bullying Goes High-Tech

By Elizabeth Landau
CNN.com, April 15, 2013

Brandon Turley didn't have friends in sixth grade. He would often eat alone at lunch, having recently switched to his school without knowing anyone.

While browsing MySpace one day, he saw that someone from school had posted a bulletin—a message visible to multiple people—declaring that Turley was a "fag." Students he had never even spoken with wrote on it, too, saying they agreed.

Feeling confused and upset, Turley wrote in the comments, too, asking why his classmates would say that. The response was even worse: He was told on MySpace that a group of twelve kids wanted to beat him up, that he should stop going to school and die. On his walk from his locker to the school office to report what was happening, students yelled things like "fag" and "fatty."

"It was just crazy, and such a shock to my self-esteem that people didn't like me without even knowing me," said Turley, now 18 and a senior in high school in Oregon. "I didn't understand how that could be."

A pervasive problem

As many as 25 percent of teenagers have experienced cyberbullying at some point, said Justin W. Patchin, who studies the phenomenon at the University of Wisconsin-Eau Claire. He and colleagues have conducted formal surveys of 15,000 middle and high school students throughout the United States, and found that about 10 percent of teens have been victims of cyberbullying in the last thirty days.

Online bullying has a lot in common with bullying in school: Both behaviors include harassment, humiliation, teasing, and aggression, Patchin said. Cyberbullying presents unique challenges in the sense that the perpetrator can attempt to be anonymous, and attacks can happen at any time of day or night.

There's still more bullying that happens at school than online, however, Patchin said. And among young people, it's rare that an online bully will be a total stranger.

"In our research, about 85 percent of the time, the target knows who the bully is, and it's usually somebody from their social circle," Patchin said.

Patchin's research has also found that, while cyberbullying is in some sense easier to perpetrate, the kids who bully online also tend to bully at school.

"Technology isn't necessarily creating a whole new class of bullies," he said.

Long-lasting consequences

The conversations that need to be happening around cyberbullying extend beyond schools, said Thomas J. Holt, associate professor of criminal justice at Michigan State University.

"How do we extend or find a way to develop policies that have a true impact on the way that kids are communicating with one another, given that you could be bullied at home, from 4 p.m. until the next morning, what kind of impact is that going to have on the child in terms of their development and mental health?" he said.

Holt recently published a study in the International Criminal Justice Review using data collected in Singapore by his colleague Esther Ng. The researchers found that 27 percent of students who experienced bullying online, and 28 percent who were victims of bullying by phone text messaging, thought about skipping school or skipped it. That's compared to 22 percent who experienced physical bullying.

Those who said they were cyberbullied were also most likely to say they had considered suicide—28 percent, compared to 22 percent who were physically bullied and 26 percent who received bullying text messages.

Although there may be cultural differences between students in Singapore and the United States, the data on the subject of bullying seems to be similar between the two countries, Holt said.

A recent study in the journal JAMA Psychiatry suggests that both victims and perpetrators of bullying can feel long-lasting psychological effects. Bullying victims showed greater likelihood of agoraphobia, where people don't feel safe in public places, along with generalized anxiety and panic disorder.

People who were both victims and bullies were at higher risk for young adult depression, panic disorder, agoraphobia among females, and the likelihood of suicide among males. Those who were only bullies showed a risk of antisocial personality disorder.

Reporting cyberbullying

Since everything we do online has a digital footprint, it is possible to trace anonymous sources of bullying on the Internet, he said. Patchin noted that tangible evidence of cyberbullying may be more clear-cut than "your word against mine" situations of traditional bullying.

Patchin advises that kids who are being cyberbullied keep the evidence, whether it's an e-mail or Facebook post, so that they can show it to adults they trust. Historically, there have been some issues with schools not disciplining if bullying didn't strictly happen at school, but today, most educators realize that they have the responsibility and authority to intervene, Patchin said.

Adults can experience cyberbullying also, although there's less of a structure in place to stop it. Their recourse is basically to hire a lawyer and proceed through the courts, Patchin said.

Even in school, though, solutions are not always clear.

Turley's mother called the school on his behalf, but the students involved only got a talking-to as punishment. Cyberbullying wasn't considered school-related behavior, at least at that time, he said.

"I was just so afraid of people," says Turley, explaining why he went to different middle schools each year in sixth, seventh, and eighth grade. He stayed quiet through most of it, barely speaking to other students.

Fighting back by speaking out

Turley started slowly merging back into "peopleness" in eighth grade when he started putting video diaries on YouTube. Soon, other students were asking him to help them film school project videos, track meets, and other video projects.

In high school, Turley discovered an organization called WeStopHate.org, a non-profit organization devoted to helping people who have been bullied and allow them a safe space to share their stories.

Emily-Anne Rigal, the founder of the organization, experienced bullying in elementary school, getting picked on for her weight. Although she and Turley lived on opposite sides of the country, they became friends online, united by their passion for stopping bullying.

WeStopHate.org has achieved a wide reach. Rigal has received all sorts of honors for her efforts, from the Presidential Volunteer Service Award to a TeenNick HALO Award presented by Lady Gaga.

Turley designed the WeStopHate.org website and most of its graphics and is actively involved in the organization. In addition to Rigal, he has many other friends in different states whom he's met over the Internet.

"I got cyberbullied, and I feel like, with that, it made me think, like, well, there has to be somebody on the Internet who doesn't hate me," he said. "That kind of just made me search more."

> **People who were both victims and bullies were at higher risk for young adult depression, panic disorder, agoraphobia among females, and the likelihood of suicide among males.**

Parental controls

Ashley Berry, 13, of Littleton, Colorado, has also experienced unpleasantness with peers online. When she was 11, a classmate of hers took photos of Ashley and created an entire Facebook page about her, but denied doing it when Ashley confronted the student whom she suspected.

"It had things like where I went to school, and where my family was from and my birthday, and there were no security settings at all, so it was pretty scary," she said.

The page itself didn't do any harm or say mean things, Ashley said. But her mother, Anna Berry, was concerned about the breach of privacy and viewed it in the context of what else was happening to her daughter in school: Friends were uninviting her to birthday parties and leaving her at the lunch table.

"You would see a girl who should be on top of the world coming home and just closing herself into her bedroom," Berry said.

Berry had to get police involved to have the Facebook page taken down. For seventh grade, her current year, Ashley entered a different middle school than the one her previous school naturally fed into. She says she's a lot happier now and does media interviews speaking out against bullying.

These days, Berry has strict rules for her daughter's online behavior. She knows Ashley's passwords, and she's connected with her daughter on every social network that the teen has joined (except Instagram, but Ashley has an aunt there). Ashley won't accept "friend" requests from anyone she doesn't know.

Technical solutions to technical problems

Parents, extended relatives, Internet service providers, and technology providers can all be incorporated in thinking about how children use technology, Holt said.

Apps that control how much time children spend online and other easy-to-use parental control devices may help, Holt said. There could also be apps to enable parents to better protect their children from certain content and help them report bullying.

Scientists at Massachusetts Institute of Technology are working on an even more automated solution. They want to set up a system that would give bullying victims coping strategies, encourage potential bullies to stop and think before posting something offensive, and allow onlookers to defend victims, said Henry Lieberman.

Lieberman's students Birago Jones and Karthik Dinakar are working on an algorithm that would automatically detect bullying language. The research group has broken down the sorts of offensive statements that commonly get made, grouping them into categories such as racial/ethnic slurs, intelligence insults, sexuality accusations, and social acceptance/rejection.

While it's not all of the potential bullying statements that could be made online, MIT Media Lab scientists have a knowledge base of about 1 million statements. They've thought about how some sentences, such as "you look great in lipstick and a dress," can become offensive if delivered to males specifically.

The idea is that if someone tries to post an offensive statement, the potential bully would receive a message such as "Are you sure you want to send this?" and some educational material about bullying may pop up. Lieberman does not want to automatically ban people, however.

"If they reflect on their behavior, and they read about the experience of others, many kids will talk themselves out of it," he said.

Lieberman and colleagues are using their machine learning techniques on the MTV-partnered website "A Thin Line," where anyone can write in their stories of cyberbullying, read about different forms of online disrespect, and find resources for getting help. The researchers' algorithm tries to detect the theme or topic of each story and match it to other similar stories. They're finding that the top theme is sexting, Lieberman said.

"We're trying to find social network sites that want to partner with us, so we can get more of this stuff out into the real world," Lieberman said.

Turley and Rigal, who is now a freshman at Columbia University, are currently promoting the idea of having a "bully button" on Facebook so that people can formally report cyberbullying to the social network and have bullies suspended for a given period of time. They haven't gotten a response yet, but they're hopeful that it will take off.

In the meantime, Turley is feeling a lot safer in school than he used to.

"Times have changed definitely, where people are becoming slowly more aware," he said. "At my school, at least, I'm seeing a lot less bullying and a more acceptance overall. People just stick to their own."

Digital Harassment Is the New Means of Domestic Abuse

By Keli Goff
The Daily Beast, February 10, 2014

When most hear the words "domestic violence," the image of someone physically battered comes to mind. But technology is increasingly replacing fists as the weapon of choice in abusive relationships.

Katie Ray-Jones, president of the National Domestic Violence Hotline, explained that one of the goals of Teen Dating Violence Awareness Month this February is to educate teens and their parents about the perils of dating abuse in all its forms. Ray-Jones explained that in recent years they have seen a significant increase in the number of girls contacting the hotline to report treatment by their boyfriends that didn't fit traditional definitions of violence but certainly constituted abuse.

"What we're hearing a lot on the hotline and prompted us to engage in a digital abuse awareness strategy was a lot of young people were talking about their part-ner—boyfriend or girlfriend—constantly texting them and if they don't respond in appropriate time there are repercussions and a fight breaks out," she said. Others reported their partners "constantly texting them to know where they are and who they are talking to."

Some reported their boyfriends threatened to post demeaning photos of them on social media if the teens disobeyed their commands. Others said their boyfriends set up fake Facebook accounts to test whether or not they were interacting with members of the opposite sex without permission. In what sounded like a particular-ly extreme case of technology being used as a form of control, one teen reported her boyfriend would text her on a designated schedule so he could be sure she wasn't with someone else cheating. When he would sleep, he had his friends continue texting her on the schedule, and whether she was trying to sleep or not she was ex-pected to reply or face physical violence. This story sounded hard to believe until I spoke with Brittny Henderson a twenty-three-year-old victim of dating abuse, much of it carried out through technology before allegedly escalating to physical violence.

Henderson was a freshman at the University of Wisconsin when she attended a speech on dating abuse. The speaker was sharing the story of his daughter who had been in an abusive relationship. "Everything he said about her had happened to me," she said. "That presentation hit home and it hit hard. It opened my eyes to the fact that I had been in abusive relationship." It was also "the first time I'd even heard the term dating abuse," she said.

As a shy high-school freshman, Henderson was pursued by senior who was a popular football star. She felt so in awe that he expressed interest in her that she never questioned the appropriateness of some of his behavior. Initially it began with him regularly critiquing her appearance, reminding her that many girls wondered why he had chosen to be with "someone like her." But the real warning sign she now realizes was the amount of time he expected her to be available to him by phone. Henderson explained that he would often spend time at her home when they weren't at school together, and after her parents would ask him to leave, he would call her and ask to stay on the phone with him for the entire drive home. After both dressed for bed, he would call her again. "I would wake up to his voice screaming at me on the phone because I had fallen asleep," she said.

Despite her friends and family expressing alarm, the relationship continued for years and, his abuse escalated. After becoming upset she was spending too much time at a summer job and not enough with him, Henderson said he locked her car keys in his trunk. When that didn't work, he put her work uniform in a running shower so she was unable to wear it that day. Henderson's boss then reported strange calls. Some days a family emergency required her to leave work immediately. These behaviors, while disturbing, never seemed to fit the traditional definitions of abuse as Henderson and others knew it. But one incident did. "He pinned me against the wall by my throat," Henderson said, after he interpreted her laughter as directed at him.

> **Those working in the domestic violence nonprofit space are hopeful there will be more that can be done from a law enforcement standpoint eventually, particularly with efforts to seriously address cyber-stalking.**

After Henderson's father put his foot down and demanded they stop seeing each other, she continued the relationship—until she heard the speech on dating violence at her university. She now tries to educate other teens on dating abuse as a member of the Youth Advisory Board for LoveIsRespect.org. Her advice to other girls: "You deserve to be treated with respect and you deserve to be in a relationship that empowers you." Henderson also encourages girls to "Have your own friends and your own goals." The advice given to friends and family worried someone they love is in an abusive relationship is to tread lightly. Henderson said her ex-boyfriend worked to drive a wedge between her and her friends and family, and their criticism of him played into the idea that they were Romeo and Juliet against the world.

"What's really important is if your friend is going through an abusive relationship, just listen to them. Be there for them," Henderson said. But she also suggested visiting resources like LoveIsRespect.org or confiding in an adult you trust who is not necessarily your friend's parent, which she believes would simply have pushed her further away.

Henderson also expressed concern that while schools stay virtually silent on the issue of teen relationship abuse, pop culture is perpetuating dating violence. [Some example are the] mega-hit *Twilight* franchise and MTV's *Jersey Shore*.

Katie Ray-Jones said she is hoping to educate parents and teens on some signs to look out for. One is being conscious of the amount of time teens spend on the phone as well as social media, as well as establishing boundaries and consent. For instance, spending a lot of time texting is not unusual, but doing so because teens are expected to by a significant other is a warning sign. They also want to educate teens on the fact that they have a right not to give your boyfriend or girlfriend passwords to social media accounts or to take photos that make them uncomfortable.

Roberta Valente, a consultant who works with the hotline, said laws are struggling to keep up with the changing digital landscape. "This is a new world for legislators," she wrote in an email. Valente also wrote that those working in the domestic violence nonprofit space are hopeful there will be more that can be done from a law enforcement standpoint eventually, particularly with efforts to seriously address cyber-stalking.

In Henderon's case, her boyfriend eventually served a short amount of time in jail for another crime but never faced any penalties for his alleged treatment of her. "It took me until I was 18 to learn there was such as thing as dating abuse." Her hope is that by speaking out she can reach another girl earlier.

The Downfall of the Most Hated Man on the Internet

By Emily Greenhouse
The New Yorker, January 28, 2014

In October, 2011, Kayla Laws, a twenty-four-year-old actress, photographed herself in front of a bedroom mirror and stashed the photos in her inbox for safekeeping. The following January, she was waiting tables when she received a phone call: a topless image of her had been posted on a Web site called Is Anyone Up?. It was one of the selfies that Kayla had taken three months prior. She was frantic, then confused, since she had never shown the pictures to anyone.

Last week, the owner of Is Anyone Up?, Hunter Moore, and a collaborator, Charles Evens—who often went by the name Gary Jones—were arrested by federal authorities and charged with multiple counts of conspiracy, unauthorized access to a protected computer to obtain information, and aggravated identity theft. According to the indictment, Moore paid Evens upwards of two hundred dollars a week to break into women's e-mail accounts and steal nude photos of them, which he posted for personal gain.

Hunter Moore's Website, isanyoneup.com, trafficked in images like Laws's: nude pictures taken in private, usually of women. They were typically posted alongside screenshots from Facebook, Twitter, or Tumblr—or any other social network that identified the person in the photo—perhaps with a snarky comment, or animated GIF. The photos were often submitted by bitter and jilted exes, a practice known as "revenge porn," or obtained through more mysterious circumstances. Some women sent their photos directly to Moore, though in the end he didn't care about their provenance.

Before it effectively shut down in April, 2012, the site received some three hundred to three hundred and fifty thousand visitors a day and made thousands of dollars a month, helping Moore become, in the words of *Rolling Stone,* "the most hated man on the Internet." It was not an undeserved accolade. Billing himself as a "professional life ruiner," Moore caused some women to quit their jobs and change their names; victims who spoke out were regularly mocked on a section of the Web site set up for that purpose. When Brandi Passante, a star of A&E's reality show *Storage Wars,* sued Moore for defamation, he responded by sending her lawyer a picture of a penis. In March, on a radio morning show appearance, he threatened a morning radio d.j., "I'll rape your f**king cohost in front of you."

It is currently not a distinct federal offense to post nude photos of a person online without his or her permission, so Laws continues to press for federal and state legislation that would formally criminalize "revenge porn."

How does one grow up to become Hunter Moore? *The Daily Beast* reported that, as a child, Moore was expelled from Woodland Christian School, then dropped out altogether at thirteen and launched a series of businesses. He told the writer, Marlow Stern, "I just didn't think I needed school. Now I do because I'm kind of retarded." When Moore was fifteen, he says, he suffered his first heartbreak, at the hand of a girl named Rachel, which he frames as a pivotal moment in his development: "The only way to get to a point where you have no feelings, you have to have your heart ripped out and shit on. I hate to use the term 'heartless,' but you have to have something traumatic happen to get there." Several years later, Moore found himself "hosting sex parties around New York, catering to middle-aged white businessmen." At that point, Moore claims, his sister intervened, and he purchased the domain name isanyoneup.com, which he initially used to review night clubs. Then, in late 2010, as Moore told the *Daily Beast*, "I was having sex with this girl who was getting engaged to a member of an emo band, and everyone wanted to see her naked." A friend convinced him to post a nude photo of her on the site; the fourteen thousand visitors it garnered in a single day insured that while she was the first victim, she would be far from the last.

By January of 2012, when Kayla Laws explained to her mother, Charlotte, that a topless photo of her was posted on Is Anyone Up?, Moore's site was making up to thirteen thousand dollars a month, so he likely didn't think twice about brushing off Charlotte Laws's letter requesting the removal of Kayla's photo. When Moore refused, Laws contacted the L.A.P.D. "The detective was pretty condescending, and blamed Kayla for taking pictures of herself," Laws told me this weekend, from Los Angeles. "So I called the F.B.I." While her contacts at that agency were initially hesitant to pursue a case against Moore, Laws pressured them until they opened an investigation, later that month. By then, she had also begun reaching out to other women whose pictures were on Moore's site, in order to compile a thick dossier for the F.B.I. She held a victims' meeting, attended by F.B.I. agents, during which many of the women spoke of being hacked by a "Gary Jones." That investigation led to the arrest of Moore and Evens last week.

This past Thursday, Laws attended the arraignment of Evens, who pleaded not guilty. It turns out that he went to high school down the street, says Laws, and shares several of Kayla's Facebook friends. Laws also says that she spoke briefly with Evens's mother, though she didn't reveal who she was. (She insinuated that she was a journalist.) She told me with a laugh that she can't stand confrontation, though she gave me, without prompting, the addresses of both Evens and Moore. She also intends to be at Hunter Moore's next court date, on February 7th, when he is expected to enter a plea. If convicted, he and Evens could both potentially face decades in federal prison.

It is currently not a distinct federal offense to post nude photos of a person online without his or her permission, so Laws continues to press for federal and state legislation that would formally criminalize "revenge porn." "It's cyber rape," she told me. Laws was involved in California Governor Jerry Brown's recent criminalization of the practice, and she told me that she's met with California Senator Barbara Boxer's office and spoken with New Jersey Senator Cory Booker. Laws wants the United States to follow the lead of Israel, which earlier this month enacted legislation that threatens people found guilty of "the dissemination of sexual pictures or videos on the Internet without permission" with up to five years in prison.

I asked Laws if she didn't consider "revenge porn" a misnomer, since "revenge" implies a kind of justice against someone who inflicted injury. "I don't know," she answered, granting that the term may not be exactly right. "But then, I suppose, even if you don't know the person, you are getting revenge against them—because you hate women."

Minnesota Detectives Crack the Case with Digital Forensics

By Shannon Prather
Star Tribune, October 6, 2014

In the world of law enforcement, it's a game changer nearly as profound as the advent of DNA testing.

When two thirteen-year-old Andover girls went missing last week, the first place detectives looked was for the digital clues in their iPods and smartphones. It worked. The girls were soon found in the basement of a twenty-three-year-old Burnsville man, Casey Lee Chinn, who is now charged with felony criminal sexual conduct, kidnapping, and solicitation of a child.

Digital forensics—the examination of cellphones, tablets, and personal electronics in criminal investigations—are dramatically changing the way cases are worked and solved. While technology has created new portals for predators searching for victims, it's also leaving telltale trails for police.

The number of smartphones, tablets, and personal devices examined by the Anoka County Sheriff's Office has tripled in the past three years. In 2013, detectives searched 300 phones and devices in a wide array of cases. It's now often the first piece of evidence detectives seek out.

"That [missing girls] case was solved by a detective in the lab, not by any field work or eyewitness accounts. It was digital forensics," said Commander Paul Sommer. "It's become an investigation imperative. You try to find the personal electronics."

With 90 percent of American adults now carrying a cellphone—58 percent with a smartphone, according to the Pew Research Center—the devices have become the one constant in many people's lives—in their pocket or purse all day, on their bedside table at night. It's the alarm clock, home phone line, camera, chat forum, e-mail, and social media terminal. Police use that almost constant phone activity to verify a suspect's or witness' statement and provide a log of a person's movements and activities. Smartphones can even be an eyewitness, recording a crime in progress.

.The Hennepin County Sheriff's Office crime lab analyzes thousands of phones and personal electronic devices each year for its own investigations as well as for other police agencies. It also contracts with an outside digital forensic expert to keep up with the constantly changing technology.

"Electronic devices are just a treasure trove of information," said Hennepin County Sheriff Rich Stanek. "The digital evidence is one of the first things we go to. They leave footprints all over the place: Who the girls were last talking with, who they were tweeting with. They offer up a lot of clues about what has been happening in these young girls' lives in the past few hours and days."

Ramsey County Sheriff Matt Bostrom said his investigators increasingly rely on digital evidence to break cases in addition to older investigative methods.

"It is one of the best advancements in the last decade in being able to quickly respond to crime," Bostrom said. "It has changed the way we are capable of responding to citizens that are in trouble."

With potential access to so much personal information, police also face a big responsibility to not misuse data or violate the privacy rights of innocent people, since lawmakers could still throttle back law enforcement's access to digital data.

The Anoka County Sheriff's Office has set up a digital forensics lab with computers and about eight tools that can download cellphone data, useful because the sheriff handles all death investigations in the county and most of the sex crimes.

This year the Sheriff's Office hired two new detectives, bringing the total to seventeen to help handle the increased digital forensic caseload.

Digital forensics—the examination of cellphones, tablets, and personal electronics in criminal investigations—are dramatically changing the way cases are worked and solved.

The office also is setting up the first mobile digital forensic lab in the state. It's still in the early stages but when it's outfitted, detectives can take the unit—an old ambulance donated by Allina Emergency Medical Services —to a crime scene or a missing person's home and quickly copy evidence from cellphones. Now detectives have to take phones back to the lab—something that witnesses can resist.

"You are going to have witnesses taking video. The Boston bombing is a prime example of that," said Anoka County detective Brian Hill.

Detectives want immediate access to that evidence, "but who wants to be without their phone for twenty-four hours?" Hill said.

And in cases of suspected online solicitation where a child is missing, it saves precious minutes by eliminating a drive back to the sheriff's department.

"There is a huge sense of urgency," Hill said.

Hill is one of five Anoka County detectives trained to download and search data from cellphones and devices. He traveled to Washington, D.C., this summer to testify before a subcommittee of Congress to discuss how cellphones and spyware are the newest ways domestic abusers terrorize their victims. But it also leaves a trail that police can use to help prosecute them.

Hill said about half his work time is now spent on digital forensics. That's a dramatic change from when he started with the sheriff's office in 2000.

When deputies are called to a crime scene, the first question is: "Where's the phone? Can we get access to the phone?" Hill explained. "Virtually every crime today involves technology and that is usually a cellphone."

Detectives often get witnesses, victims, or suspects' consent to search a phone. Hill said he and his colleagues are cognizant of the personal nature of phones. He said he doesn't snoop through pictures, e-mails, and other information unrelated to the case.

If necessary, detectives obtain a search warrant.

Hill said there are many ways smartphone data can corroborate or poke holes in a suspect's statement to police.

First, phones record a user's physical movements, which can help break a case.

"They track where you go. Smartphones are constantly reaching out to towers," Hill said.

Text messages, e-mails, and even photos stored on smartphones can help detectives flesh out the truth especially if someone's statement doesn't add up. There have been cases where text messages have exonerated suspects.

"Text messages can tell a whole different story," Hill said.

A pause in phone use also can tell detectives something. Detectives look to see if someone shuts their smartphone off or even simply leaves it at home and fails to check e-mails and texts during the period when a crime was committed.

In the case of the missing Andover girls, parents reported their disappearance at 9:36 p.m. Monday. Detective Pat O'Hara searched one of the girl's iPods found in her room and discovered two weeks of sexually explicit texts with the final text "Be there" received at 8:31 p.m. Monday.

Police were searching the suspect's home by the next morning.

Hollywood-Style Surveillance Technology Inches Closer to Reality

By GW Schultz
The Center for Investigative Reporting, April 11, 2014

COMPTON, Calif.—When sheriff's deputies here noticed a burst of necklace snatchings from women walking through town, they turned to an unlikely source to help solve the crimes: a retired Air Force veteran named Ross McNutt.

McNutt and his Ohio-based company, Persistent Surveillance Systems, persuaded the Los Angeles County Sheriff's Department to use his surveillance technology to monitor Compton's streets from the air and track suspects from the moment the snatching occurred.

The system, known as wide-area surveillance, is something of a time machine—the entire city is filmed and recorded in real time. Imagine Google Earth with a rewind button and the ability to play back the movement of cars and people as they scurry about the city.

"We literally watched all of Compton during the time that we were flying, so we could zoom in anywhere within the city of Compton and follow cars and see people," McNutt said. "Our goal was to basically jump to where reported crimes occurred and see what information we could generate that would help investigators solve the crimes."

McNutt, who holds a doctorate in rapid product development, helped build wide-area surveillance to hunt down bombing suspects in Iraq and Afghanistan. He decided that clusters of high-powered surveillance cameras attached to the belly of small civilian aircraft could be a game-changer in U.S. law enforcement.

"Our whole system costs less than the price of a single police helicopter and costs less for an hour to operate than a police helicopter," McNutt said. "But at the same time, it watches 10,000 times the area that a police helicopter could watch."

McNutt's airborne cameras are just one part of a new digital movement in law enforcement. The Hollywood version of American policing is made up of darkened command centers where a wellspring of digital data about criminals always seems just a few clicks away.

In cities across the country, that fiction is inching closer to reality.

The FBI is rolling out a sprawling data complex that contains over 147 million mug shots and sets of fingerprints, many of which belong to people who are not criminals. Local law enforcement analysts are using surveillance centers to monitor video feeds and reported crimes minute by minute.

The Center for Investigative Reporting and KQED teamed up to take an inside look at the emerging technologies that could revolutionize policing—

> **The system, known as wide-area surveillance, is something of a time machine—the entire city is filmed and recorded in real time.**

and how intrusively the public is monitored by the government. The technology is forcing the public and law enforcement to answer a central question: When have police crossed the line from safer streets to expansive surveillance that threatens to undermine the nation's constitutional values?

In one city, law enforcement officials don't need to see your identification: They just need your face. Police officers in Chula Vista, near San Diego, already have used mobile facial recognition technology to confirm the identities of people they suspect of crimes. After using a tablet to capture the person's image, an answer is delivered in eight seconds. (About 1 percent of the time, the system retrieves the wrong name, according to the manufacturer, FaceFirst.)

Chula Vista is now part of a larger trend in law enforcement to use unique biological markers like faces, palm prints, skin abnormalities, and the iris of eyes to identify people.

"You can lie about your name, you can lie about your date of birth, you can lie about your address," said Officer Rob Halverson. "But tattoos, birthmarks, scars don't lie."

The FBI, meanwhile, is finalizing plans this year to make 130 million fingerprints digital and searchable.

Many of the fingerprints belong to people who have not been arrested but simply submitted their prints for background checks while seeking jobs. Civil libertarians worry that facial images for these individuals could be next. The FBI already maintains a collection of some 17 million mug shots.

This personal information is now housed in a West Virginia-based storage facility the size of two football fields containing row after row of blinking and buzzing server stacks. These machines are the heart of the FBI's Next Generation Identification program, which seeks to make it easier for police officers and investigators around the nation to distinguish one human being from another based on biological traits.

"What it potentially means is that we're able to catch bad guys faster, and we're able to get them off the streets a lot faster with the technologies we have so they don't commit another crime," said Jeremy Wiltz, acting assistant director of the FBI's Criminal Justice Information Services Division.

Such technology, he said, also could exonerate innocent people and keep them from being held in a jail cell for days or longer. Audits have been conducted to ensure Next Generation Identification isn't accessed by local police for conducting inappropriate searches, Wiltz added.

The potential for misuse nonetheless troubles civil libertarians.

Jennifer Lynch, a senior staff attorney at the Electronic Frontier Foundation, said she's concerned the government will eventually collect and store face images like it does now with the tens of millions of fingerprints submitted by people seeking certain jobs. She's worried such data will be merged with criminal records that are currently kept separate – resulting in innocent people being placed under suspicion.

"Once the nation has a facial recognition database, and once facial recognition capabilities improve to the point that we can identify faces in a crowd, it will become possible for authorities to identify people as they move through society," Lynch said.

As for wide-area surveillance, McNutt said that ground-based cameras offer higher resolutions and that his technology cannot zoom in on faces or other particular details. But cameras on the ground are limited in range, and a seemingly infinite number would be necessary to blanket an entire city. McNutt believes his technology will be good enough in a few years to cover twice as much area—perhaps as large as the entire city of San Francisco.

In the case of a Compton necklace snatching, the suspects eventually drove out of camera range without being identified, said L.A. County sheriff's Sgt. Doug Iketani, who supervised the project. He added that McNutt's system can't provide the kind of detailed, close-up images that would survive in court. But Iketani said the technology did give police useful leads.

So why have the people of Compton heard little about this experiment until now?

"The system was kind of kept confidential from everybody in the public," Iketani said. "A lot of people do have a problem with the eye in the sky, the Big Brother, so in order to mitigate any of those kinds of complaints, we basically kept it pretty hush-hush."

Elsewhere in the Los Angeles area, police are facing similar challenges at a command center near downtown where law enforcement analysts observe a video surveillance feed aimed at the iconic Hollywood sign, which police say is sometimes targeted by vandals and is vulnerable to fires.

Policing the Hollywood sign is one of many tasks of the Los Angeles Police Department's Real-Time Analysis and Critical Response Division—looking not unlike other high-tech law enforcement centers that have sprung up around the country as part of a post-9/11 trend known as predictive or intelligence-led policing. The goal: speed up reaction times or, better yet, intercede before new crimes, including potential precursors to terrorism, occur.

The center has access to 1,000 surveillance cameras spread across the city. Also available, through a feed to the center, are social media sites, news broadcasts and data captured by license-plate recognition devices.

There's also a wall-mounted digital map of real-time reported crimes around Los Angeles that could provide analysts with valuable insight into when and where crimes are most likely to occur, where trends are emerging, and where officers should be patrolling.

Like many cities around the country, Los Angeles is grappling with unease from residents over thousands of networked cameras that can peer into many corners of our lives, often without our being fully aware of it.

The center's commanding officer, Capt. John Romero, recognizes the concerns but equates them with public resistance to street lights in America's earliest days.

"People thought that this is the government trying to see what we're doing at night, to spy on us," Romero said. "And so over time, things shifted, and now if you try to take down street lights in Los Angeles or Boston or anywhere else, people will say no."

Hacker or Spy? In Today's Cyberattacks, Finding the Culprit Is a Troubling Puzzle

By Bruce Schneier
The Christian Science Monitor, March 4, 2015

The vigorous debate after the Sony Pictures breach pitted the Obama administration against many of us in the cybersecurity community who didn't buy Washington's claim that North Korea was the culprit.

What's both amazing—and perhaps a bit frightening—about that dispute over who hacked Sony is that it happened in the first place.

But what it highlights is the fact that we're living in a world where we can't easily tell the difference between a couple of guys in a basement apartment and the North Korean government with an estimated $10 billion military budget. And that ambiguity has profound implications for how countries will conduct foreign policy in the Internet age.

Clandestine military operations aren't new. Terrorism can be hard to attribute, especially the murky edges of state-sponsored terrorism. What's different in cyberspace is how easy it is for an attacker to mask his identity—and the wide variety of people and institutions that can attack anonymously.

In the real world, you can often identify the attacker by the weaponry. In 2006, Israel attacked a Syrian nuclear facility. It was a conventional attack—military airplanes flew over Syria and bombed the plant—and there was never any doubt who did it. That shorthand doesn't work in cyberspace.

When the U.S. and Israel attacked an Iranian nuclear facility in 2010, they used a cyberweapon and their involvement was a secret for years. On the Internet, technology broadly disseminates capability. Everyone from lone hackers to criminals to hypothetical cyberterrorists to nations' spies and soldiers are using the same tools and the same tactics. Internet traffic doesn't come with a return address, and it's easy for an attacker to obscure his tracks by routing his attacks through some innocent third party.

And while it now seems that North Korea did indeed attack Sony, the attack it most resembles was conducted by members of the hacker group Anonymous against a company called HBGary Federal in 2011. In the same year, other members of Anonymous threatened NATO, and in 2014, still others announced that they were going to attack ISIS. Regardless of what you think of the group's capabilities, it's a new world when a bunch of hackers can threaten an international military alliance.

Get Monitor cybersecurity news and analysis delivered straight to your inbox.

Follow Passcode

Even when a victim does manage to attribute a cyberattack, the process can take a long time. It took the U.S. weeks to publicly blame North Korea for the Sony attacks. That was relatively fast; most of that time was probably spent trying to figure out how to respond. Attacks by China against U.S. companies have taken much longer to attribute.

This delay makes defense policy difficult. Microsoft's Scott Charney makes this point: When you're being physically attacked, you can call on a variety of organizations to defend you—the police, the military, whoever does antiterrorism security in your country, your lawyers. The legal structure justifying that defense depends on knowing two things: who's attacking you and why. Unfortunately, when you're being attacked in cyberspace, the two things you often don't know are who's attacking you and why.

Whose job was it to defend Sony? Was it the U.S. military's, because it believed the attack to have come from North Korea? Was it the FBI, because this wasn't an act of war? Was it Sony's own problem, because

> We're living in a world where we can't easily tell the difference between a couple of guys in a basement apartment and the North Korean government with an estimated $10 billion military budget.

it's a private company? What about during those first weeks, when no one knew who the attacker was? These are just a few of the policy questions that we don't have good answers for.

Certainly Sony needs enough security to protect itself regardless of who the attacker was, as do all of us. For the victim of a cyberattack, who the attacker is can be academic. The damage is the same, whether it's a couple of hackers or a nation-state.

In the geopolitical realm, though, attribution is vital. And not only is attribution hard, providing evidence of any attribution is even harder. Because so much of the FBI's evidence was classified—and probably provided by the National Security Agency—it was not able to explain why it was so sure North Korea did it. As I recently wrote: "The agency might have intelligence on the planning process for the hack. It might, say, have phone calls discussing the project, weekly PowerPoint status reports, or even Kim Jong-un's sign-off on the plan." Making any of this public would reveal the NSA's "sources and methods," something it regards as a very important secret.

Different types of attribution require different levels of evidence. In the Sony case, we saw the U.S. government was able to generate enough evidence to convince itself. Perhaps it had the additional evidence required to convince North Korea it was sure and provided that over diplomatic channels. But if the public is expected to support any government retaliatory action, they are going to need sufficient evidence made public to convince them. Today, trust in U.S. intelligence agencies is low, especially after the 2003 Iraqi weapons-of-mass-destruction debacle.

What all of this means is that we are in the middle of an arms race between attackers and those that want to identify them: deception and deception detection. It's an arms race in which the US—and, by extension, its allies—has a singular advantage. We spend more money on electronic eavesdropping than the rest of the world combined, we have more technology companies than any other country, and the architecture of the Internet ensures that most of the world's traffic passes through networks the NSA can eavesdrop on.

In 2012, then U.S. Secretary of Defense Leon Panetta said publicly that the US—presumably the NSA—has "made significant advances in ... identifying the origins" of cyberattacks. We don't know if this means they have made some fundamental technological advance, or that their espionage is so good that they're monitoring the planning processes. Other U.S. government officials have privately said that they've solved the attribution problem.

We don't know how much of that is real and how much is bluster. It's actually in America's best interest to confidently accuse North Korea, even if it isn't sure, because it sends a strong message to the rest of the world: "Don't think you can hide in cyberspace. If you try anything, we'll know it's you."

Strong attribution leads to deterrence. The detailed NSA capabilities leaked by Edward Snowden help with this, because they bolster an image of an almost-omniscient NSA.

It's not, though—which brings us back to the arms race. A world where hackers and governments have the same capabilities, where governments can masquerade as hackers or as other governments, and where much of the attribution evidence intelligence agencies collect remains secret, is a dangerous place.

[...] So is a world where countries have secret capabilities for deception and detection deception, and are constantly trying to get the best of each other. This is the world of today, though, and we need to be prepared for it.

The Dark Web Remains

By Russell Berman
The Atlantic, February 5, 2015

The Wednesday conviction of Silk Road creator Ross Ulbricht on seven felony charges demonstrated at least one thing pretty clearly: U.S. law enforcement can not only find, but successfully prosecute online operators of the drug market who cloak their criminal dealings behind hidden web addresses—especially when those operators slip up by, say, talking about their drug deals in messages linked to a personal Gmail account.

Yet beyond sending a thirty-year-old to prison, what does Ulbricht's conviction mean for the so-called "dark web," which continues to grow even after the government shut down both the original Silk Road and its immediate successor? That's far murkier, say experts on cybercrime and privacy issues.

In many ways, the largest shift came when federal agents arrested Ulbricht in October 2013 and accused him of being the mastermind of Silk Road, the $1.2 billion criminal enterprise that operated on the hidden Tor network and used Bitcoin as its currency. With Ulbricht in the headlines, the price of Bitcoin plummeted, and the closures of Silk Road and Silk Road 2.0 forced other major hubs of the dark web to add new levels of security to evade law enforcement.

Ulbricht's arrest and conviction was a victory for the feds, which had caught him "literally with his fingers on the keyboard" at a San Francisco library after a Department of Homeland Security agent had infiltrated Silk Road and posed as one of Ulbricht's employees. Using his laptop, journal, chat logs, and the network's servers in Iceland and Pennsylvania, prosecutors unloaded a mountain of evidence against Ulbricht and identified him as the man behind the pseudonym, Dread Pirate Roberts. Ulbricht, they said, had even asked applicants to his "bitcoin startup" to use his eponymous Gmail address. A college friend testified that Ulbricht had confided to him that he created Silk Road, and the FBI traced $13.4 million in bitcoins back to Ulbricht's e-wallet, according to *Wired.* The jury took less than four hours to convict him.

At the same time, however, the high-profile trial gave a lot of publicity to the dark web, and both the number of sites and the volume of people using them have increased since Silk Road was shuttered, notes *The Dark Net* author Jamie Bartlett, director of the Centre for the Analysis of Social Media at Demos. "I think it's a mixed bag for law enforcement," Bartlett said by phone on Thursday. "The long-term impact was the sites got smarter. They got more careful."

> **"The long-term impact was the sites got smarter. They got more careful."**

The cat-and-mouse game may shift as well. Newer dark sites (two major ones are Agora and Evolution) are likely to protect their servers by basing them in countries "hostile to U.S. law enforcement," said Nicholas Weaver of the International Computer Science Institute in Berkeley, California. "The markets will keep moving overseas, but law enforcement will keep going after the dealers," he said, referring to the people who actually ship and deliver the drugs sold online.

On another front—the Fourth Amendment concerns raised by the FBI's discovery of the Silk Road server—Ulbricht's case may set less of a precedent than Internet-freedom advocates originally feared. To the surprise of Weaver and other close observers of the trial, Ulbricht's defense team never fully challenged the government's seizure of the Silk Road server on constitutional grounds, because to have legal standing under the Fourth Amendment, he would first have had to state definitively that the server belonged to him—in other words, he would have had to admit to being the mastermind of Silk Road. Yet as Weaver writes, such an admission would not have been as devastating as it sounds, because it would not have come out in open court, with the jury present.

Such a declaration is not an admission of guilt: It can only be used by the prosecution if the defendant testifies. So as long as Ulbricht doesn't testify, the jury never learns that Ulbricht admits to controlling the server.

The judge tossed Ulbricht's motion to suppress the government's evidence from the server, and he did not end up testifying in his own defense. While not denying Ulbricht's involvement with Silk Road, his lawyer, Joshua Dratel, had argued he was framed and that he was not the site's creator. Dratel said he'll appeal the conviction over the judge's decision not to allow the presentation of certain evidence and witnesses, *The Wall Street Journal* reported. In an interview Thursday, Weaver said the judgment against Ulbricht was sound even if the investigation was not. "It is fortunate for us that it looks like this case will have no legal precedent," he said.

For now, Ulbricht sits in jail, awaiting both his sentence and his appeal* (and a second, related trial on murder-for-hire charges). The dark web that he helped to build and popularize goes on, with the FBI attempting to track increasingly sophisticated hidden drug, munitions, and hacking markets. "How will law enforcement try to strategically undermine these sites?" Bartlett asked. The answer, he said, might lie in the same undercover methods of monitoring and infiltration the government has used to take down vast child pornography networks, as well as Silk Road. "It becomes a little more like good, old-fashioned policing," Bartlett said, "but in a new space."

Editor's Note

* Ulbricht was later sentenced to life in prison and is in the process of appealing the sentence and his conviction.

Eyes Wide Open to Problems Experienced by Black Men

By Dan Rodricks
The Baltimore Sun, April 20, 2015

"Innocent people don't run from cops," a follower posted on my Facebook page, a comment on the circumstances that ultimately led to the death of Freddie Gray. To which I respond: "Easy for a white man to say."

Any white American who has not had eyes opened by the citizen-captured videos of Gray's arrest in West Baltimore or the killing of Walter Scott in South Carolina or the chokehold death of Eric Garner in New York must live in the nation's 51st state—the state of denial.

For decades, verbal or written complaints by African-American men about police harassment might have gone in one white ear and out the other. But there's no way videos can be dismissed. In the digital age, they have the raw force of now, the power to make the most skeptical old cynic agree that something is deeply wrong.

I didn't know Gray. I don't know the cops who were involved in stopping and arresting him. I know that he was black, and that historically, twenty-five-year-old black men in Baltimore have far more contacts with police than twenty-five-year-old white men.

According to a court document, Gray "fled unprovoked upon noticing police presence."

And that was enough for the Facebook poster to presume guilt.

Until recently, I might have agreed with him.

Now I can just as easily think this: Maybe Freddie Gray had reason to fear the police. Maybe his last encounter with them didn't go well. Maybe he thought he could outrun them and avoid a confrontation on a pleasant Sunday morning in spring.

Of course, that's speculation on my part. But there's a lot of that going around, and for good reason.

Until Monday, we had little information about what happened during Gray's encounter with police in West Baltimore on April 12.

Thanks to a court document obtained by *Baltimore Sun* reporters Justin Fenton and Jessica Anderson, we have the first bit of light about why police arrested Freddie Gray. It took more than a week.

But while charging documents mention that Gray was carrying a switchblade-like knife, we have nothing more on why he came to the attention of police to begin with, and we still know precious little about how he received the severe injuries that contributed to his death.

Given that Gray's arrest was videotaped by an onlooker, and given the present atmosphere in Baltimore—with a Justice Department inquiry into police misconduct opening deep and festering wounds—you'd think the mayor and police commissioner would want to get answers a lot faster than at the present pace. And if they have answers, you'd think they would share them with an angry public.

Given the atmosphere in the nation—with distrust of police forged in Ferguson and other places where encounters have led to the deaths of unarmed citizens—you'd think we'd have more information by now.

Obviously, it is prudent for the police to conduct a thorough investigation.

Transparency is good. But some situations call for transparency a whole lot faster than we've seen here. A delay of this length fosters more distrust—not only among the immediate family of the deceased, but among those of us who have had our eyes opened by these disturbing cellphone videos.

In the Gray case, it's hard to believe that it takes more than a week to come up with some straightforward answers: Why did police stop him? What explains his apparently painful condition, as seen in the citizen-captured video of his arrest, when he was led to a police wagon? (Some might say he was carried, others that he was dragged.)

> **Social and mainstream news media quickly push these stories in front of our eyes, as never before, and a plodding pace of explanation doesn't work.**

And what happened to Gray during his transport in the police wagon?

Police have provided a timeline of events, but not much else. The fact that officers found Gray with a knife was not volunteered during the last week; the reference was found in a District Court document. The document says Gray was arrested "without force or incident," but the citizen video challenges that assertion as well as the mayor's claim that what happened to Gray occurred inside the police wagon and not on the street.

A few years ago, I might have suggested that we all just be quiet and patiently wait for the investigation to be completed.

But the Freddie Gray video, and others like it, announce the new reality for police departments, for all of us: Eyes are everywhere; citizens are watching and recording, and their videos travel fast. Social and mainstream news media quickly push these stories in front of our eyes, as never before, and a plodding pace of explanation doesn't work. It compounds distrust.

People see a disturbing image, and they want to know what it means.

Earnest as the mayor and police commissioner might seem, this week of mystery about Gray's arrest did nothing to restore public confidence in the Police Department's ability to police itself. And it makes you wonder what might have happened in the old days, before the prevalence of video cameras.

5
Economy and the Workforce

© Noah Berger/Reuters/Corbis

Kiva robots move inventory at an Amazon fulfillment center in Tracy, CA on December 1, 2014. Amazon.com Inc. installed more than 15,000 robots across ten US warehouses, in an effort to cut operating costs by one-fifth and get packages out the door more quickly in the run-up to the holiday season.

Surf and Spend Economics

In 1969, economic theorist Peter F. Drucker theorized in his book, *The Age of Discontinuity*, that the world economy was shifting towards a "knowledge economy," in which data would become the primary resource.[1] The digital age has proven many of Drucker's theories correct as the ownership and management of data created industries that rival the industrial giants of the twentieth century. This transformation has provided massive economic, social, recreational, educational, and professional benefits for consumers, but this period has also destabilized many of the former economic pillars of the industrial economy.

The Techno-industrial Complex

The first layer of the digital economy consists of the hardware needed to participate in the digital marketplace and the infrastructure that physically connects computers and devices. This is the arena in which the digital economy overlaps with the industrial economy because the development of new hardware and infrastructure relies on labor and physical innovation. Though economic studies of the digital age often focus on virtual services and innovation, like web browsers and social media, the new economy is still built on physical networks that provide electricity and the physical transport of signals. In the 1990s, the Internet became a utility, in the same vein as home phone or cable television and by the 2010s had become the most important telecommunications service in the world.[2] The companies that built Internet infrastructure and sell Internet services, like Verizon, Charter, Comcast, and Time Warner, constitute the first essential pillar of the digital economy, as they the raw resource of virtual economics: data.

Since the 1980s, new companies have emerged while established tech giants and telecommunications corporations have adapted to provide digital technology. Companies like Apple/Mac, Microsoft, Dell, IBM, Hewlett-Packard, Acer, and Samsung, many of which were already tech leaders, expanded their dominance through the personal computer market. Personal computers and devices that can access the Internet through cellular or wireless networks are the essential tools of the new economy and companies that manufacture these devices have grown into industry leaders in the digital age.

However, hardware and data are useless without an interface and one of the most innovative and fastest growing segments of the digital economy is composed of companies that provide digital service platforms including web browsers and digital communications, like email, voice, and video chat. While tech companies like Microsoft and Apple also provide Internet communication and web browsing services, the innovators in this field came from companies that focused entirely on providing innovative web application and tools. This industry includes Yahoo and Google, which have dominated the search engine and email business since the mid-2000s and have grown to offer an increasingly complex series of services to Internet users, ranging from entertainment and connectivity to finance and cartography.[3]

Digital Data in the Marketplace

As infrastructure, hardware, and software developed, the next step in the evolution of the digital economy was the development of online shopping and e-commerce. The first companies to succeed as online retailers were still rooted in the traditional supply chain. The web giant Amazon, for instance, began as a digital version of the venerable bookstore business model. Online vendors grew rapidly as customers responded to the convenience and the ability to access a global inventory of products from their home computers or devices.[4]

In addition to online vendors, the digital equivalent of brick and mortar businesses, a new wave of companies emerged in the 2000s that abandoned the supply chain altogether, using data as their only product and their primary asset. Social media companies, like Facebook, YouTube, Twitter, and Instagram provide examples of this phenomenon. These companies invest only in the development of an interface application that can be used by consumers to store, manipulate, and share data. Web service companies like Google provide another example, as these companies' primary "product" is data, though filtered through various applications. Social media companies and web service providers like Google are able to provide their services for "free" to consumers because they also use data as their primary currency. Facebook and Google, for instance, sell consumer data to advertisers, and this pays the cost of developing applications and providing free services.[5]

A newer example of the data-first business model can be seen in what economists have called the "sharing economy," in which companies provide a way to link buyers and sellers. Amazon, for instance, which still maintains large physical warehouses called "fulfillment centers" to store thousands of products, has begun to evolve their business by incorporating "user to user" sales. In 2015, Amazon offered the ability for stores to create "shops" within their website in return for a monthly fee and also offered general customers the ability to sell their products through the website, paying an average of $.99 per sale to Amazon for access to the company's enormous customer base.[6] Many other successful Internet businesses, like Ebay and Etsy, essentially do the same thing: linking buyers and sellers and earning fees from successful transaction. A new dimension to this model has emerged with companies like AirBnB, which allows property owners to rent property like a hotel, and Uber, which encourages car owners to use their vehicles to provide alternative taxi services. Uber and AirBnB offer users cheaper access to room and transportation, while at the same time providing a new source of potential revenue for home and car owners. Both companies benefit from limited expenditures, as they maintain no infrastructure beyond providing users with a web interface and so can concentrate most of their revenue towards improving their services and attracting customers.[7]

In general, forming an Internet business requires less investment in terms of infrastructure and capital, and this has opened the possibility of entrepreneurship to a much larger portion of the population and has also placed innovation at a premium. The success of social networking and the new innovations of the sharing economy provide evidence of how an innovative idea can transform markets and lead to major evolutionary changes in the economy. Perhaps one of the most unusual and innovative examples has been the development of "cryptocurrency," like "bitcoin," over the past decade. Cryptocurrency is a new approach to money in which certain vendors and service providers conduct business through the exchange of digital vouchers that can then be exchanged with other vendors that choose to accept the alternative form of payment. The idea of cryptocurrency is new, and has only begun to become widely accepted, but it does highlight the innovative dimension of the digital economy in which even currency itself may come to be radically redefined.[8]

Disruptors and Inequity

One of the economic buzzwords of the digital age is "disruption," defined as ideas or companies that "disrupt" the existing model for a certain business or industry. At the 2015 World Economic Forum in Davos, Switzerland, John Chambers, CEO of Cisco Systems, estimated that 40 percent of the businesses in the modern world will not survive through the next decade. Chambers' argument was simple: the digital exchange of goods and services will continue to make many existing business models obsolete by offering the same or similar services through innovative digital platforms.[9]

For all the innovation and creativity of the digital economy, the shift from traditional to digital markets has also been a destructive force. Amazon put bookstores out of business, and Uber has significantly reduced traditional taxi markets in San Francisco and several other states.[10] The loss of these industries is far from trivial. The taxi business, for instance, provides employment for immigrants and other groups at a disadvantage in other industries. The unfortunate repercussion of the digital shift in economics has been felt most acutely by small businesses that lack the resources to compete with online retailers. There is little question that innovative digital platforms like Uber and other ride-share platforms provide advantages to consumers but each step forward in the digital economy has resulted in the loss of service, labor, and other jobs that were once the backbone of the industrial economy.

Another example of this trend can be seen in the creative industries. Sharing data through digital platforms and streaming services had led to a situation in which many consumers increasingly feel that music, movies, and literature are products that should be "free." Writing in the *New York Times* in 2013, columnist Jaron Lanier argues that most creative professionals are living on "false hope," in a world where their services are devalued because of the ease with which free information and art are available, while a small elite builds wealth by facilitating the process that allows for the exploitation of artistic and trade jobs.[11] In some ways, the digital economy has empowered consumers, primarily by providing access to a much larger range of vendors and services. The expansion of the marketplace for certain products and services has forced companies to become more innovative and competitive, often translating into savings for consumers. For entrepreneurs and small business owners, online markets and digital marketing provide the potential benefit of access to a global consumer base. However, there is a growing inequality around the world between countries that have been able to keep abreast of digital economics and those that have not.[12]

The inequity of the digital economy is compounded by biases in education and training that continue to exclude women and many minorities from many of the essential industries in the new economy. For instance, government programs that promote female interest in scientific and technological fields (STEM careers) have been successful in increasing the percentage of women in STEM fields from 9 percent in 1970 to nearly 40 percent in 2013. However, the distribution of income and control remains fundamentally unequal. Surveys from 2013 indicate that women own or manage only 5 percent of tech start-ups and hold a similarly small percentage of leadership jobs in tech companies.[13] In 2011, surveys of the engineering field found that 73 percent of scientists and engineers are white. By contrast, African American men and women, though comprising 34 percent of the US population, hold less than 3 percent of science and engineering jobs.[14]

Returning to Drucker's prescient 1969 economic predications, he argued that democratic societies could become "class societies" unless workers are able to earn "...both income and dignity."[15] The 2010s have seen waves of protests in western nations against the idea of the "1 percent," the relatively small number of predominantly white male executives and business owners who control an inordinate percentage of the world's wealth, and this growing sense of economic disparity and dwindling opportunity is also a defining characteristic of the digital economy.

Micah L. Issit

Notes

1. Drucker, The Age of Discontinuity, 247-258.
2. "Working Paper: Digital Economy – Facts and Figures," 4-5.
3. Williams, "Web Browsers: A Brief History."
4. Webley, "A Brief History of Online Shopping"
5. Eggers, Hamill, Ali, "Data as the New Currency."
6. Wohlsen, "Amazon Could Finally Grow Its Profits."
7. Fisher, "The Big Question With Uber, Airbnb And the Rest of the 'Sharing Economy': Who to Sue?"
8. Davis, "The Crypto-Currency."
9 Wall, "How to Reign Over the New 'Digital Economy'."
10. Davidson, "Uber Has Pretty Much Destroyed Regular Taxis in San Francisco."
11. Lanier, "Fixing the Digital Economy."
12. Wakefield, "World Wakes Up To Digital Divide."
13. Foroohar, "The Digital Economy is Profoundly Unequal."
14. McPhail, "The 'New' American Dilemma: STEM and Minorities."
15. Wartzman, "What Peter Drucker Knew About 2020."

Gross Domestic Freebie

By James Surowiecki
The New Yorker, November 25, 2013

Twitter's recent I.P.O. bonanza gave us all some striking numbers to consider. There's the company's valuation: an astounding twenty-four billion dollars. And its revenue: just five hundred and thirty-five million. It has more than two hundred and thirty million active users, and a hundred million of them use the service daily. They collectively send roughly half a billion tweets every day. And then there's the starkest number of all: zero. That's the price that Twitter charges people to use its technology. Since the company was founded, ordinary users have sent more than three hundred billion tweets. In exchange, they have paid Twitter no dollars and no cents.

Ever since Netscape made the decision to give away its browser, free has been more the rule online than the exception. And even though traditional media companies have been erecting paywalls to guard revenue, a huge chunk of the time we spend online is spent consuming stuff that we don't pay for. Economically, this makes for an odd situation: digital goods and services are everywhere you look, but their impact is hard to see in economic statistics.

Our main yardstick for the health of the economy is G.D.P. growth, a concept devised in the nineteen-thirties by the economist Simon Kuznets. If it's rising briskly, we know that the economy is doing well. If not, we know it's time to worry. The basic assumption is simple: the more stuff we're producing for sale, the better off we are. In the industrial age, this was a reasonable assumption, but in the digital economy that picture gets a lot fuzzier, since so much of what's being produced is available free. You may think that Wikipedia, Twitter, Snapchat, Google Maps, and so on are valuable. But, as far as G.D.P. is concerned, they barely exist. The M.I.T. economist Erik Brynjolfsson points out that, according to government statistics, the "information sector" of the economy—which includes publishing, software, data services, and telecom—has barely grown since the late eighties, even though we've seen an explosion in the amount of information and data that individuals and businesses consume. "That just feels totally wrong," he told me.

Brynjolfsson is the co-author, with Andrew McAfee, of the forthcoming book *The Second Machine Age*, which examines how digitization is remaking the economy. "We're underestimating the value of the part of the economy that's free," he said. "As digital goods make up a bigger share of economic activity, that means we're likely getting a distorted picture of the economy as a whole." The issue is that, as Kuznets himself acknowledged, "the welfare of a nation . . . can scarcely be inferred

---

> **The enormous gains for consumers in the digital age often come at the expense of workers.**

from a measure of national income." For instance, most Web sites are built with free, open-source applications. This makes running a site cheap, which has all sorts of benefits in terms of welfare, but G.D.P. ends up lower than it would be if everyone had to pay for Microsoft's server software. Digital innovation can even shrink G.D.P.: Skype has reduced the amount of money that people spend on international calls, and free smartphone apps are replacing stand-alone devices that once generated billions in sales. The G.P.S. company Garmin was once one of the fastest-growing companies in the U.S. Thanks to Google and Apple Maps, Garmin's sales have taken a severe hit, but consumers, who now have access to good directions at no cost, are certainly better off.

New technologies have always driven out old ones, but it used to be that they would enter the market economy and thus boost G.D.P.—as when the internal-combustion engine replaced the horse. Digitization is distinctive because much of the value it creates for consumers never becomes part of the economy that G.D.P. measures. That makes the gap between what's actually happening in the economy and what the statistics are measuring wider than ever before.

Figuring out the invisible value created by the Internet is no easy task. One strategy that economists have used is to measure how much time we spend online (on the assumption that time is money). A recent study by Brynjolfsson and Joo Hee Oh concluded that in 2011 the value of free goods on the Internet was hundreds of billions of dollars and that it was increasing at a rate of more than forty billion dollars annually. Another study, by the economist Michael Mandel, contended that the government had underestimated the value of data services (mobile apps and the like) by some three hundred billion dollars a year. These are rough estimates, but they give a sense of how much better off the digital economy has made us.

There's a catch, though. The enormous gains for consumers in the digital age often come at the expense of workers. Wikipedia is great for readers. It's awful for the people who make encyclopedias. Although the digital economy creates new ways to make money, digitization doesn't require a lot of workers: you can come up with an idea, write a piece of software, and distribute it to hundreds of millions of people with ease. That's fundamentally different from physical products, which require much more labor to produce and distribute. And while digitization has already transformed the media and entertainment businesses, it's not going to stop there. "There are very few industries that are going to be unaffected," Brynjolfsson told me. The value that the digital economy is creating is real. But so is the havoc.

What the Sharing Economy Takes

By Doug Henwood
The Nation, January 27, 2015

Sharing is a good thing, we learned in kindergarten, but that wisdom was soon called into question by the grown-up world of getting and spending. Now, New Age capitalism has spun out a wonderful invention: the "sharing economy," which holds out the promise of using technology to connect disparate individuals in mutually profitable enterprise, or at least in warm feelings.

The most prominent examples of the sharing economy are a taxi-hailing service called Uber and a real-estate-subletting service called Airbnb. As with most enterprises emerging from Silicon Valley, they come with a very ambitious vocabulary. Brian Chesky, the co-founder of Airbnb, uses words like "revolution" and "movement" to describe his company, which is now valued at $13 billion—a bit less than the price at which the stock market values Starwood, a company that operates 1,200 properties in 100 countries, under names like W, Westin and Sheraton—making Airbnb the best-capitalized revolutionary movement in history. The term "sharing economy" has been making the rounds for about a decade, but the phenomenon has roots in the 1990s: all of its trademark enthusiasms—the flattening of stodgy old hierarchies, the rise of peer-to-peer networks, the decentering of everything—were concepts imported into middlebrow culture by the likes of Thomas Friedman. Then as now, the structure of the Internet was taken as a model for society: a network of peers rather than a gray-suited hierarchy. But in its last iteration, during the dot-com boom, techno-utopianism was more about the production side of the economy—transforming the world of work into a flexible, hip space for creativity and collaboration.

The updated version is more about the consumption side; in fact, another name for it is "collaborative consumption." In a 2010 article in the *Harvard Business Review,* Rachel Botsman, formerly of the Clinton Foundation, and venture capitalist Roo Rogers applied the term to Zipcar and Netflix, though it seems like a grand appellation for gussied-up rental operations. "Collaborative consumption," they wrote, "gives people the benefits of ownership with reduced personal burden and cost and also lower environmental impact—and it's proving to be a compelling alternative to traditional forms of buying and ownership." Less famous names in the "space," as business professors like to say, included Zilok.com, a peer-to-peer rental scheme for tools and appliances (which offered me a jackhammer for $18.75 a day);

UsedCardboardBoxes.com, for the "rescue" and resale of used cardboard boxes (which brags that it's saved over 900,000 trees); and the then-new Airbnb.

* * *

Airbnb, which seems universally loved by both hosts and renters, has since become the most appealing example of this profitably collective ethos. I spoke with hosts (who universally crave anonymity) who pick up anywhere from $15,000 to $75,000 a year by renting out parts of their houses. It's not quite free money; one host in Los Angeles, whose annual earnings are at the high end of that range, estimates that it takes from one to three hours a day to maintain the space (which would work out to $125 an hour or more). And guests love the service, too—it's much cheaper than a hotel.

But the model isn't blemish-free: there's a real, if hard-to-measure, impact on housing availability and affordability in desirable cities. In October, New York State Attorney General Eric Schneiderman issued a report tracing the rapid growth of Airbnb in New York City. It found many of the rentals illegal, which wouldn't necessarily be something to worry about if they didn't stretch an already-taut housing market. Schneiderman also found that many of the units are rented out not by individuals, but by large commercial operations that do nothing but let out units via Airbnb, taking them off the regular rental market. Airbnb's response is that the company has put an end to the commercial operators and that its footprint is too small in any event—25,000 hosts in a rental market of 2.2 million units—to make much of a difference.

That may sound reasonable, but it's not fully convincing. Yes, 25,000 hosts is tiny next to a 2.2 million rental inventory—but there were only 68,000 vacancies as of the city's most recent survey. And more subtle displacements go on as well: one graduate student I spoke with took a two-bedroom apartment in a gentrifying Brooklyn neighborhood that he otherwise couldn't afford, knowing that he could rent out the empty room and cover his rent. He feels guilty, but what's an impecunious grad student to do? He added that he had a friend who rented a four-bedroom apartment, also in a gentrifying neighborhood, and Airbnb'd three of the rooms. Such practices take units off the rental market and grease the wheels of gentrification by making rapidly rising rents "affordable." My Los Angeles source said similar things about her neighborhood. And she dismissed Airbnb's claim about getting commercial operators out of the business; she's recognized houses previously run by professionals who have simply recast themselves as private individuals.

Airbnb would rather we see it as a community, not merely commerce, even as it hastens the breakup of working-class neighborhoods in cities like New York and Los Angeles. Airbnb's head of community, Douglas Atkin, wrote a book about how brands such as Apple are like a religion to their loyalists. The aim is to turn a business, whose overriding aim is to make a profit, into "radical belonging organizations."

* * *

Writing three years after Botsman and Rogers's "collaborative consumption" article in the *Harvard Business Review,* and with Airbnb firmly established as a leading "sharing" company, Arun Sundararajan announced in the same journal that collaborative-consumption models had surpassed Zipcar in the ride-sharing sphere. Zipcar was still burdened with a dedicated fleet, while outfits like RelayRides and GetAround allowed car owners to rent out vehicles they weren't using. Sundararajan said that while

> **The sharing economy looks like a classically neoliberal response to neoliberalism: individualized and market-driven, it sees us all as micro-entrepreneurs fending for ourselves in a hostile world.**

collaborative consumption was "more reminiscent of flower power than of Gordon Gekko," big business was going to have to adapt to its challenge. We're not there yet: last year, RelayRides reported on Monday of Thanksgiving week that I could rent a Camry for $80 a day, or an Escalade for $300 over the holiday weekend, in New York. Avis's Brooklyn location was out of cars.

But in ride sharing, there's really only one victor: Uber, a company with a knack for breaking laws, because the march of disruption can't be bothered with legalities. Uber is the headline-grabber of the moment because, at a dinner party in New York last November, a company VP suggested to BuzzFeed's Ben Smith that it might be a good idea to spend $1 million hiring opposition researchers to dig up dirt on the lives of journalists who had been writing critically about them—especially *Pando's* Sarah Lacy.

But that's only one of Uber's problems. As Lacy noted, singling her out was just the latest in the company's string of offenses against women. In June, an Uber driver kidnapped an inebriated woman in Los Angeles and drove her to a motel with the presumed intent of raping her, according to the charges. Driver screening seems minimal, and in Lacy's words, the Uber PR team has a habit of "discrediting female passengers who accuse drivers of attacking them by whispering that they were 'drunk' or 'dressed provocatively.'" Founder Travis Kalanick—whom colleagues call a "douche" and an "a**hole"—bragged to a *GQ* reporter that his success had made him such a magnet for women that he should rename the company "Boob-er." In France, Uber ran an ad promoting drivers who were also *"avions de chasse,"* which translates literally as "fighter planes" but colloquially as "hot chicks."

According to legend, Kalanick founded Uber in 2009 one snowy evening in Paris after a brainstorming session with co-founder Garrett Camp. It launched in San Francisco—a city where it's notoriously difficult to get a cab because of strict limits on their numbers—in 2010. It was far from Kalanick's first venture. A youthful coder, he founded Scour.com, a Napsterish file-sharing site, in 1999, while still a student at UCLA; it was quickly sued out of business by the entertainment industry for copyright violations. (Apparently, he has a thing for sharing other people's stuff.) A second venture, Red Swoosh, moved media files around legally for pay; it was sold in 2007 and made Kalanick a small-time millionaire. He's a big-time billionaire now.

After its San Francisco launch, Uber was immediately slapped with a cease-and-desist order by city authorities for running an unlicensed cab service. Kalanick found this opposition energizing: the company quickly expanded to other cities, sometimes with official blessings and sometimes without. At first, Uber featured high-end cars for a little taste of luxury, booked via a smartphone app. As Kalanick told an early Uber gathering, the experience was: "I pushed a button, and a car showed up, and now I'm a pimp." Uber soon faced competition at the low end from the now-second-banana ride-sharing service Lyft, however, and began recruiting regular people with regular cars as drivers. Its growth has been explosive: it now has hundreds of thousands of drivers in over 200 cities.

But there's a lot of discontent among drivers, both those who work for Uber and those who work for what are derisively called "incumbent" companies. Traditional drivers have staged protests against Uber and its rivals in Los Angeles, Washington, and across Europe, although none have gone to the same lengths as Parisian cabbies, who have attacked the cars, smashing windows and slashing tires. And while Kalanick et al. have a point about the restricted taxi availability in major cities, it's the fleet owners who are profiting, not the drivers facing a low-cost rival.

Uber drivers often complain about the low (and declining) pay and miserable conditions. S., a driver in Chicago (who, like everyone I spoke with, wanted to remain anonymous for fear of reprisals), says that full-timers put in sixty hours a week for an hourly rate that comes to $12 or $13 after expenses. He says the company is constantly scheming to cut pay. A., a driver in Los Angeles (and one of the few women in the trade), says she gets $11 to $12 an hour after expenses (daily expenses like gas, not depreciation of the car), which is around the twenty-fifth percentile of the city's hourly earnings, though about in line with typical taxi-driver pay. That's a sharp contrast with the $35-an-hour rate that was dangled in front of her when she signed up. A. describes Uber as "a port in the storm," a way to pick up some cash while, Angeleno that she is, she works on some movie and web projects. Uber's a different story in New York, where all drivers have to be certified by the Taxi and Limousine Commission, and the cars are all regular cabs or car-service vehicles. Every Uber-hailed driver I've spoken with in New York likes the service, because it delivers more paying riders than they'd otherwise have.

Drivers are rated by their passengers, and if your rating isn't high enough, the company will "deactivate" you—which is how they say "fire," since you're just another node in the app to them. J., another LA driver whose name was passed along to me by an organizer with the California App-Based Drivers Association (a project of the Teamsters Union), says passengers love to wield this power over drivers: one insisted that he run a red light or lose his five-star rating. And J. says there's no appeal process for a bad rating or deactivation.

You need a newish car to drive for Uber; if your car gets too old, that's grounds for deactivation. But the company is ready to help: it's entered into a partnership with Santander, a Spanish bank, to offer car loans to drivers, with the payments conveniently deducted from their paycheck. According to the terms posted on Uberpeople.net, a chat board for drivers, the payments work out to an interest rate of around 21 percent. They get you coming and going.

Earlier this year, Uber hired former Obama campaign manager David Plouffe to handle its PR, strategy, and lobbying. Kalanick describes a politico like Plouffe as a perfect fit with Uber, because there are daily "primaries going on with folks in the ride-sharing space." Well-capitalized revolutions need such high-end strategists.

* * *

The sales pitch that accompanies this revolution is an update of what Richard Barbrook and Andy Cameron, writing almost twenty years ago, called the "Californian Ideology," a "new faith [that] emerged from a bizarre fusion of the cultural bohemianism of San Francisco with the hi-tech industries of Silicon Valley.... [T]he Californian Ideology," they added, "promiscuously combines the free-wheeling spirit of the hippies and the entrepreneurial zeal of the yuppies"—a marriage sealed by a common anti-statism. Its promise was that, in time, everyone will be "hip and rich."

For Barbrook and Cameron, the techno-utopia promised in the mid-1990s was very much a product of the baby boom, with roots in a 1970s artisanal hippie/New Leftish capitalism, subsequently leavened with the rising libertarian ideology of the New Right in the 1980s. Individualism and techno-utopianism were merged into a single, seductive package. The latest update of the Californian Ideology is the product of a different cohort, one more comfortable with Ayn Rand than Charles Reich. Its enterprises are less associated with garages than with venture capitalists. It traffics in one of Silicon Valley's favorite words, "disruption," but it's a bit short on the intense utopian promises of the New Economy era of the late '90s. Then, technology was going to make work meaningful, end recessions, and promote human understanding. Now, technology is making it easier for you to hail a taxi—in a way that's taking down the already low incomes of "incumbent" cabbies. It may make you feel hip, if that's something you're longing for, but it's going to make only a few people rich.

Of course, "sharing" entrepreneurs aren't entirely lacking a utopian line, as Chesky's exuberant language demonstrates. But despite the appeal to a green communitarianism, it just doesn't have the verve of its dot-com ancestor. That may be because in the 1990s bubble, jobs were easy to come by and real wages were rising across the board, so optimism was easily transmissible. Now, despite over five years of official recovery, the sharing economy offers some people, like cab drivers, the prospect of real wage cuts, and others, like people with a spare bedroom, a way to supplement stagnant incomes. The sharing economy is a nice way for rapacious capitalists to monetize the desperation of people in the post-crisis economy while sounding generous and to evoke a fantasy of community in an atomized population.

Perhaps nothing exemplifies this growing desperation like the smaller, production-oriented side of the sharing economy. Here, the labor of people is shared in an arrangement that looks increasingly feudal. There's the venerable TaskRabbit, founded in 2008, which was described by *Wired* as an "eBay for real-world labor." It matches "Taskers" with "Clients"—firms or people with errands to run. Financially, TaskRabbit is a pipsqueak next to the giants of the sharing space; according to CrunchBase, it's received just $38 million in financing.

CrunchBase's bio for TaskRabbit hits all the right notes: "It was a cold night in Boston in February of 2008 when Leah Busque realized she was out of dog food for her 100-lb yellow lab, Kobe. Leah thought to herself, 'Wouldn't it be nice if there was a place online I could go to connect with my neighbors—maybe one who was already at the store at that very moment—who could help me out?'" Thanks to the magic of this "curated" website, lugging a bag of dog food on a cold winter night gets recast as an act of neighborly generosity, even though money will change hands and the "neighbor" is unlikely to be seen again. Many Taskers are people who had good jobs until the recession hit; as of last year, 70 percent had a bachelor's degree, and 5 percent a PhD. Now they're running around town fetching stuff. Comparable services like Amazon's Mechanical Turk allow workers to bid for the privilege of doing piecework online—filling out spreadsheets, doing graphic design, checking code for errors—at low rates with no accountability from companies, which can reject their work (and their invoice) if they deem it insufficient for any reason.

The sharing economy looks like a classically neoliberal response to neoliberalism: individualized and market-driven, it sees us all as micro-entrepreneurs fending for ourselves in a hostile world. Its publicists seek to transform the instability of the post–Great Recession economy into opportunity. Waiting for your script to sell? Drive an Uber on the weekend. Can't afford a place to live while attending grad school? Take a two-bedroom apartment and rent one room out. You may lack health insurance, sick days, and a pension plan, but you're in control.

As Airbnb's Chesky said in a McKinsey & Company interview, today's generation sees ownership as "a burden." People aren't proud of their homes or cars; they're proud of their Instagram feed. As Chesky predicts, "in the future, people will own whatever they want responsibility for. And I think what they're going to want responsibility for the most is their reputation, their friendships, their relationships, and the experiences they've had." Affect triumphs over material lack. You may not have a job, Chesky adds, citing Thomas Friedman, but you'll have an ever more complex "income stream"—which in most cases is more likely to be a trickle than a torrent.

Cryptocurrency Exchanges Emerge as Regulators Try to Keep Up

By Larry Greenemeier
Scientific American, April 8, 2015

Digital cryptocurrencies—including bitcoin and litecoin, along with dozens of others—have struggled to win mainstream acceptance in the U.S. Interest in this so-called "Internet money" is not going away, however, which is why regulators are developing rules that that they hope can avert a repeat of last year's Mt. Gox meltdown, when the world's largest bitcoin exchange unexpectedly shut down after losing hundreds of thousands of bitcoins in a cyber attack.

The U.S. government has largely sat on the sidelines, leaving states to regulate digital cryptocurrency exchanges. The exchanges, with names such as BitPay and Coinbase, are Web sites for buying, selling, and exchanging digital currency. Bitcoin and its ilk are referred to as cryptocurrencies for their use of cryptography to secure transactions and mint new virtual coins.

More than a dozen states and Puerto Rico already issue licenses for bitcoin exchanges, which represent the lion's share of the world's cryptocurrency transactions. California is working out the details of its own licensing guidelines while New York State's Department of Financial Services plans to finalize its BitLicense regulatory framework in the coming weeks. Other countries are likewise grappling with the legal status of such currencies. The U.K., for example, recently announced it would police digital currencies by applying anti-money laundering rules to these exchanges.

Regulations are good for cryptocurrency exchanges, says Campbell Harvey, a Duke University professor of finance. The rules will lend them a sense of legitimacy that should help reduce the volatility that has kept merchants and investors out of the action. The volatility comes from people seeing virtual currency as operating just outside the law, Harvey adds.

Coinbase is licensed in sixteen states and claims that eight other states—including California and New York—allow access to the exchange without the need for a license. Part of Coinbase's success comes from allowing investors to change U.S. dollars into bitcoins and vice versa, an important feature because of bitcoins' fluctuating value. A single bitcoin is currently worth about $250; a couple of years ago they were trading at more than $1,100 apiece.

Cameron and Tyler Winklevoss, venture capitalist siblings best known for their

> **The U.S. has a lot of ground to make up if banks and businesses here want to cash in on cryptocurrency—80 percent of all Bitcoin volume is exchanged into and out of Chinese yuan.**

legal battle with Mark Zuckerberg over the origin of Facebook, are awaiting New York's licensing regulations to their Gemini Bitcoin exchange in the state. Gemini will be a place to buy and sell bitcoins, akin to the way NASDAQ lets investors trade stocks, the Winklevosses said at last month's South by Southwest Interactive conference in Austin, Texas. Bitcoin is a harbinger of the "cashless society" that will be here by 2025, they said, adding that they believe in the cryptocurrency so much that they currently own 1 percent of the world's more than 14 million bitcoins.

Bitcoin operates on a peer-to-peer network that consists of computers run by people known as "miners." Their computers are set up specifically to verify the validity of a transaction and record it in a digital public ledger system called a "blockchain." The first computer to solve a cryptographic puzzle accompanying each transaction wins bitcoins for its miner. Other computers in the network check the solution, creating a redundancy designed to guard against transaction fraud. Once a transaction is entered into the blockchain ledger, it cannot be deleted or changed. The idea behind the blockchain is to prevent fraudulent transactions. And the peer-to-peer nature of the Bitcoin network means there is no bank or clearinghouse to charge a large fee per transaction.

Although Apple Pay, Paypal, and other digital payment services are improvements over credit cards and other online options, they are not a "breakaway" technology on par with the Bitcoin Network, Cameron Winklevoss said at SXSW

Regardless of such endorsements, Bitcoin exchanges continue to be a risky proposition. Start-up exchange Buttercoin will shut down on April 10 after failing to raise sufficient funding. Even high-profile financial backing from the likes of investors Y Combinator, Google Ventures and Reddit co-founder Alexis Ohanian was not enough to keep the lights on. Part of the problem is the nascent technology's history as a volatile investment as well as an enabler of anonymous cybercriminal activity, including the infamous Silk Road online market for illegal drugs.

The U.S. has a lot of ground to make up if banks and businesses here want to cash in on cryptocurrency—80 percent of all Bitcoin volume is exchanged into and out of Chinese yuan, according to a March 10 Goldman Sachs report. The report estimates that more than 100,000 merchants worldwide—including Overstock.com, TigerDirect.com, and Expedia—accept bitcoins as payment.

A sign that these companies do not completely trust their finances to cryptocurrencies, however: many convert these payments into more stable currencies rather than hold them as bitcoins.

Silicon Valley Gender Gap is Widening

By Jessica Guynn
USA Today, March 26, 2015

Najla Bulous wants to change the face of Silicon Valley.

The daughter of immigrants from Mexico and Egypt, Bulous is a Harvey Mudd College-trained software engineer. After graduation in May, she's starting a new job at a Silicon Valley technology giant.

Bulous knows she isn't the stereotypical Silicon Valley geek. She didn't study computer science until college and never intended to major in it. But after just one introductory course, Bulous was hooked on the challenge of mastering problems with lines of code.

Now this 21-year-old is not just planning a career in technology. She wants a hand in re-engineering the culture of Silicon Valley to be more inclusive of women and people from underrepresented groups.

She has her work cut out for her.

Despite the rise of tech superstars such as Sheryl Sandberg and Marissa Mayer, Silicon Valley is still a man's world.

Girls graduate high school on par with boys in math and science, but boys are more likely to pursue engineering and computing degrees in college. That disparity only grows at the graduate level and in the workforce where women are dramatically underrepresented in engineering and computing. Even those women who pursue this kind of technical career drop out at much higher rates than men.

A report released Thursday by the American Association of University Women (AAUW) is sounding a wake-up call for the industry. It warns that the gender gap in technology is widening as women are being held back by stereotypes and biases.

"What we found is that not only are the numbers low, they are headed in the wrong direction," says Catherine Hill, AAUW's vice president for research.

From college curriculum to hiring and retention practices, changes must be made across the board to encourage more women to see themselves as technologists and explore careers in the industry, Hill says.

Women made up just 26 percent of computing professionals in 2013, substantially less than thirty years earlier and about the same percentage as in 1960. In engineering, women are even less well represented, making up just 12 percent of working engineers in 2013.

Anemic Numbers

The statistics for women of color are even more anemic.

Although African-American, Hispanic, American Indian, and Alaskan Native women together were 18 percent of the population ages twenty to twentyfour in 2013, they were awarded just 6 percent of computing and 3 percent of engineering bachelor's degrees that year.

Those statistics are reflected in the workforce of leading companies in Silicon Valley which say 20 percent or less of their technical staff are women.

Also in a distinct minority inside major tech companies: Women in non-technical roles. Seven out of ten employees in these companies are men. And few women reach the senior executive level or the boardroom at major companies and start-ups alike.

Women don't fare any better as entrepreneurs. A sliver of venture capital funding goes to women and a tiny percentage of venture capital investors are women.

The only place women seem to be gaining representation is in the courts. A high-profile courtroom showdown between prominent venture capital firm Kleiner Perkins Caufield & Byers and former partner Ellen Pao has Silicon Valley buzzing over allegations of sexism and discrimination. And, in just the last couple weeks, Facebook and Twitter each were sued for discrimination.

All of which has fueled momentum to bring more women and minorities into the industry—and for good reason.

Research shows diversity in the workforce sparks productivity and innovation. Women's views and experiences are crucial to shaping twenty-first-century technology, Hill says.

It's also crucial for women to gain more access to one of the nation's highest-paying careers in one of the economy's fastest-growing sectors.

"I believe engineers and computer scientists are made, not born," Hill says. "It's a question of exposure and opportunity."

As early as first grade, children begin to associate math with boys. In college, women frequently report they don't feel they belong.

Women face major hurdles in landing jobs.

One study found that scientists were more likely to choose a male candidate over an identical female candidate for a hypothetical job opening at a lab. They also offered the male candidate a higher salary.

Facing Implicit Bias, Explicit Harassment

Kate Heddleston, a software engineer in San Francisco who has held titles such as Head Mugwump and Software Warrior Princess, says women routinely face implicit bias and explicit harassment in the workplace.

"We need to realize that we have created workspaces that don't welcome everyone equally and we need to change that," Heddleston says. "Large-scale change might seem daunting, but it is possible. Diversity problems can be solved the same way that challenging engineering problems can be solved— one small step at a time. By recognizing problems, isolating them, and coming up with creative solutions, we can make more inclusive and productive environments."

> **Despite the rise of tech superstars such as Sheryl Sandberg and Marissa Mayer, Silicon Valley is still a man's world.**

As a summer intern, Bulous says she initially struggled as the only woman on the engineering team at a small tech company in New York before finding her comfort zone.

"The tech industry should actively be trying to dismantle systemic biases that push out anyone who doesn't fit the tech guy image," Bulous said. "What's the point of trying to recruit people from underrepresented backgrounds if they're forced to assimilate into an unwelcoming culture?"

Technology companies here are experimenting with new approaches to combating bias and transforming work cultures, from unconscious bias training to gender-blind hiring and performance evaluations.

Google is one of the companies funneling money and resources into recruiting and retaining women.

Angela Navarro, 23, is a software engineer who works on the YouTube Android app. She says she's often the only woman in a meeting or on a team.

A women's group at Google has helped "tremendously" in providing a support system and mentors.

"It's great to meet other women and not feel like you are the only person here in this building," Navarro says.

Navarro belongs to a new generation of women scaling the ramparts of the tech world.

Lynn Root, 29, is a software engineer for streaming music service Spotify in San Francisco.

It's a second career for Root, who has a business degree in finance and economics and was working in banking when she fell in love with programming in 2011.

Root says she wakes up every day ready to sprint to the office.

"I discovered I loved programming, being able to create something with my bare hands or from nothing in a technical way," Root says. "It's just so beautiful to come up with an elegant solution."

Programming is the kind of career that offers endless challenges, she says.

"There is so much you can learn in software engineering," Root says. "I am chipping away at this huge mountain ahead of me."

But, Root says, she first had to overcome anxiety to tackle "a subject that is universally known as difficult."

"What has worked for me is essentially becoming comfortable with making yourself uncomfortable," she said.

Jenny Jensen, 27, says she came from a small town and studied theater in college. She wasn't encouraged to pursue technology as a career.

She was inspired to give up her job at a non-profit and learn how to code while scraping old wallpaper from her guest bedroom and watching a livestream of Google's software developer conference I/O in 2012.

Now Jensen works as a Web production analyst for a software firm in Michigan. She's a die-hard hockey fan and in her spare time she is building a searchable database for fines and suspensions in the NHL.

"I like to solve the puzzle to make things work," Jensen says.

Layne McNish, 27, says coding helped her unravel the puzzle of what she wanted to do with her life. She was a professional cellist and a Broadway publicist before she started coding a year ago.

At first she thought coding would be too "technical and boring." But after immersing herself, she says she discovered coding is more creative and empowering than anything else she has ever done.

McNish is one of two women on an engineering team for a tech company in Portland, Ore.

"It's something I really love doing and I can have a good life," McNish says. "I liked what I did before, but I was working a million hours a week and it was miserable and I didn't get paid barely anything. Now I like what I am doing with my life, and it can offer the flexibility that many women want out of a job. ... It seems like the perfect place for women."

Net Neutrality:
How the Government Finally Got It Right

By Tim Wu
The New Yorker, February 5, 2015

For years, the federal government supported the principle of net neutrality: the idea that broadband providers should treat all Internet traffic the same. Verizon and Comcast, for example, shouldn't be able to block you from accessing sites that they consider competitive or threatening, and they shouldn't be able to accelerate your access to sites that have paid them. But the legal authority supporting these rules was flawed, and last January a federal court struck them down.

Following the ruling, it seemed unlikely that the regulations would be replaced with a strong, or "battleship," net-neutrality law. Tom Wheeler, the chairman of the Federal Communications Commission, or F.C.C., was said to be the cable companies' man, and his first proposal was not very promising. It would have allowed for so-called slow lanes, giving cable companies the right to de-prioritize the speed of some Web sites in favor of others. Additionally, the Obama Administration hadn't shown much willingness to argue with people who claimed, however speciously, that new laws would cause stocks to plummet. And nearly everyone agreed that companies like Comcast and A. T. & T., some of the largest donors in Washington, had long ago bought off Congress and maybe the F.C.C. as well.

But, on Wednesday, Wheeler confessed to a change of heart. It was a Nixon-goes-to-China moment. He wrote, in *Wired* magazine, "Originally, I believed that the FCC could assure Internet openness through a determination of 'commercial reasonableness.'" But, he said, he had come to fear that a weak rule would "be interpreted to mean what is reasonable for commercial interests, not consumers." Instead, he continued, "I am submitting to my colleagues the strongest open Internet protections ever proposed by the F.C.C." With those words, Tom Wheeler became a net-neutrality hero.

How exactly did this come to be? Whatever opponents may think, there is no conspiracy; there was no shady or powerful actor pushing for this outcome. In fact, large companies like Google and Facebook, which favor net neutrality, decided to sit on their hands. And while startups, which have the most to lose because they're likely to end up in slow lanes, did make strong net neutrality their cause, they have little influence in Washington. The real reason for the shift was something that occasionally happens in a democracy: enough of the population caught wind of what was going on and said they didn't like it. And then the chairman of the F.C.C. and the President noticed. All of which his begs another question: The public doesn't usually react so passionately to telecom rules—what caused so many people to care about this particular issue?

For one thing, net neutrality, particularly when cast as the prospect of "Internet slow lanes" tapped into strong anxieties about inequality. Would the Internet become dominated by just a handful of wealthy companies that could afford to pay for fast connections to users? The link between financial inequality and net neutrality reached the President. And so, in November, when he finally demanded a strong net-neutrality rule, he framed his argument as way of allowing for a fair fight between large and small, rich and poor: "An entrepreneur's fledgling company should have the same chance to succeed as established corporations," he said. "Access to a high-school student's blog shouldn't be unfairly slowed down to make way for advertisers with more money."

> **The real reason for the shift was something that occasionally happens in a democracy: enough of the population caught wind of what was going on and said they didn't like it.**

Polls show that more than three-quarters of Americans don't like the idea of slow lanes for certain online content. The idea that the Internet would be tiered like so much else—for instance, boarding an airplane—is appealing to few people other than those who run cable companies. Citizens may not have much faith in the government, but it's clear that they have even less faith in the companies that provide broadband.

It is also true that open Internet, though far from perfect, has come to represent a somewhat unpredictable and exciting frontier, a place where people can invent and explore new things. The cable companies, by demanding the right to control access, seemed to want to block off that frontier. For the past ten years, the cable-and-telephone industry has been saying that it needs fast lanes to help technology evolve. But the Internet continued to progress despite the absence of fast lanes. Net neutrality, the de-facto rule, seemed to be working, and the industry's demands for fast lanes became a solution looking for a problem.

All of these factors, in some combination, managed to convince the public, and then President Obama and the chairman of the F.C.C., that net neutrality was important. And there's a lesson to be learned here: the equalitarian instinct reflected in the campaign to protect net neutrality doesn't seem likely to just go away, and it may not bode well for some of the largest Internet firms, like Facebook and Amazon, should they be perceived as straying too far from the ideals of openness and egalitarianism. Of course, balls can be intercepted on the one-yard line. There will be a last-minute lobbying effort against Wheeler's proposal. Congress could also overrule him, and, of course, in an age in which suing agencies has become a corporate reflex, someone will likely ask the courts to overturn his handiwork. But, barring any surprises, Wheeler's strong version of net neutrality will soon be the law of the land. And that is something that our democracy can be proud of.

How Robots & Algorithms Are Taking Over

By Sue Halpern
The New York Review of Books, April 2, 2015

In September 2013, about a year before Nicholas Carr published *The Glass Cage: Automation and Us*, his chastening meditation on the human future, a pair of Oxford researchers issued a report predicting that nearly half of all jobs in the United States could be lost to machines within the next twenty years. The researchers, Carl Benedikt Frey and Michael Osborne, looked at seven hundred kinds of work and found that of those occupations, among the most susceptible to automation were loan officers, receptionists, paralegals, store clerks, taxi drivers, and security guards. Even computer programmers, the people writing the algorithms that are taking on these tasks, will not be immune. By Frey and Osborne's calculations, there is about a 50 percent chance that programming, too, will be outsourced to machines within the next two decades.

In fact, this is already happening, in part because programmers increasingly rely on "self-correcting" code—that is, code that debugs and rewrites itself—and in part because they are creating machines that are able to learn on the job. While these machines cannot think, per se, they can process phenomenal amounts of data with ever-increasing speed and use what they have learned to perform such functions as medical diagnosis, navigation, and translation, among many others. Add to these self-repairing robots that are able to negotiate hostile environments like radioactive power plants and collapsed mines and then fix themselves without human intercession when the need arises. The most recent iteration of these robots has been designed by the robots themselves, suggesting that in the future even roboticists may find themselves out of work.

The term for what happens when human workers are replaced by machines was coined by John Maynard Keynes in 1930 in the essay "Economic Possibilities for our Grandchildren." He called it "technological unemployment." At the time, Keynes considered technical unemployment a transitory condition, "a temporary phase of maladjustment" brought on by "our discovery of means of economizing the use of labour outrunning the pace at which we can find new uses for labour." In the United States, for example, the mechanization of the railways around the time Keynes was writing his essay put nearly half a million people out of work. Similarly, rotary phones were making switchboard operators obsolete, while mechanical harvesters, plows, and combines were replacing traditional farmworkers, just as the first steam-engine tractors had replaced horses and oxen less than a century before.

Machine efficiency was becoming so great that President Roosevelt, in 1935, told the nation that the economy might never be able to reabsorb all the workers who were being displaced. The more sanguine *New York Times* editorial board then accused the president of falling prey to the "calamity prophets."

In retrospect, it certainly looked as if he had. Unemployment, which was at nearly 24 percent in 1932, dropped to less than 5 percent a decade later. This was a pattern that would reassert itself throughout the twentieth century: the economy would tank, automation would be identified as one of the main culprits, commentators would suggest that jobs were not coming back, and then the economy would rebound and with it employment, and all that nervous chatter about machines taking over would fade away.

When the economy faltered in 1958, and then again in 1961, for instance, what was being called the "automation problem" was taken up by Congress, which passed the Manpower Development and Training Act. In his State of the Union Address of 1962, President Kennedy explained that this law was meant "to stop the waste of able-bodied men and women who want to work, but whose only skill has been replaced by a machine, moved with a mill, or shut down with a mine." Two years later, President Johnson convened a National Commission on Technology, Automation, and Economic Progress to assess the economic effects of automation and technological change. But then a funny thing happened. By the time the commission issued its report in 1966, the economy was approaching full employment. Concern about machines supplanting workers abated. The commission was disbanded.

That fear, though, was dormant, not gone. A *Time* magazine cover from 1980 titled "The Robot Revolution" shows a tentacled automaton strangling human workers. An essay three years later by an MIT economist named Harley Shaiken begins:

> As more and more attention is focused on economic recovery, for 11 million people the grim reality is continued unemployment. Against this backdrop the central issue raised by rampant and pervasive technological change is not simply how many people may be displaced in the coming decade but how many who are currently unemployed will never return to the job.

Unemployment, which was approaching 10 percent at the time, then fell by half at decade's end, and once more the automation problem receded.

Yet there it was again, on the heels of the economic collapse of 2008. An investigation by the Associated Press in 2013 put it this way:

> Five years after the start of the Great Recession, the toll is terrifyingly clear: Millions of middle-class jobs have been lost in developed countries the world over.

> And the situation is even worse than it appears.

> Most of the jobs will never return, and millions more are likely to vanish as well, say experts who study the labor market....

They're being obliterated by technology.

Year after year, the software that runs computers and an array of other machines and devices becomes more sophisticated and powerful and capable of doing more efficiently tasks that humans have always done. For decades, science fiction warned of a future when we would be architects of our own obsolescence, replaced by our machines; an Associated Press analysis finds that the future has arrived.

Here is what that future—which is to say now—looks like: banking, logistics, surgery, and medical recordkeeping are just a few of the occupations that have already been given over to machines. Manufacturing, which has long been hospitable to mechanization and automation, is becoming more so as the cost of industrial robots drops, especially in relation to the cost of human labor. According to a new study by the Boston Consulting Group, currently the expectation is that machines, which now account for 10 percent of all manufacturing tasks, are likely to perform about 25 percent of them by 2025. (To understand the economics of this transition, one need only consider the American automotive industry, where a human spot welder costs about $25 an hour and a robotic one costs $8. The robot is faster and more accurate, too.) The Boston group expects most of the growth in automation to be concentrated in transportation equipment, computer and electronic products, electrical equipment, and machinery.

Meanwhile, algorithms are writing most corporate reports, analyzing intelligence data for the NSA and CIA, reading mammograms, grading tests, and sniffing out plagiarism. Computers fly planes—Nicholas Carr points out that the average airline pilot is now at the helm of an airplane for about three minutes per flight—and they compose music and pick which pop songs should be recorded based on which chord progressions and riffs were hits in the past. Computers pursue drug development—a robot in the UK named Eve may have just found a new compound to treat malaria—and fill pharmacy vials.

Since replacing human labor with machine labor is not simply the collateral damage of automation but, rather, the point of it, whenever the workforce is subject to automation, technological unemployment, whether short- or long-lived, must follow.

Xerox uses computers—not people—to select which applicants to hire for its call centers. The retail giant Amazon "employs" 15,000 warehouse robots to pull items off the shelf and pack boxes. The self-driving car is being road-tested. A number of hotels are staffed by robotic desk clerks and cleaned by robotic chambermaids. Airports are instituting robotic valet parking. Cynthia Breazeal, the director of MIT's personal robots group, raised $1 million in six days on the crowd-funding site Indiegogo, and then $25 million in venture capital funding, to bring Jibo, "the world's first social robot," to market.

What is a social robot? In the words of John Markoff of *The New York Times*, "it's a robot with a little humanity." It will tell your child bedtime stories, order takeout when you don't feel like cooking, know you prefer Coke over Pepsi, and snap photos of important life events so you don't have to step out of the picture. At the other end of the spectrum, machine guns, which automated killing in the nineteenth century, are being supplanted by Lethal Autonomous Robots (LARs) that can operate without human intervention. (By contrast, drones, which fly without an onboard pilot, still require a person at the controls.) All this—and unemployment is now below 6 percent.

Gross unemployment statistics, of course, can be deceptive. They don't take into account people who have given up looking for work, or people who are underemployed, or those who have had to take pay cuts after losing higher-paying jobs. And they don't reflect where the jobs are, or what sectors they represent, and which age cohorts are finding employment and which are not. And so while the pattern looks familiar, the worry is that this time around, machines really will undermine the labor force. As former Treasury Secretary Lawrence Summers wrote in *The Wall Street Journal* last July:

> The economic challenge of the future will not be *producing* enough. It will be providing enough *good jobs*.... Today...there are more sectors losing jobs than creating jobs. And the general-purpose aspect of software technology means that even the industries and jobs that it creates are not forever.

To be clear, there are physical robots like Jibo and the machines that assemble our cars, and there are virtual robots, which are the algorithms that undergird the computers that perform countless daily tasks, from driving those cars, to Google searches, to online banking. Both are avatars of automation, and both are altering the nature of work, taking on not only repetitive physical jobs, but intellectual and heretofore exclusively human ones as well. And while both are defining features of what has been called "the second machine age," what really distinguishes this moment is the speed at which technology is changing and changing society with it. If the "calamity prophets" are finally right, and this time the machines really will win out, this is why. It's not just that computers seem to be infiltrating every aspect of our lives, it's that they *have* infiltrated them and *are* infiltrating them with breathless rapidity. It's not just that life *seems* to have sped up, it's that it has. And that speed, and that infiltration, appear to have a life of their own.

Just as computer hardware follows Moore's Law, which says that computing power doubles every eighteen months, so too does computer capacity and functionality. Consider, for instance, the process of legal discovery. As Carr describes it,

> computers can [now] parse thousands of pages of digitized documents in seconds. Using e-discovery software with language-analysis algorithms, the machines not only spot relevant words and phrases but also discern chains of events, relationships among people, and even personal emotions and motivations. A single computer can take over the work of dozens of well-paid professionals.

Or take the autonomous automobile. It can sense all the vehicles around it, respond to traffic controls and sudden movements, apply the brakes as needed, know when the tires need air, signal a turn, and never get a speeding ticket. Volvo predicts that by 2020 its vehicles will be "crash-free," but even now there are cars that can park themselves with great precision.

The goal of automating automobile parking, and of automating driving itself, is no different than the goal of automating a factory, or pharmaceutical discovery, or surgery: it's to rationalize the process, making it more efficient, productive, and cost-effective. What this means is that automation is always going to be more convenient than what came before it—for someone. And while it's often pitched as being most convenient for the end user—the patient on the operating table, say, or the Amazon shopper, or the Google searcher, in fact the rewards of convenience flow most directly to those who own the automated system (Jeff Bezos, for example, not the Amazon Prime member).

Since replacing human labor with machine labor is not simply the collateral damage of automation but, rather, the point of it, whenever the workforce is subject to automation, technological unemployment, whether short- or long-lived, must follow. The MIT economists Erik Brynjolfsson and Andrew McAfee, who are champions of automation, state this unambiguously when they write:

> Even the most beneficial developments have unpleasant consequences that must be managed....Technological progress is going to leave behind some people, perhaps even a lot of people, as it races ahead.[1]

Flip this statement around, and what Brynjolfsson and McAfee are also saying is that while technological progress is going to force many people to submit to tightly monitored control of their movements, with their productivity clearly measured, that progress is also going to benefit perhaps just a few as it races ahead. And that, it appears, is what is happening. (Of the fifteen wealthiest Americans, six own digital technology companies, the oldest of which, Microsoft, has been in existence only since 1975. Six others are members of a single family, the Waltons, whose vast retail empire, with its notoriously low wages, has meant that people are much cheaper and more expendable than warehouse robots. Still, Walmart has benefited from an automated point-of-sale system that enables its owners to know precisely what is selling where and when, which in turn allows them to avoid stocking slow-moving items and to tie up less money than the competitors in inventory.)

As Paul Krugman wrote a couple of years ago in *The New York Times*:

> Smart machines may make higher GDP possible, but they will also reduce the demand for people—including smart people. So we could be looking at a society that grows ever richer, but in which all the gains in wealth accrue to whoever owns the robots.

In the United States, real wages have been stagnant for the past four decades, while corporate profits have soared. As of last year, 16 percent of men between eighteen and fifty-four and 30 percent of women in the same age group were not working, and more than a third of those who were unemployed attributed their joblessness to technology. As *The Economist* reported in early 2014:

Recent research suggests that... substituting capital for labor through automation is increasingly attractive; as a result owners of capital have captured ever more of the world's income since the 1980s, while the share going to labor has fallen.

> Carr makes a convincing case for the ways in which automation dulls the brain, removing the need to pay attention or master complicated routines or think creatively and react quickly.

There is a certain school of thought, championed primarily by those such as Google's Larry Page, who stand to make a lot of money from the ongoing digitization and automation of just about everything, that the elimination of jobs concurrent with a rise in productivity will lead to a leisure class freed from work. Leaving aside questions about how these lucky folks will house and feed themselves, the belief that most people would like nothing more than to be able to spend all day in their pajamas watching TV—which turns out to be what many "nonemployed" men do—sorely misconstrues the value of work, even work that might appear to an outsider to be less than fulfilling. Stated simply: work confers identity. When Dublin City University professor Michael Doherty surveyed Irish workers, including those who stocked grocery shelves and drove city buses, to find out if work continues to be "a significant locus of personal identity," even at a time when employment itself is less secure, he concluded that "the findings of this research can be summed up in the succinct phrase: 'work matters.'"[2]

How much it matters may not be quantifiable, but in an essay in *The New York Times*, Dean Baker, the codirector of the Center for Economic and Policy Research, noted that there was a 50 to 100 percent increase in death rates for older male workers in the years immediately following a job loss, if they previously had been consistently employed.

One reason was suggested in a study by Mihaly Csikszentmihalyi, the author of *Flow: The Psychology of Optimal Experience* (1990), who found, Carr reports, that "people were happier, felt more fulfilled by what they were doing, while they were at work than during their leisure hours."

Even where automation does not eliminate jobs, it often changes the nature of work. Carr makes a convincing case for the ways in which automation dulls the brain, removing the need to pay attention or master complicated routines or think creatively and react quickly. Those airline pilots who now are at the controls for less than three minutes find themselves spending most of their flight time staring at computer screens while automated systems do the actual flying. As a consequence, their overreliance on automation, and on a tendency to trust computer data even in the face of contradictory physical evidence, can be dangerous. Carr cites a study by Matthew Ebbatson, a human factors researcher, that found a direct correlation between a pilot's aptitude at the controls and the amount of time the pilot had spent flying without the aid of automation.... The analysis indicated that "manual flying skills decay quite rapidly towards the fringes of 'tolerable' performance without relatively frequent practice."

Similarly, an FAA report on cockpit automation released in 2013 found that over half of all airplane accidents were the result of the mental autopilot brought on by actual autopilot.

If aviation is a less convincing case, since the overall result of automation has been to make flying safer, consider a more mundane and ubiquitous activity, Internet searches using Google. According to Carr, relying on the Internet for facts and figures is making us mindless sloths. He points to a study in *Science* that demonstrates that the wealth of information readily available on the Internet disinclines users from remembering what they've found out. He also cites an interview with Amit Singhal, Google's lead search engineer, who states that "the more accurate the machine gets [at predicting search terms], the lazier the questions become."

A corollary to all this intellectual laziness and dullness is what Carr calls "deskilling"—the loss of abilities and proficiencies as more and more authority is handed over to machines. Doctors who cede authority to machines to read X-rays and make diagnoses, architects who rely increasingly on computer-assisted design (CAD) programs, marketers who place ads based on algorithms, traders who no longer trade—all suffer a diminution of the expertise that comes with experience, or they never gain that experience in the first place. As Carr sees it:

> As more skills are built into the machine, it assumes more control over the work, and the worker's opportunity to engage in and develop deeper talents, such as those involved in interpretation and judgment, dwindles. When automation reaches its highest level, when it takes command of the job, the worker, skillwise, has nowhere to go but down.

Conversely, machines have nowhere to go but up. In Carr's estimation, "as we grow more reliant on applications and algorithms, we become less capable of acting without their aid…. That makes the software more indispensable still. Automation breeds automation."

But since automation also produces quicker drug development, safer highways, more accurate medical diagnoses, cheaper material goods, and greater energy efficiency, to name just a few of its obvious benefits, there have been few cautionary voices like Nicholas Carr's urging us to take stock, especially, of the effects of automation on our very humanness—what makes us who we are as individuals—and on our humanity—what makes us who we are in aggregate. Yet shortly after *The Glass Cage* was published, a group of more than one hundred Silicon Valley luminaries, led by Tesla's Elon Musk, and scientists, including the theoretical physicist Stephen Hawking, issued a call to conscience for those working on automation's holy grail, artificial intelligence, lest they, in Musk's words, "summon the demon." (In Hawking's estimation, AI could spell the end of the human race as machines evolve faster than people and overtake us.) Their letter is worth quoting at length, because it demonstrates both the hubris of those who are programming our future and the possibility that without some kind of oversight, the golem, not God, might emerge from their machines:

[Artificial intelligence] has yielded remarkable successes in various component tasks such as speech recognition, image classification, autonomous vehicles, machine translation, legged locomotion, and question-answering systems.

As capabilities in these areas and others cross the threshold from laboratory research to economically valuable technologies, a virtuous cycle takes hold whereby even small improvements in performance are worth large sums of money, prompting greater investments in research....

The potential benefits are huge, since everything that civilization has to offer is a product of human intelligence; we cannot predict what we might achieve when this intelligence is magnified by the tools AI may provide, but the eradication of disease and poverty are not unfathomable. Because of the great potential of AI, it is important to research how to reap its benefits while avoiding potential pitfalls.

The progress in AI research makes it timely to focus research not only on making AI more capable, but also on maximizing the societal benefit.... [Until now the field of AI] has focused largely on techniques that are neutral with respect to purpose. We recommend expanded research aimed at ensuring that increasingly capable AI systems are robust and beneficial: our AI systems must do what we want them to do.

Just who is this "we" who must ensure that robots, algorithms, and intelligent machines act in the public interest? It is not, as Nicholas Carr suggests it should be, the public. Rather, according to the authors of the research plan that accompanies the letter signed by Musk, Hawking, and the others, making artificial intelligence "robust and beneficial," like making artificial intelligence itself, is an engineering problem, to be solved by engineers. To be fair, no one but those designing these systems is in a position to build in measures of control and security, but what those measures are, and what they aim to accomplish, is something else again. Indeed, their research plan, for example, looks to "maximize the economic benefits of artificial intelligence while mitigating adverse effects, which could include increased inequality and unemployment."

The priorities are clear: money first, people second. Or consider this semantic dodge: "If, as some organizations have suggested, autonomous weapons should be banned, is it possible to develop a precise definition of autonomy for this purpose...?" Moreover, the authors acknowledge that "aligning the values of powerful AI systems with our own values and preferences [may be] difficult," though this might be solved by building "systems that can learn or acquire values at run-time." However well-meaning, they fail to say what values, or whose, or to recognize that most values are not universal but, rather, culturally and socially constructed, subjective, and inherently biased.

We live in a technophilic age. We love our digital devices and all that they can do for us. We celebrate our Internet billionaires: they show us the way and deliver us to our destiny. We have President Obama, who established the National Robotics Initiative to develop the "next generation of robotics, to advance the capability and usability of such systems and artifacts, and to encourage existing and new communities to focus on innovative application areas." Even so, it is naive to believe that government is competent, let alone in a position, to control the development and deployment of robots, self-generating algorithms, and artificial intelligence. Government has too many constituent parts that have their own, sometimes competing, visions of the technological future. Business, of course, is self-interested and resists regulation. We, the people, are on our own here—though if the AI developers have their way, not for long.

Note

*Carr discusses integrated development environments (IDEs), which programmers use to check their code, and quotes Vivek Haldar, a veteran Google developer: "'The behavior all these tools encourage is not 'think deeply about your code and write it carefully,' but 'just write a crappy first draft of your code, and then the tools will tell you not just what's wrong with it, but also how to make it better.'"

1. *The Second Machine Age: Work, Progress, and Prosperity in a Time of Brilliant Technologies* (Norton, 2014), pp. 10–11.

2. Michael Doherty, "When the Working Day Is Through: The End of Work As Identity?" *Work, Employment and Society*, Vol. 23, No. 1 (March 2009).

6
Politics and Globalism

Missy Ryan/The Washington Post via Getty Images

On June 16, 2015, an Air Force pilot conducted a training flight at Creech Air Force Base, Nevada, which oversees drone operations overseas.

6

Politics and Globalism

Virtual War and Peace

The battlegrounds for warfare and political dialogue are increasingly fought in the digital domain. Digital technology has tremendous potential to foster and enhance communication and has been a driving force in political transformation. At the same time, the shift to the digital age has also revealed new threats to national security and has created a competitive information environment in which harnessing and maintaining the interest of the people has become increasingly difficult to achieve.

News and Political Engagement

The digital age has provided a variety of new ways for people around the world to engage in the political process. From grass roots civic activism organized through social media to Twitter feeds from prominent politicians, digital communication provides the potential for a nearly constant stream of political information and involvement. However, in the United States, civic and political involvement increases with age in the population, while the use of Internet and social media is more prevalent among youth.

A 2012 Pew report, for instance, found that political involvement among voters under 30 years old fell from 35 percent to 18 percent between 2008 and 2012. The 2008 presidential election was unique in the level of popular support that the election generated, in part because it was the first election to feature an African American candidate.[1] Without the intense pop-cultural appeal of the 2008 election, political parties have had a difficult time maintaining interest among younger voters. There have been a variety of suggestions for how to encourage youth involvement in politics, including adopting online or same day registration. As younger generations are increasingly attuned to digital tools, there has been a push in the United States to legalize online voting. Cybersecurity experts, however, are leery, citing the potential for fraud and other security issues.[2]

According to a 2013 Pew Research report, between 2008 and 2012 individuals increasingly followed political candidates or joined political parties through social media. The number of US social media users also grew from 33 percent of the online population to over 69 percent in the same period.[3] However, the 2013 report also found that more than 60 percent of political donations come through traditional rather than digital channels and that most people in surveys say that they have political discussions "offline" rather than through social media. These conflicting findings indicate a change in the process of political involvement, but also that political action may still rely on traditional methods of reaching voters and citizens.

One major change to political strategy has been in attempting to adjust to the rapid news cycle of digital media. At a national agenda speaker series at the

University of Delaware in 2014, CNN digital reporter Peter Hanby said that Twitter has changed the 24-hour news cycle into a 24-minute news cycle. After the 2012 presidential campaign, Hanby argued, political candidates have become increasingly wary of interacting with the media, realizing that any mistake or gaff can become a major embarrassment through viral social media. As a result, political parties are increasingly protecting candidates from the media.[4]

From Slacktivism to Digital Activism

Digital activism is a relatively new phenomenon in which social media tools and street level organization are used together to generate interest in political or civic issues. The Occupy Wall Street protests of 2011 and Black Lives Matter protests in 2014 and 2015 provide examples of cases in which online organization resulted in widespread interest and involvement.

The "Black Lives Matter" slogan was invented in Facebook exchanges between friends Patrisse Cullors and Alicia Garza about the trial in which George Zimmerman was acquitted of murder charges in the shooting death of Trayvon Martin. The slogan went viral as a "hashtag" attached to Twitter posts dealing with racism and cases of alleged police abuse directed at African Americans. The 2014 shooting death of Michael Brown in Ferguson, Missouri and the choking death of Eric Garner in Long Island, New York, both incidents in which white police officers were accused of using unnecessary lethal force, made Black Lives Matter a national movement. Protests organized in New York, Philadelphia, Los Angeles, Chicago, San Francisco, were partially organized through online groups like Black Lives Matter.[5]

Social media has also been used to gather support for feminist activism in the United States and the UK and has become a powerful force for organization around the world. Most notably, the "Arab Spring," of 2011, a series of protests in Tunisia, Egypt, and across the Middle East, has been seen as a harbinger of how social media and digital organizing may be changing the political landscape. In 2013, Oxford University Press published a collaborative scholarly volume in which specialists asked if the growing dominance of digital media represented a "fourth wave" of democracy through virtual organization and involvement.[6] Another example has been the growing online youth movement in China. In a 2013 article in *The Atlantic*, for instance, Yunqian Wang reported that Chinese youth activists, first meeting and organizing through an online platform called CAPE, are now gathering in cafes and meeting halls to discuss their issues and problems with the Chinese political system. Wang and other analysts suspect that such online movements could become a major political force in China, even though the Chinese government continues to exert strong censorship controls over Internet use and communication.[7]

A November 2014 study of digital activism, conducted by researchers at the University of Washington, found that the most successful digital activist movements use multiple modes of communication and organization simultaneously, including both digital and traditional methods. According to the researchers, none of the widely available digital tools can be said to be the most effective and combining methods of organizations. For instance, successful digital activist groups typically rely on local organization, through word of mouth and paper postings, and then engage in a multi-modal social media campaign using Twitter, Facebook, YouTube, Snapchat, Instagram, and a variety of other social sites, and creating what the researchers called "social media stew."[8]

Another popular political buzzword of the 2010s is "slacktivism," a derisive term that refers to the superficial level of political involvement among some social media users. Critics argue that there has been an increase in individuals simply "liking" a post or "retweeting" a political message, but without any deeper level of commitment or involvement. Superficial political involvement is not a new phenomenon for American youth. At the height of the political movements of the 1960s, for instance, there were many young Americans who wore t-shirts or hung posters because such things were in fashion, and without taking a deeper interest in the underlying issues. Though now called "slactivism," the term "armchair activism," has also been used to describe this level of social, superficial political motivation.[9]

In a *Huffington Post* article in 2012, Evan Bailyn argued that even passing political interest can make a major difference to a grassroots political movement. Even simply sharing or retweeting helps increase the spread of a media campaign, potentially reaching others who might make donations or become more deeply involved in the movement.[10] However, though digital activism provides new avenues for political involvement, studies of traditional civic engagement indicate flagging interest among most segments of the population. For instance, a 2013 report from the US Bureau of Labor Statistics (BLS) indicated that volunteering with civil, social, and charitable organizations fell to the lowest levels measured since the BLS started measuring volunteer statistics in 2002. Between 2012 and 2013, for instance, nearly one million fewer people became volunteers.[11]

National Security and Digital Warfare

As digital media plays an increasingly important role in political activism, governments have had to face the issue of coping with digital organizations that foster violence and terrorism. Though indications have been that digital activism, as a broader phenomenon, is largely focused on non-violent activism, the social media recruitment of the Islamic terrorist organization ISIS shows a darker side to digital organization. The power of the digital medium is that it is difficult to stop, both because of the challenges of locating individuals through cyberspace and because social media expression is not, in itself, a crime. Since the revelation that ISIS has been using social media for recruitment, the US military has organized social media and digital campaigns to disrupt and reduce the effectiveness of ISIS recruitment efforts. As of June 2015, US efforts to slow or reverse ISIS social media gains had been unsuccessful, and some worry that ISIS has begun making social media inroads into western nations as well.[12]

Videos showing the execution of ISIS hostages were released on the Internet in 2014, revealing a new dimension of what has been called "cyberterrorism," the use of digital media and technology to further terrorist goals.[13] The ISIS videos are a form of psychological cyberterrorism, messages meant to evoke fear and "terror" among a targeted group, but national security organizations are concerned about a different form of cyberterrorism, the use of computer hacking, viruses, and destructive programs called "malware" to disrupt the digital systems of a business or government. Cybersecurity experts agreed in 2015 that ISIS was unlikely to develop the capability to launch a cyberterrorist attack against their enemies, but the potential for a terrorist organization to develop digital tools remains a pressing concern.[14] In 2014, President Barack Obama called "cyberterrorism" one of the nation's most immediate threats, and the Obama administration has assembled a team of security experts to enhance security and create countermeasures for foreign cyberattacks.[15]

Related to "cyberterrorism" is "cyberwarfare," an evolving military field centered on the development and use of digital weapons against hostile nations. As of 2015, the United States is a leader in the development of both cyberwarfare technology and cybersecurity measures to protect against digital attacks. The US government's StuxNet virus, for instance, has been described as the world's first "cyberweapon." The US military released the StuxNet virus in 2010, and used it to disrupt computer-controlled systems in Iranian nuclear laboratories, effectively disrupting the nation's controversial nuclear development program.[16]

Increasingly, the United States uses high tech digital weaponry to protect the lives of US soldiers, but these new technological innovations have been controversial as well. For instance, the US government's controversial use of automated drones to attack terrorist targets in Afghanistan, Iraq, and Pakistan has raised serious ethical and moral questions. Amnesty International has argued that drone attacks might be considered "war crimes" as the attacks are indiscriminate and more likely to lead to civilian casualties.[17] Like cyberweapons, drones can be deployed from a distance, essentially removing the direct human element from warfare, and critics therefore worry that the ease and detachment with which these new weapons can be used may be escalating the use of violence as opposed to negotiation and diplomacy.

While some use the threat of cyberterrorism and cyberwarfare to justify the US government's controversial surveillance programs, others have criticized those programs as a violation of constitutional protections. Nevertheless, while digital privacy activists criticize government surveillance, the US government at least to date has protected the open exchange of information through the Internet and has largely resisted lobbies calling for Internet censorship or restricting traffic based on national security or corporate interests. Protecting the democratic nature of the Internet while addressing ever more technologically advanced threats will likely remain a major governmental issue for the next generation.

Micah L. Issit

Notes

1. "Youth Engagement Falls; Registration Also Declines."
2. Gross, "Why Can't Americans Vote Online?"

3. Smith, "Civic Engagement in the Digital Age."

4. Rhodes, "National Agenda 2014."

5. Kurwa, "'Black Lives Matter' Slogan Becomes a Bigger Movement."

6. Howard and Hussian, "Democracy's Fourth Wave?"

7. Wang, "In China, Digital Activists Are Starting to Meet Up in Person."

8. Kelley, "Study Shines Light on What Makes Digital Activism Effective."

9. Seay, "Does Slacktvism Work?"

10. Bailyn, "The Difference Between Slacktivism and Activism."

11. Kurtzleben, "Volunteering Hits Lowest Rate in More than 10 Years."

12. Mazzetti and Gordon, "ISIS Is Winning the Social Media War, U.S. Concludes."

13. Press Association, "Timeline: Isis Hostage Killings."

14. Frizell, "Experts Doubt ISIS Could Launch Major Cyberattack Against the U.S."

15. Harress, "Obama Says Cyberterrorism is Country's Biggest Threat."

16. Zetter, "An Unprecedented Look at Stuxnet, the World's First Digital Weapon."

17. Boone, "US Drone Strikes Could be Classed as War Crimes, Says Amnesty International."

Welcome to the Age of Digital Imperialism

By Bill Wasik
The New York Times, June 4, 2015

In March, the Culture Ministry of Thailand sent out an unusual communiqué. Women, it seems, both locals and tourists, were snapping pictures of their breasts from beneath, in an act known colloquially as the "underboob selfie." The ministry reminded women that sharing such images was banned under the Computer Crime Act of 2007 and that offenders could face five years in prison. Since the shots were cropped below the face, a ministry spokesman acknowledged to Reuters, prosecuting the scofflaws would be difficult. But this flaunting of flesh, the spokesman feared, might tempt others toward the same indelicacy. "We can only warn people to not take it up," he said. "They are inappropriate actions."

Some foreign observers saw this as another reactionary move by Thailand's military junta, which took power a year ago in a bloodless coup. But in fact, the ministry has long policed images of nudity in the country, in keeping with a longstanding uneasiness in Thai culture around public displays of sexuality. For at least a century, despite Thailand's famously (or infamously) laissez-faire attitude toward prostitution, the mainstream Thai stance on pornography has been markedly more conservative than the West's. Production, distribution, and possession of porn, widely defined, are all outlawed. In 2011, when three teenage girls danced bare-breasted at a spring festival, a video of the event sparked a national scandal, and the police —under what was then a democratically elected government—began a search for the culprits. (The girls, thirteen to sixteen, eventually turned themselves in and paid fines of $16 each.)

During the twentieth century, for governments that hoped, as Thailand's did and does, to beat back undesirable values from outside, the main culprit was what sometimes is called "cultural imperialism." Pop-culture products like rock 'n' roll and Hollywood films were seen, no doubt correctly, as smuggling within them not just a licentiousness but a dangerous individualism, a hatred of authority, a love of consumerism and wealth. In Thailand, the banning of foreign films stretches back at least as far as 1925, when an Indian-German production called "The Lion of India" was barred for its depiction of the Buddha's life. Today the country continues to repel big-screen indecency (e.g., *Zack and Miri Make a Porno*, from 2008) as well as sins against the Thai royal family like *The King and I*, whose most recent Hollywood rendition, *Anna and the King* (from 1999, starring Jodie Foster), got no further with the Culture Ministry than any previous version.

The underboob selfie, though, represents a rather different form of cultural incursion. Call it digital imperialism, perhaps, in that the values are arriving not inside artworks made by others but through a tool that locals can use themselves. As Thailand is discovering, the smartphone—for all its indispensability as a tool of business and practicality—is also a bearer of values; it is not a culturally neutral device. On the matter of privacy, for example, the pull toward sharing more and concealing less begins with the mere existence of the camera, tucked in every pocket, available whenever the impulse arises. It continues through the design of the apps we use, which have been calibrated to make our uploading seamless, to make our posts default to public, to make the less private choice always and everywhere more attractive to us in a cycle of escalating self-revelation. Thanks to the Internet's ability to find for us, in an instant, hordes of other people with the same impulse as ours—to photograph, say, the underside of a taboo body part—we can feel secure in that impulse, even if it's not shared by anyone else within a hundred or a thousand miles. We Americans might praise this shift as liberatory, or laugh it off as harmless, but we cannot pretend that it is somehow value-free.

> For individual users, everything about the smartphone nudges them by design to reveal more, to express and connect more. But all the resulting revelations then get rolled up as data that can be offered to governments and corporations—which feel practically compelled, once they know they can obtain it, to parse it all for usable intelligence.

And if digital imperialism is happening—if smartphones and other gadgets are bearing cultural freight as they cross borders—there is little doubt as to which nation's values are hiding in the hold. As of 2013, eight of the world's top ten Internet companies by audience were based in the United States, though 81 percent of their online visitors were not. (This fact was made painfully obvious to those users and their governments that same year, when Edward Snowden's trove of N.S.A. documents showed just how low these American Internet giants had stooped to cooperate with surveillance demands.) Smartphones themselves, from their precision-milled exteriors to their tiled grids of apps on-screen, are patterned largely on Apple's blueprint, even when designed and made by companies based in South Korea or China. The question is not whether the spread of technology is promulgating, as Hollywood once did, an American vision of what the world should be. Rather, the question is how the rest of the world will respond. . . .

. . . In Silicon Valley, the notion that technology spreads values is part of the corporate culture—as evidenced in the manifesto that Facebook published, rather incongruously, in the filing papers for its $16 billion I.P.O. three years ago. Declaring at the outset that Facebook was "built to accomplish a social mission," the document goes on to promise a sort of Facebook revolution: "By giving people the power to share, we are starting to see people make their voices heard on a different scale from what has historically been possible." It continues: "Through this process, we believe that leaders will emerge across all countries who are pro-Internet and fight for the rights of their people, including the right to share what they want and the right to access all information that people want to share with them." This evangelical stance, pervasive in the Valley, explains why a major part of Facebook's and Google's philanthropic efforts in the past two years has been concentrated on taking Internet access to the developing world. Executives of these companies genuinely believe that over the long run, information technology—including, naturally, the services they themselves provide—is crucial to bettering society.

From the Valley's perspective, that is, the "power to share" looks less like an imposition of American values and more like a universal social good. But even if we agree with this proposition—as Thailand's Culture Ministry, for one, might not—there is the more fraught question of what all that sharing adds up to. For individual users, everything about the smartphone nudges them by design to reveal more, to express and connect more. But all the resulting revelations then get rolled up as data that can be offered to governments and corporations—which feel practically compelled, once they know they can obtain it, to parse it all for usable intelligence. For institutions, as with consumers, all resistance recedes once they understand what is possible, once it's all made to seem not merely acceptable but inevitable and desirable.

This double-edged quality is a hallmark of so many technological innovations today. The same facial recognition software that autotags your photos can autoflag dissidents at the border. The machine-translation engine that lets you flirt in passable French can help spy on multiple continents from a single cubicle. The fitness data you use to adjust your workout might soon forcibly adjust your health-insurance premium. And the stakes have risen considerably as the Valley's ambitions, during the past few years, have clambered into physical space; in a phenomenon that the venture capitalist Marc Andreessen has famously called "software eating the world," a new generation of tech companies has encroached on industries like hospitality (Airbnb), transportation (Uber and Lyft), office space (WeWork), and more, bringing a set of tech-inflected values with them.

In old-fashioned nineteenth-century imperialism, the Christian evangelists made a pretense of traveling separately from the conquering colonial forces. But in digital imperialism, everything travels as one, in the form of the splendid technology itself: salvation and empire, missionary and magistrate, Bible and gun. For all that the world-changing talk of Silicon Valley gets parodied, it is not just empty rhetoric. Over the past decade, it has helped draw so many of the nation's most driven college graduates to Silicon Valley, the one place in twenty-first-century America that promises to satisfy both their overweening ambition and their restless craving for social uplift. These unquiet Americans have gone on to design tools that spread values as they create value—a virtuous circle for all who share their virtues.

The Mobile Election: How Smartphones Will Change the 2016 Presidential Race

By Dylan Byers
Politico, April 1, 2015

Four years ago today, President Barack Obama was gearing up to announce his reelection campaign, Mitt Romney was leading Newt Gingrich in the polls, and roughly one out of every three American adults owned a smartphone.

You read that right: In the spring of 2011, just 35 percent of American adults owned a smartphone, according to Pew Research. The Internet and social media may have been changing politics in myriad ways, but news consumption was mostly a sedentary experience.

Today, as Hillary Clinton prepares for the formal launch of her campaign, and as Jeb Bush and Scott Walker are neck and neck in the polls, roughly two out of every three American adults, or 64 percent, own a smartphone, according to a new report from Pew.

The new mobile reality is changing the state of news and advertising, and it will also change the dynamic of American politics—especially during the 2016 campaign season, journalists and political operatives said.

"Mobile is going to be the big thing in 2016," Chris Lehane, the Democratic strategist and Clinton White House alum, told the *On Media* blog. "It is what any sophisticated campaign will be trying to figure out and then maximize in 2016—and all the campaigns from both parties will be in a race to see who can figure out the tools to best lever the power of mobile."

On the consumption side, the rise in mobile will "change politics the same way it is changing American life broadly," said Ben Smith, the editor-in-chief of BuzzFeed. "People will organize and persuade on mobile devices and apps, the same way they live on them more broadly."

68 percent of smartphone owners now use their phone to follow along with breaking news events, while 33 percent say that they do this "frequently," according to the Pew report. Though mobile usage is highest among younger Americans, news consumption is "common even among older smartphone owners," as "four-in-ten smartphone owners ages 65 and older use their phone at least occasionally to keep up with breaking news."

On the media side, the rise in mobile usage will increase the number of citizen reporters, whose influence on recent political campaigns has been quite significant. Video footage of an errant remark—from George Allen's "Macaca" moment in 2006

"The Mobile Election: How Smartphones Will Change the 2016 Presidential Race" by Dylan Byers. Originally published by Politico, April 1, 2015.

to Mitt Romney's "47 percent" moment in 2012—can have more influence on a political campaign than any traditional news report.

"In 2011, one-third of Americans were essentially campaign trackers. Now two-thirds are," said Tommy Vietor, a former Obama spokesperson. "As we learned from the 47 percent video, catching a politician speaking bluntly in what they think is a private setting can change the course of a campaign."

> **"Gaffes will blow up even faster. Partisan rooting will be even quicker and more intense"**

New livestreaming applications like Periscope and Meerkat, which allow smartphone owners to stream live video footage directly to their Twitter followers, will now allow voters to witness such events in real time. "Every minute—literally every minute—of every day of the campaign will be available live to anyone who wants it, no matter where they are," former Obama adviser Dan Pfeiffer wrote last month. Pfeiffer focused on the benefits of these services—greater engagement opportunities for Millennials, the importance of Twitter followers—but there is also potential for the rise in mobile usage to exacerbate the already fractious and fractured state of American politics.

"Gaffes will blow up even faster. Partisan rooting will be even quicker and more intense," Henry Blodget, the editor and C.E.O. of *Business Insider*, predicted. "Anonymous trolls will swarm Twitter and brand any news story that is not highly flattering to their team as 'bias.'"

On the campaign side, the rise in mobile usage will create new ways for campaigns to advertise and target voters, down to highly specified demographic groups.

"The ability to really translate the power and opportunity of big data to allow for nano-targeting communications with precision-targeted messaging is dependent on the ability to lever the power of mobile," Lehane explained. "There will be an explosion of mobile advertising in 2016; an explosion in using mobile to share campaign content; an explosion in using mobile to organize."

Lehane mapped out one scenario, in the fall of 2016, where "a voter identified by a campaign based on its data analytics will be nano-targeted via addressable mobile with ads, with social messages from their friends who have been engaged by the campaigns to reach out to their social network." On election day, Lehane predicted, campaigns will have information about the voter "based on GPS data, to both determine whether they have visited a voting poll and/or [provide] step by step directions of how to find the poll in their precinct."

At the most basic level, the rise in mobile usage will speed up the entire political process. Voters will have faster and more frequent access to campaign news and information, and campaigns will have better access to voters and their data.

"Mobile is really this generation's version of their car," Lehane said. "It is the platform where they spend much of their time; it is their TV, radio, movie screen, phone and computer all in one; it is what allows them to, in effect, travel beyond their current location by connecting them to various outlets from social to content to communications."

Activism or Slacktivism? How Social Media Hurts and Helps Student Activism

By Kate Essig
St. Louis Public Radio, January 2, 2014

On Oct. 1, 1964, hundreds of University of California-Berkeley students surrounded a police car to protest the arrest of a student. Students stood on top of the car to deliver speeches and sing, "We Shall Overcome," to a crowd that grew to include roughly two thousand students.

Years later, on Nov. 21, 2013, students gathered in Saint Louis University's student union for "The State of St. Louis," an event planned by a SLU's Political Roundtable. Students sat around tables instead of standing on cars, but that's not the only difference between student activism today and the sit-ins of the past. Student activists today can use social media to promote their organizations online.

While Political Roundtable has 126 supporters on Facebook, roughly thirty students attended their event. Their absence could be attributed to studying for tests or having another commitment, but it could be because of a different phenomenon: slacktivism.

What Is "Slacktivism"?

Slacktivism is a term for giving token support for a cause, like wearing a pin or "liking" something on Facebook, without being willing to engage in more meaningful support, like donating time or money. And with the presence of social media, being a slacktivist is easier now than ever.

A recent study from the University of British Columbia found that when people participate in a form of public token support, they aren't any more likely to participate in a form of more meaningful support in the future. Someone who "likes" a cause on Facebook wouldn't be any more likely to donate in the future than someone who had no exposure to the cause at all.

Kirk Kristofferson is one of the authors of the study.

"What we found is that the social observability of the token support really impacted how likely consumers were to follow up and provide real support for that charity," Kristofferson said. "We found that when consumers gave public support, they were no more likely to provide more meaningful support for the cause than if someone was just randomly asked for the larger request."

Studies have shown that when people support a cause with some effort, they're

---

more likely to support a cause with an even larger effort in the future. For example, someone who participates in a 5k run for a charity is more likely to donate in the future than someone who has no familiarity with the cause at all or has done something minimal like joining their page on Facebook.

> **"Raising awareness is a lazy objective. Awareness is a given, action is what you want to promote."**

If college students choose to be activists by sharing a link or liking a status, they may not feel more compelled to take real, tangible effort towards social change.

"Drawing back from the 60s and sit ins, that was real action. That was people putting forth a strong effort," Kristofferson said. "Conversely, what social media has done is remove that effort. So, our findings would suggest that it (social media) would be making it more difficult to make a difference."

How Do Students See Social Media With Social Causes?

Back at SLU, T.K. Smith is on the executive board of Saint Louis University's Political Round Table. He thinks that social media can convince users they're doing something good even if all they're doing is pressing a button.

"Because we can like something, because we can read an article online, it kind of changes how you feel like you are doing something," Smith said. "You kind of feel like being more in the know that you are doing more than if you hadn't 'liked' it."

Another student at Saint Louis University, Christina LaFon, created a Facebook group with the purpose of sharing articles about feminism with like-minded people.

But raising awareness, LaFon said, isn't the end goal of social justice, or her own end goal for the group.

"Raising awareness is a lazy objective. Awareness is a given, action is what you want to promote," LaFon said. "Eventually, I'd really like for us to be able to provide resources for people to start their own movements."

'Slacktivism' Still Means Activism... When It's Done Right

Advocating for a cause on social media does not automatically make you a slacktivist. LaFon, for instance, has been involved in political campaigning and offline advocacy in addition to the awareness she tries to raise online.

Julie Dixon is Deputy Director of the Georgetown Center for Social Impact Communication and one of the authors of *Digital Persuasion*, a study that looks at how social media users use their influence to promote social change.

"It's unfair to write off everyone who supports on social media as being a slacktivist," Dixon said. "Because as we've seen in other research, there are folks who are active on social media who are deeply involved in other ways."

Despite the potential effects of slacktivism, student protests do still occur on college campuses. Just last year SLU students helped organize a sit-in and teach-in in protest of then-President Father Lawrence Biondi, and within the last couple years student protests have gained global attention in Egypt, England and Chile.

In many ways, Dixon said, social media makes it easier for students to organize in a way that can lead to offline engagement.

Most importantly, Dixon said to remember that social media isn't a fundraising tool; it's a relationship-building tool. Social causes are helped by social media when you see what your network cares about and decide to care about that, too.

"How people hear about causes and how people decide to support and care about them it comes a lot more often from their friends," Dixon said. "It doesn't come from this blanket post from the organization—that doesn't work as much as having a friend say, 'Hey this is an organization that I really care about and it's impacted my life, and you should care about this as well.'"

Social media allows users to organize, network, and share what they're passionate about in a way that wasn't available to student protestors in the 60s. It's now easier than ever to learn about causes and share information, but it's also easier than ever to be a slacktivist.

Through research, experts like Dixon and Kristofferson continue to work towards connecting users and organizations in a way that will combat slacktivism and lead to meaningful support that both users and organizations could "like."

Hashtag Activism Isn't a Cop-Out

By Noah Berlatsky
The Atlantic, January 7, 2015

Mainstream-media figures often portray social media as a buzzing hive of useless outrage. Thinkpieces present hashtag activism as vanity activism, in which narcissistic pronouncements substitute for actual engagement, and anger is leveraged at best for petty entertainment and at worst for coordinated harassment.

Yet activists themselves often argue that social media is important to their work. DeRay Mckesson, who has emerged as one of a number of leading organizers and activists against police brutality, has spoken on his feed about how vital Twitter is for boosting a movement. When he first drove from his home in Minneapolis—where he works as a school administrator, traveling for protests mainly on weekends—to Ferguson to participate in the protests, Mckesson knew no one; he didn't even know where he would sleep. Facebook networks found him a couch, and social media was vital in connecting him with the community of protestors. Mckesson reports live from protests through Twitter, where his following has ballooned from 800 followers to more than 61,000 since he began his activism. He's also used social networks to raise awareness and to organize, by for example creating a text-message alert that informed thousands the instant the grand jury in Ferguson returned a no-indictment verdict in the Michael Brown case.

I talked to Mckesson about social media, protest, and the connections between the two. This interview has been edited for length and clarity.

Noah Berlatsky: What role has social-media activism played in the movement against police brutality that started in Ferguson?

DeRay Mckesson: Missouri would have convinced you that we did not exist if it were not for social media. The intensity with which they responded to protestors very early—we were able to document that and share it quickly with people in a way that we never could have without social media. We were able to tell our own stories.

The history of blackness is also a history of erasure. Everybody has told the story of black people in struggle except black people. The black people in the struggle haven't had the means to tell the story historically. There were a million slaves but you see very few slave narratives. And that is intentional. So what was powerful in the context of Ferguson is that there were many people able to tell their story as the story unfolded.

The other thing I will add is that Twitter specifically has been interesting because we're able to get feedback and responses in real time. If we think about this as community building, and we think of community building as a manifestation of love, and we think about love being about accountability, and accountability about justice, what's interesting is that Twitter has kept us honest. There's a democracy of feedback. I've had really robust conversations with people who aren't physically in the space, but who have such great ideas. And that's proven to be invaluable.

Berlatsky: The civil-rights movement of the '60s obviously didn't have Twitter or social media or the Internet, but it was able to get its message out to the media in other ways. Why wouldn't traditional media be adequate now?

Mckesson: Ferguson exists in a tradition of protest. But what is different about Ferguson, or what is important about Ferguson, is that the movement began with regular people. There was no Martin, there was no Malcolm, there was no NAACP, it wasn't the Urban League. People came together who didn't necessarily know each other, but knew what they were experiencing was wrong. And that is what started this. What makes that really important, unlike previous struggle, is that—who is the spokesperson? The people. The people, in a very democratic way, became the voice of the struggle.

Our access to information is also so much greater than in the past. For instance, there's an officer in Ferguson who is really aggressive with protestors for no reason. And I was able to take a picture of him—he would cover his badge with his hand, he would not show his name. So I took a picture of him, put it online, and within 30 minutes they knew everything about him. And that's a different way of empowering people.

Berlatsky: It sounds like you're saying that Twitter allowed the movement to be a lot more decentralized. Is that an advantage or a disadvantage? It seems like it might be a disadvantage in terms of settling on specific goals, for example.

Mckesson: It is not that we're anti-organization. There are structures that have formed as a result of protest, that are really powerful. It is just that you did not need those structures to begin protest. *You* are enough to start a movement. Individual people can come together around things that they know are unjust. And they can spark change. Your body can be part of the protest; you don't need a VIP pass to protest. And Twitter allowed that to happen.

I think that what we are doing is building a radical new community in struggle that did not exist before. Twitter has enabled us to create community. I think the phase we're in is a community-building phase. Yes, we need to address policy, yes, we need to address elections; we need to do all those things. But on the heels of building a strong community.

Berlatsky: You also publish—along with Johnetta (Netta) Elzie—an online newsletter about the protest movement called Words to Action. Do you see yourself as a journalist? Or as an activist? Or both? How important is social media to those roles, or to combining them?

Mckesson: I see myself as a protestor who is also telling the story as it happens. The newsletter started—I remember when Trayvon [Martin] died, I wanted to fol-low the case, but I didn't know what was fact or fiction. I didn't want that to be the

> **"What we are doing is building a radical new community in struggle that did not exist before. Twitter has enabled us to create community....Yes, we need to address policy, yes, we need to address elections; we need to do all those things. But on the heels of building a strong community."**

story of Mike Brown. There was so much news; there was so much stuff that was unclear. There were so many questions. The goal was to create a space where people could go to get true news.

Now the movement has spread beyond St. Louis, we cover stories from around the country. So the goal was to be a hub of information. I think the first newsletter that went out had 400 subscribers, and we're at a little bit less than 14,000 now. And we did a text-message alert for the no-indictment—you could sign up to get a text when the decision came out. And 21,000 people signed up in 10 days, which was wild. So the work is focused on, how can we use the tools we have access to in order to create infrastructure for the movement.

And that's what Netta and I have been focused on. None of this takes away from our protesting. We don't put the newsletter out when we're out until 4 in the morning protesting. The trade-off always veers in the favor of protest. It's rooted in the confrontation and disruption that is protest. We want to make structures to empower people. The newsletter is a way to empower people. Because we believe that the truth is actually so damning that we can just tell you all the news that's happening and you should be radicalized. We believe that.

Berlatsky: I saw you talking about Iggy Azalea and issues of appropriation on Twitter a little bit back. That's the sort of cultural issue that I think many people would say is just a distraction, or is just a way for people to express outrage without working for social change. Do you see cultural conversations around Iggy, or similar issues, as a distraction from your work as an organizer? Or are they complementary?

Mckesson: Good lord. Iggy. (*laughs*) You're really trying to get me in trouble.

When people think about protest, they think that protest is always confrontation, protest is always disruption. But protest is also intellectual confrontation and disruption. So part of what we do when the police speak is that we question. The thing about people like Iggy is that we also question. We question what it means to have your success be on a medium and a platform that was born of black struggle, like hip-hop or rap, and what does it mean that you identify with everything but the struggle part? Which is the Iggy issue.

We question these issues of race and struggle and white privilege, because we know that those issues are real, and because those issues have real implications in black communities. And white supremacy is not only dangerous but it is deadly. We know this to be true.

Berlatsky: Do you get a lot of harassment on social media?

Mckesson: Yeah, the death threats aren't fun. They put my address out there, that's not fun. I get called a nigger more than I've ever been called that in my entire life. I've blocked over 9,000 people, so I don't personally see it as much anymore, but my friends do. So that sort of stuff I don't love.

But what social media has done is that it has exposed the intensity of hatred in America. People who you wouldn't expect to be racist ... some of the tweets are from people who are well-intentioned but racist. And I appreciate that that's exposed. People now understand where you're coming from. And it's deeply problematic. But we don't have to guess anymore; we get it.

The harassment is never a good thing. But there's something valuable in making sure you're not surrounded by people who think like you. It helps you understand what you think better. And I appreciate that about Twitter. It's a cacophony of voices. Even when you don't agree, you at least understand different perspectives. The medium itself sets that up.

Scholars Re-Examine Arab World's "Facebook Revolutions"

By Ursula Lindsey
The Chronicle of Higher Education, March 13, 2015

In January 2011, Laila Shereen Sakr realized something momentous was happening in the Middle East when her server crashed.

Ms. Sakr, at that time a graduate student in the University of Southern California's media arts and practice program, had been monitoring digital activism in the Middle East for several years. When protests began in Tunisia, she says, "I began collecting data immediately." After the incident with her server, she quickly transferred it all to the cloud and kept on building the database that would eventually become her dissertation.

Today R-Shief (the site's name is the Arabic pronunciation of "archive") contains 18 billion tweets in English and Arabic and years' worth of Facebook, YouTube, and website data. Every month, it processes about 100,000 million new tweets. Ms. Sakr compares English and Arabic hashtags, as well as different hashtags referring to the same events, looking for interesting patterns. Anyone can log onto the R-Shief site and do a number of searches and comparisons, using tools developed by Ms. Sakr and several collaborators.

At the moment, Ms. Sakr doesn't have the resources to make the full archive available to a large public. If she did, she says, she'd turn it into a tool that anyone could use to answer the many shifting questions regarding the relationship between social media and political mobilization in the Arab world.

"It's difficult to tell the story of the Arab Spring without talking about social media," says Philip N. Howard, a professor in the department of communications at the University of Washington. But "after years of excitement and effervescence," he notes, "we're in a much more jaded or critical stage of inquiry."

Working on his book (with Muzammil M. Hussain) *Democracy's Fourth Wave? Digital Media and the Arab Spring*, Mr. Howard developed a causal model that weighed access to new communication technology in Arab countries alongside other socioeconomic factors. He concluded that access was part of the basic infrastructure needed for collective action to take place.

But by the time the book was published, in 2013, those mass mobilizations for change had seemingly collapsed. Today, out of half a dozen Arab countries that witnessed uprisings, only Tunisia has managed to see its democratic transition through.

Across the region, the bloggers and activists who helped plan and publicize protests were sidelined by Islamist parties and military regimes. They have been silenced, imprisoned, or driven into exile.

Knowing What to Do Next

Scholars are now asking a different set of questions: How did these huge and hopeful social movements fizzle? Why were they unable to achieve political gains? How is social media being used today by resurgent autocratic governments and by terrorist groups?

Zeynep Tufekci, an assistant professor at the University of North Carolina at Chapel Hill's School of Information and Library Science, argued in a recent paper that the ability to "scale up" quickly that social media offers to protest movements means they don't have to do the hard and necessary work of building traditional organizations that know how to make decisions collectively, change strategies, and persevere. In a TED talk she gave in October, Ms. Tufekci compared today's social movements, in the Arab world and elsewhere, to "start-ups that got very big without knowing what to do next."

Clay Shirky, whose 2008 book *Here Comes Everybody: The Power of Organizing Without Organizations* focused on the transformative power of new communication technologies, now says he underestimated the need for traditional organizations. Mr. Shirky, an associate arts professor at New York University, interviewed the Egyptian blogger and activist Alaa Abd El Fattah for the book and says he considers Mr. Abd El Fattah's status a "benchmark" of political freedom. On February 23, the activist was sentenced to a five-year jail term for breaking a ban on protests; he is one of many convicted recently on similar charges.

"It's not enough to just show up in Tahrir Square when you're angry," says Mr. Shirky. "It's not enough when you are up against other organizations who have long-term horizons and significant resources."

Nevertheless, he emphasizes that the autocracies of the Middle East are less secure than they were five years ago. "Every autocratic state is now terrified by social media, as it should be," he says.

"Part of the problem is we tend to expect too much of social media," says Rasha A. Abdulla, an associate professor of journalism and mass communication at the American University in Cairo. "It's not there to cause uprisings. It was a good facilitator in 2011 because the environment was ripe."

Ms. Abdulla is collaborating with researchers from the University of Amsterdam to analyze the content of the We Are All Khaled Said Facebook page, which was created in honor of a young Egyptian beaten to death by police in 2010 and was instrumental in encouraging the protests. The page was a site for political discussions and even decision making (it regularly polled its millions of followers). Ms. Abdullah hopes to learn more about the page's readers and commenters and their political leanings, to find out how social media can "best be used now to create more social and political change."

'The Elites Have Learned'

"The protesters used information technology to catch political elites off-guard," says Mr. Howard. Today "the elites have learned, and started investing very heavily in using social technology as a means of social control rather than conversation." He has been looking at the way regimes use automated scripts ("bots") to neutralize their opponents online (they can do so, for example, by flooding a critical Twitter hashtag with extraneous material).

Dalia Othman, a research fellow and visiting scholar at Harvard University's Berkman Center for Internet and Society, is helping to update the center's landmark 2009 report on the Arab blogosphere. She is interested in observing the biggest differences pre- and post-uprisings and in figuring out what the main online communities in Arab countries are today and how they communicate with each other.

> The ability to "scale up" quickly that social media offers to protest movements means they don't have to do the hard and necessary work of building traditional organizations that know how to make decisions collectively, change strategies, and persevere.

Ms. Othman also studies how different kinds of narrative are created and disseminated, or hijacked and smothered. The Arab Spring "was always a war of narratives," she says. Now, with more government censorship and pro-government groups joining platforms to dilute revolutionary messages, "activists are being drowned out."

Unfortunately, "social media can become an effective tool not only in the hands of proponents but opponents of democracy as well," notes Imad Salamey, an associate professor of political science and international affairs at the Lebanese American University. He believes that the online campaign of fear being waged by terrorist groups is another blow to the chances of democratization in the region.

Studying ISIS

Mr. Salamey wonders how social-media users build resilience against antidemocratic images and avoid infatuation with images of violence. "What kind of counter campaign can balance this out, to allow people to still believe in peaceful protest and peaceful mobilization?"

Other scholars are analyzing the online activities of the Islamic State in Iraq and Syria to try to understand its ideology and strategy, or to figure out how effective social media really is as a recruitment tool. British authorities recently announced that they were searching for three teenage girls believed to have traveled to join the group. Ms. Sakr warns against thinking that one can easily answer questions like "Who is ISIS?" just by looking at social media. But she says R-Shief has been used as a resource to study, for example, whether ISIS spreads its ideology differently according to gender.

This fall, Ms. Sakr will join the faculty of the University of California at Santa

Barbara's film-and-media-studies program. She hopes to find the funds to make all of R-Shiefs data publicly available, to turn it into an interactive resource "where everybody could build their own archive."

And she is interested in posing creative questions. She is working on an experimental documentary in which she will use the data she has collected as a basis to envisage different scenarios: What if Egypt's President Mubarak hadn't turned off the Internet? What if the Houthi party hadn't taken power in Yemen? What if—as so many people have wondered by now—things had turned out differently?

How ISIS Succeeds on Social Media
Where #StopKony Fails

By J.M. Berger
The Atlantic, March 16, 2015

Social networks offer an incredible tool for tapping into the collective unconscious, a virtual Jungian arena in which competition might be expected to amplify the critical values and anxieties of millions of people in real time.

In early 2015, these critical issues included the ambiguous color of a random dress, the so-called Islamic State, and llamas—in that order.

How did we get here?

The answer to this question is, predictably, complex. Divining the mood of the masses has always been a tricky business. Prior to the rise of democracy, there were few consistent tools for this purpose, aside from counting how many pitchforks and torches the peasants were waving outside the gates. The vote became one way to quantify citizen priorities. But in practice, democracy is reductive. A finite number of candidates run for a finite number of offices, and the winners infer what their constituents want and need.

The explosion of affordable communications technologies allowed such inferences to become more accurate over time. Still, at every stage, reductionist influences kept whittling and shaping the raw data of public opinion. Pollsters decided what to ask and how to phrase the questions. Politicians decided which issues to exploit. News editors and producers made judgment calls about what was newsworthy.

Social media has introduced a new and profound layer of complication to how we listen to the voice of the masses. The technology has replaced the reductionism of the old world with a bafflingly dense ecosystem of echo and amplification. While this seems to cut out the middleman, the surging complexity of the system results in an unpredictable stew of dynamics that can create false impressions, such as that the rising terrorist threat in Iraq and Syria presents an existential threat to the world—despite the fact that ISIS, the terrorist group in question, possesses only tens of thousands of fighters and little popular support—or that the perceived color of a dress is more important still, if only for a day.

* * *

Highly interconnected systems like social-media networks display a phenomenon known as emergence, which can be boiled down to the idea that a system is more than the sum of its parts, especially when the parts become numerous. And a system built from many smaller

> **True virality can't be engineered, but it is possible to stack the deck. ISIS has done so expertly.**

systems, each of which is itself complex, will exhibit behaviors that could not have been predicted. Weather is an emergent property, which is why weather forecasts can never be perfect. No matter how many factors you consider—from the action of the Gulf Stream to areas of low atmospheric pressure—the weather forecast for any specific day in the future will always contain a degree of uncertainty.

Stock prices are an emergent property of the market. They may track generally with a company's health, but stocks reflect the subjective views of investors, which can include factors such as a company's failure to meet an expectation for earnings, or aggregated jobs reports that have no particular bearing on any given company's performance.

On social networks, emergent behavior can be found in spades, and we have words to describe some of its manifestations. For example, a "viral" sensation, such as that darn [is it gold and white or blue and black?] dress, creates an explosion of interest from users that can be as inexplicable as it is hard to ignore. The word "viral" is used to refer to content that becomes wildly popular online seemingly of its own accord, but it applies more broadly to a host of networked phenomena in which a small current of activity explodes into a tidal wave, whether it's a trending hashtag, a sleeper hit at the movies, a massive stock market swing, or an outbreak of mass hysteria.

A multitude of sites now actively try to make their material go "viral," but most such attempts fail precisely because emergence makes it impossible to predict how any given thing will play on social media. Most of this activity is harmless, even if it disappoints our hopes that humanity is evolving toward a higher dialogue.

But sometimes, these waves of social-media focus are pernicious, as in the case of the Islamic State, also known as ISIS. And while true virality can't be engineered, it is possible to stack the deck. ISIS has done so expertly. The number of accounts tweeting in support of ISIS numbers, at most, in the low tens of thousands—about one or two-hundredths of 1 percent of the total active Twitter accounts in any given month—but ISIS's strategic and industrious activity commands a disproportionate amount of media and policy attention, even inspiring talk of prosecution or legislation to help counter the problem.

* * *

A 2014 paper in the Proceedings of the National Academy of Sciences of the United States of America (PNAS) coined the term "femtorisk" to refer to a numerically small phenomenon capable of exerting an outsized impact on global politics ("femto" is the prefix meaning one quadrillionth). The history of ISIS is a classic example of a femtorisk. The group started as a tiny nucleus of terrorist operatives, evolved into al-Qaeda in Iraq, and erupted into a full-scale insurgency with significant local and international support. It was beaten back, under pressure from local enemies and the American "surge," devolving into a small and utterly despised terrorist group. But it rebounded again, gaining thousands of new supporters, dramatically asserting itself in 2014 with the seizure of massive swathes of Iraq and Syria.

Most quantitative approaches to ISIS show that its impact is far greater than its numerical strength. It seized Mosul, a city of 1.5 million people, with just a few thousand fighters. It has dominated the world's attention for months with just a few tens of thousands of supporters in the field and on social media. Embraced by considerably less than one-hundredth of 1 percent of the world's 1.6 billion Muslims, ISIS has nevertheless managed to spark a seemingly endless controversy about what it says about the religion of Islam. Responsible for a handful of attacks in the West, it has convinced many that it presents an existential threat to the United States. Its international expansion has been fueled in part by its ability to project an image of strength and threat beyond its actual physical capacity.

It's not just ISIS. Other examples of femtorisks abound and often carry serious consequences. The paper points to the 2008 financial crisis, the Arab Spring, and Ukraine's Euromaidan protests among several examples. The "flash crash" of 2010—in which the stock market lost 10 percent of its value in just minutes before rebounding—was caused by one tiny line of code in a trading algorithm that cascaded rapidly throughout the system. Each of these events represented a rapid and mostly unforeseen escalation from small initial catalysts into global crisis and radical change, and each was facilitated by interconnected systems. Most observers—importantly including the makers of foreign and financial policy—were blindsided. And the implications of each event were often grievously misinterpreted.

Terrorist Twitter accounts on social media may be the femto-est of femtorisks, often commanding a disproportionate amount of attention, despite their vanishingly small scale compared to the monthly Twitter user base of 288 million.

Vastly interconnected networks have tremendous power to amplify certain issues unpredictably. Increasingly, we assess risk based on virality—in the sense of an event's unexpected nature and cascading consequences—with the result that risks that we failed to anticipate often become greater when we respond to them with disproportionate force and an excessive investment of resources. Terrorism is especially impacted by this evolution, because it seeks to exploit precisely that dynamic. Al-Qaeda in the Arabian Peninsula once openly boasted it could prompt the West to spend billions of dollars on airport security with an attack that cost $4,200 and didn't even succeed.

But for every successful viral outburst, a hundred thousand memes putter away at a lower level or quietly die from neglect. The success of ISIS on social media is due in part to its shock value, but it is also owes much to the group's patient, systematic work manipulating quirks within the system, and the eagerness of policymakers and media gatekeepers to respond to the outsized perception of risk, rather than to the relatively small risk itself.

Eventually we will learn to forecast the tides of social media, much as we forecast the weather—good enough to get by most days, but bad enough that everyone will continue to complain.

Even with all these tools at its disposal, ISIS enjoys only limited success. For instance, its massive investment in social media, including a team of roughly 2,000 dedicated accounts tweeting in a coordinated manner, succeeds primarily because it generates just barely enough activity to get the attention of the mainstream media, which then creates the perception that ISIS has a larger base of supporters than it does. ISIS's advantage comes from its ability to bridge the space between a social network and network news, a leap fueled largely by its extreme sadism and its choice of media-friendly victims.

In contrast, there is little science behind the wild success of #StopKony, #BringBackOurGirls, or #JeSuisCharlie—although each campaign involved specific efforts from activists and organizers—and compelling causes with understandable appeal. But while those factors put each campaign in a position to succeed, the Twitter jet stream that turned them viral could not have been foreseen or predicted. Each nevertheless quickly faded, despite the fact that organizers made more calculated efforts to keep the momentum going.

Viral eruptions are vastly more powerful than manufactured effects, such as ISIS's army of monomaniacal tweeters or Russia's deployment of thousands of social media bots and trolls. But they are less sustainable.

ISIS can drone on and maintain a certain substantial level of noise for as long as its social network is permitted to function unimpeded. It can exploit that noise to generate media coverage that exponentially magnifies its impact and influences military and political decisions. It can even push its online performance to a level that exploits technical advantages, such as the way Twitter rates search results.

What it cannot do—not by design at least—is produce material that spontaneously engages millions of people. Fear of ISIS has indeed become viral in a metaphorical sense, but ironically, its social-media effort succeeds only well enough to push its message out to mainstream media gatekeepers, who then amplify it. Even at their peak, ISIS beheading videos never performed at a level comparable to #BringBackOurGirls. The group may stumble on to a truly viral sensation by chance, or through practice, but its daily process is plodding and methodical, patiently racking up gains on a scale of dozens, not millions.

* * *

The future is uncertain, mathematically speaking, and while this is nothing new, the nature of that uncertainty has changed. The assassination of Archduke Ferdinand 100 years ago is commonly held to have sparked World War I. While this is likely an oversimplification, the "virality" of that act greatly contributed to shaping the events that followed.

Today, similarly viral moments erupt much more regularly but with far less consequence. Most will fade as quickly as they appeared, as the failure of #StopKony and #BringBackOurGirls sadly demonstrates. Groups like ISIS will increasingly try to force their agenda on the interconnected world, using technical trickery and media gamesmanship to create the appearance of strength. While they might get lucky now and then, this is ultimately a losing game. As with websites that publish head-line after headline promising "you won't believe what happens next," the audience will soon begin to see the exaggeration.

Eventually we will learn to forecast the tides of social media, much as we fore-cast the weather—good enough to get by most days, but bad enough that everyone will continue to complain. Outside of social media, as well, we will begin to un-derstand how rapid changes cascade out from small beginnings, how we should respond when they do, and how to exploit the power of virality without being seized by irrational optimism about positive outcomes or excessive fear of inflated risks. In the meantime, there's more turbulence ahead.

When Blasphemy Goes Viral

By Christopher S. Grenda and Chris Beneke
The New Republic, January 15, 2015

It's safe to say that, until last week, only a very small percentage of the world's population had heard of *Charlie Hebdo.* But the January 7 massacre at the satirical French newspaper's offices, for which al-Qaeda's Yemen branch claimed responsibility this week, turned *Charlie Hebdo* into a household name.

The slaughter also raised an unsettling question: How does a terrorist organization in the Arabian Peninsula come to set its sights on a niche publication in Paris?

To many, the murders encapsulate perennial differences between Asia and Europe, between antiquated dogmatism on the one hand and unshackled rights of speech on the other. In the words of a *New York Times* report, the murders "crystallized the culture clash between religious extremism and the West's devotion to free expression."

But last week's horror did more than elucidate differences. It also demonstrated some very old and profound similarities between the world's cultures, while pointing to some new and perilous ways in which they are converging.

The impulse to commit sacrilege—and punish it—has marked nearly every society and every epoch in human affairs. People have always gone to great lengths to protect their sanctities. Examining the historical record, we find an aversion to blasphemy not only among the usual suspects, such as the resolute monotheists of ancient Palestine and medieval Europe, but in unlikely places and times: The ancient Athenians, those archetypal democrats who allowed citizens to criticize their cherished civic institutions, still forbade them from ridiculing the gods or the worship of them.

And so it has been ever since. In each century up to the last, western governments and churches outlawed sacrilege against their deities and their faiths. Even in the United States, which has acquired a well-deserved reputation for protecting free expression, state and local authorities were once authorized to punish anti-Christian sentiments. A 1782 Massachusetts law prescribed severe punishments, including whipping, for anyone convicted of "denying, cursing, or contumeliously reproaching God, his creation, government or final judging of the world, or by cursing, or reproaching Jesus Christ..." The Bible and the Holy Ghost were off-limits too. Periodic blasphemy indictments continued into the twentieth century.

By the latter part of that century, enforcement of blasphemy laws had tapered in Europe and North America to the point that most were simply ignored or forgotten.

Elsewhere, however, blasphemy laws proved more resilient and made a vigorous comeback beginning in the 1980s. Today in predominantly Muslim countries such as Pakistan, Iran, and Sudan, those accused of disparaging Muhammad are regularly punished for defamation. Sometimes they are murdered before any trial occurs. As terrible as these fundamentalist-inspired laws have proved to religious minorities and brave contrarians in South Asia, the Middle East, and North Africa, their main impact has been domestic.

> **Together, large-scale human migration and digital culture enable the mutual surveillance of political and cultural niches that had once existed in isolation—very little in life remains offline.**

That may be changing. One of the more disquieting aspects of the *Charlie Hebdo* massacre is that it represented an attempt to regulate sacrilege across national borders, an aggressive effort by non-state actors to carry out an abiding impulse—ferreting out and eradicating the blasphemous—across cultural and political boundaries.

The world received its first intimation that we might be on this grim trajectory in 1989. That year, Iran's Ayatollah Khomeini issued his infamous *fatwa* to avenge the publication of *The Satanic Verses*, Salman Rushdie's whimsical and derisive reinvention of Qur'anic themes. Stoked by the Ayatollah's televised entreaties, obliging Islamic extremists proceeded to murder publishers and translators across the globe.

Behind the scenes, among the world's diplomats, a parallel effort is underway to police international sacrilege in less extreme fashion. Between 1999 and 2011, for example, the fifty-seven-member Organization of Islamic Cooperation (OIC) pressed the U.N. for a resolution defining "the defamation of religions" as a human rights violation (for now, they've settled on criminalizing the expression of hatred against religious persons). The OIC made progress on the world stage in part because European states, and to a lesser extent the U.S., have conceded that there should be some limits on what we say about other people's faiths, in practice if not in law. Many Western governments, including France itself, have recently enacted their own measures against religious and racial hatred.

These agreements would not be possible if Europe and the Muslim world did not share some underlying intuitions about communal responsibility to protect religion and its believers from insults. Nor, significantly, would such strictures seem as urgent in the absence of widespread awareness of the insults. Thus, if the *Charlie Hebdo* attack reflects divisions between the pious and the secular, it also makes clear that we are living in an era of heightened cross-cultural sensitivity, when vigilance on behalf of the sacred can have deadly consequences, even in distant realms.

This week's print run of five million copies notwithstanding, *Charlie Hebdo* is a niche publication with a regular circulation of roughly sixty thousand. That makes it a lot like the Danish newspaper, *Jyllands-Posten*, which carried the infamous and widely reprinted cartoons of the Prophet Muhammad in 2005. Until that point, the paper was known well to Danes on the Jutland peninsula, and that was about it.

Charlie Hebdo's relative obscurity aligns it with another discovered outrage from the fringes of Western culture—the amateur anti-Islamic film *The Innocence of Muslims*, which fueled weeks of militant outrage throughout the Muslim world in 2012. It's not clear how many protesters watched the 14-minute YouTube trailer. What we do know [according to *Vanity Fair* writer Michael Joseph Gross] is that a "feature-length cut of the movie, retitled *The Innocence of Bin Laden*, was shown exactly once, to an audience of fewer than ten people." The very notion that a video depicting a depraved and murderous Mohammed had been produced and disseminated supplied protesters the pretense they needed to besiege American embassies and consulates throughout the Muslim world, including in Benghazi, Libya.

It is impossible to make sense of the *Charlie Hebdo* attack without considering France's sizeable immigrant population, much of which has been drawn from North Africa, the Middle East, and South Asia. Many of these migrants are not Muslims, and only a small fraction of those who are have embraced extremism. Nonetheless, the growing Muslim presence in France has created a critical mass of people inclined to take offense when Islam is mocked or otherwise insulted (on newsstands, for example), and close enough to exact vengeance when they do (as in the case of the *Charlie Hebdo* murderers, Cherif and Said Kouachi, whose parents were born in Algeria).

Then again, experiencing insult in person is old-fashioned. The Internet now connects people and cultures through crackling virtual networks of outrage. There is no bottom to the world's reserves of offensive material; one need not search long for sources of provocation, or for places to express that outrage. Fugitive thoughts (say, on Twitter) and irreverent productions (in a niche satirical publication) are now more reproducible, more communicable, and thereby more aggravatingly conspicuous to anyone with an Internet connection.

Together, large-scale human migration and digital culture enable the mutual surveillance of political and cultural niches that had once existed in isolation—very little in life remains offline. The sacrilegious now have a worldwide audience for their productions; while the self-appointed protectors of the sacred now know who the offenders are, and, on occasion, where they live and work. The two—the outraged and the outrageous—are thus bound together in a geopolitical version of what Jacques Berlinerblau calls a "profanity loop," a circle of blasphemy and vengeance wherein one side metes out irreverence and the other death.

Globalization, in its demographic and digital forms, has also given new significance to offensive imagery. It is no coincidence that the attack on *Charlie Hebdo*, like the protests that greeted the *Jyllands-Postens* drawings, were sparked by cartoons. While words are hardly exempt from accusations of sacrilege, the image is the twenty-first century's most potent catalyst of outrage. Graphic, easily reproduced images require little in the way of linguistic or cultural translation; their potency derives from the ease with which they transcend difference. The *Charlie Hebdo* cartoons were intended to offend in the most straightforward and unambiguous way, avoiding theological subtleties and capitalizing instead on Islamic prohibitions against Muhammad's representation. They succeeded.

Today we confront the paradox that irreverent expression is both less inhibited and more endangered than ever before. Thanks to the fluidity of national borders and the Internet's reach, people and organizations now possess previously unimagined powers of dissemination. Never in human history has speech been so abundant and unruly, nor have artists ever enjoyed so much freedom to exhibit what churches and states would have once prohibited. And yet, never has there been such a systematic international effort to discover and avenge offensive text and images.

We may indeed be witnessing an historic contest between religious absolutism and free speech, but we should not lose sight of the fact that it is our shared regard for sacred things coupled with the increasingly multicultural intimacy of our social and digital lives that has gotten us here. In other words, if we want to better understand what happened last week, we need attend to the things—both enduring and modern—that connect the world's cultures, as well as those that divide them.

Is Drone Warfare Fraying at the Edges?

By Pratap Chatterjee
TomDispatch.com, March 5, 2015

The U.S. drone war across much of the Greater Middle East and parts of Africa is in crisis and not because civilians are dying or the target list for that war or the right to wage it just about anywhere on the planet are in question in Washington. Something far more basic is at stake: drone pilots are quitting in record numbers.

There are roughly 1,000 such drone pilots, known in the trade as "18Xs," working for the U.S. Air Force today. Another 180 pilots graduate annually from a training program that takes about a year to complete at Holloman and Randolph Air Force bases in, respectively, New Mexico and Texas. As it happens, in those same twelve months, about 240 trained pilots quit and the Air Force is at a loss to explain the phenomenon. (The better-known U.S. Central Intelligence Agency drone assassination program is also flown by Air Force pilots loaned out for the covert missions.)

On January 4, 2015, *The Daily Beast* revealed an undated internal memo to Air Force Chief of Staff General Mark Welsh from General Herbert "Hawk" Carlisle stating that pilot "outflow increases will damage the readiness and combat capability of the MQ-1/9 [Predator and Reaper] enterprise for years to come" and added that he was "extremely concerned." Eleven days later, the issue got top billing at a special high-level briefing on the state of the Air Force. Secretary of the Air Force Deborah Lee James joined Welsh to address the matter. "This is a force that is under significant stress—significant stress from what is an unrelenting pace of operations," she told the media.

In theory, drone pilots have a cushy life. Unlike soldiers on duty in "war zones," they can continue to live with their families here in the United States. No muddy foxholes or sandstorm-swept desert barracks under threat of enemy attack for them. Instead, these new techno-warriors commute to work like any office employees and sit in front of computer screens wielding joysticks, playing what most people would consider a glorified video game.

They typically "fly" missions over Afghanistan and Iraq where they are tasked with collecting photos and video feeds, as well as watching over U.S. soldiers on the ground. A select few are deputized to fly CIA assassination missions over Pakistan, Somalia, or Yemen where they are ordered to kill "high value targets" from the sky. In recent months, some of these pilots have also taken part in the new war in the Syrian and Iraqi borderlands, conducting deadly strikes on militants of ISIL.

Each of these combat air patrols involves three to four drones, usually

---

Hellfire-missile-armed Predators and Reapers built by southern California's General Atomics, and each takes as many as 180 staff members to fly them. In addition to pilots, there are camera operators, intelligence and communications experts, and maintenance workers. (The newer Global Hawk surveillance patrols need as many as 400 support staff.)

The Air Force is currently under orders to staff 65* of these regular "combat air patrols" around the clock as well as to support a Global Response Force on call for emergency military and humanitarian missions. For all of this, there should ideally be 1,700 trained pilots. Instead, facing an accelerating dropout rate that recently drove this figure below 1,000, the Air Force has had to press regular cargo and jet pilots as well as reservists into becoming instant drone pilots in order to keep up with the Pentagon's enormous appetite for real-time video feeds from around the world.

The Air Force explains the departure of these drone pilots in the simplest of terms. They are leaving because they are overworked. The pilots themselves say that it's humiliating to be scorned by their Air Force colleagues as second-class citizens. Some have also come forward to claim that the horrors of war, seen up close on video screens, day in, day out, are inducing an unprecedented, long-distance version of post-traumatic stress [disorder] (PTSD).

But is it possible that a brand-new form of war—by remote control—is also spawning a brand-new, as yet unlabeled, form of psychological strain? Some have called drone war a "coward's war" (an opinion that, according to reports from among the drone-traumatized in places like Yemen and Pakistan, is seconded by its victims). Could it be that the feeling is even shared by drone pilots themselves, that a sense of dishonor in fighting from behind a screen thousands of miles from harm's way is having an unexpected impact of a kind psychologists have never before witnessed?

> **Some have also come forward to claim that the horrors of war, seen up close on video screens, day in, day out, are inducing an unprecedented, long-distance version of post-traumatic stress [disorder] (PTSD).**

Killing Up Close and Personal From Afar

There can be no question that drone pilots resent the way other Air Force pilots see them as second-class citizens. "It's tough working night shifts watching your buddies do great things in the field while you're turning circles in the sky," a drone instructor named Ryan told *Mother Jones* magazine. His colleagues, he says, call themselves the "lost generation."

"Everyone else thinks that the whole program or the people behind it are a joke, that we are video-game warriors, that we're Nintendo warriors," Brandon Bryant, a former drone camera operator who worked at Nellis Air Force Base, told *Democracy Now*.

Certainly, there is nothing second-class about the work tempo of drone life.

Pilots log 900–1,800 hours a year compared to a maximum of 300 hours annually for regular Air Force pilots. And the pace is unrelenting. "A typical person doing this mission over the last seven or eight years has worked either six or seven days a week, twelve hours a day," General Welsh told NPR recently. "And that one- or two-day break at the end of it is really not enough time to take care of that family and the rest of your life."

The pilots wholeheartedly agree. "It's like when your engine temperature gauge is running just below the red area on your car's dashboard, but instead of slowing down and relieving the stress on the engine, you put the pedal to the floor," one drone pilot told *Air Force Times*. "You are sacrificing the engine to get a short burst of speed with no real consideration to the damage being caused."

The Air Force has come up with a pallid interim "solution." It is planning to offer experienced drone pilots a daily raise of about $50. There's one problem, though: since so many pilots leave the service early, only a handful have enough years of experience to qualify for this bonus. Indeed, the Air Force concedes that just ten of them will be able to claim the extra bounty this year, striking testimony to the startling levels of job turnover among such pilots.

Most 18Xs say that their jobs are tougher and significantly more upfront and personal than those of the far more glamorous jet pilots. "[A] Predator operator is so much more involved in what is going on than your average fast-moving jetfighter pilot, or your B-52, B-1, B-2 pilots, who will never even see their target," Lieutenant Colonel Bruce Black, a former Air Force drone pilot says. "A Predator pilot has been watching his target[s], knows them intimately, knows where they are, and knows what's around them."

Some say that the drone war has driven them over the edge. "How many women and children have you seen incinerated by a Hellfire missile? How many men have you seen crawl across a field, trying to make it to the nearest compound for help while bleeding out from severed legs?" Heather Linebaugh, a former drone imagery analyst, wrote in *The Guardian*."When you are exposed to it over and over again it becomes like a small video, embedded in your head, forever on repeat, causing psychological pain and suffering that many people will hopefully never experience."

"It was horrifying to know how easy it was. I felt like a coward because I was halfway across the world and the guy never even knew I was there," Bryant told KNPR Radio in Nevada. "I felt like I was haunted by a legion of the dead. My physical health was gone, my mental health was crumbled. I was in so much pain I was ready to eat a bullet myself."

Many drone pilots, however, defend their role in targeted killings. "We're not killing people for the fun of it. It would be the same if we were the guys on the ground," mission controller Janet Atkins told Chris Woods of the Bureau of Investigative Journalism. "You have to get to [the enemy] somehow or all of you will die."

Others like Bruce Black are proud of their work. "I was shooting two weeks after I got there and saved hundreds of people, including Iraqis and Afghanis," he told his hometown newspaper in New Mexico. "We'd go down to Buffalo Wild Wings, drink beer and debrief. It was surreal. It didn't take long for you to realize how important the work is. The value that the weapon system brings to the fight is not apparent till you're there. People have a hard time sometimes seeing that."

Measuring Pilot Stress

So whom does one believe? Janet Atkins and Bruce Black, who claim that drone pilots are overworked heroes? Or Brandon Bryant and Heather Linebaugh, who claim that remotely directed targeted killings caused them mental health crises?

Military psychologists have been asked to investigate the phenomenon. A team of psychologists at the School of Aerospace Medicine at Wright-Patterson Air Force Base in Ohio has published a series of studies on drone pilot stress. One 2011 study concluded that nearly half of them had "high operational stress." A number also exhibited "clinical distress"—that is, anxiety, depression, or stress severe enough to affect them in their personal lives.

Wayne Chappelle, a lead author in a number of these studies, nonetheless concludes that the problem is mostly a matter of overwork caused by the chronic shortage of pilots. His studies appear to show that post-traumatic stress levels are actually lower among drone pilots than in the general population. Others, however, question these numbers. Jean Otto and Bryant Webber of the Armed Forces Health Surveillance Center and the Uniformed Services University of the Health Sciences, caution that the lack of stress reports may only "reflect artificial under-reporting of the concerns of pilots due to the career-threatening effects of [mental health] diagnoses, [which] include removal from flying status, loss of flight pay, and diminished competitiveness for promotion."

Seeing Everything, Missing the Obvious

One thing is clear: the pilots are not just killing "bad guys", and they know it because, as Black points out, they see everything that happens before, during, and after a drone strike.

Indeed, the only detailed transcript of an actual Air Force drone surveillance mission and targeted killing to be publicly released illustrates this all too well. The logs recorded idle chatter on February 21, 2010, between drone operators at Creech Air Force base in Nevada coordinating with video analysts at Air Force special operations headquarters in Okaloosa, Florida, and with Air Force pilots in a rural part of Daikondi province in central Afghanistan. On that day, three vehicles were seen traveling in a pre-dawn convoy carrying about a dozen people each. Laboring under the mistaken belief that the group were "insurgents" out to kill some nearby U.S. soldiers on a mission, the drone team decided to attack.

Controller: "We believe we may have a high-level Taliban commander."

Camera operator: "Yeah, they called a possible weapon on the military-age male mounted in the back of the truck."

Intelligence coordinator: "Screener said at least one child near SUV."

Controller: "Bullshit! Where? I don't think they have kids out this hour. I know they're shady, but come on!"

Camera operator "A sweet [expletive]! Geez! Lead vehicle on the run and bring the helos in!"

Moments later, Kiowa helicopter pilots descended and fired Hellfire missiles at the vehicle.

Controller: "Take a look at this one. It was hit pretty good. It's a little toasty! That truck is so dead!"

> **"Technology can occasionally give you a false sense of security that you can see everything, that you can hear everything, that you know everything."**

Within 20 minutes, after the survivors of the attack had surrendered, the transcript recorded the sinking feelings of the drone pilots as they spotted women and children in the convoy and could not find any visual evidence of weapons.

A subsequent on-the-ground investigation established that not one of the people killed was anything other than an ordinary villager. "Technology can occasionally give you a false sense of security that you can see everything, that you can hear everything, that you know everything," Air Force Major General James Poss, who oversaw an investigation into the incident, later told the *Los Angeles Times*.

Of course, Obama administration officials claim that such incidents are rare. In June 2011, when CIA Director John Brennan was still the White House counterterrorism adviser, he addressed the issue of civilian deaths in drone strikes and made this bold claim: "Nearly for the past year, there hasn't been a single collateral death, because of the exceptional proficiency, precision of the capabilities that we've been able to develop."

His claim and similar official ones like it are, politely put, hyperbolic. "You Never Die Twice," a new report by Jennifer Gibson of Reprieve, a British-based human rights organization, settles the question quickly by showing that some men on the White House "kill list" of terror suspects to be taken out have "'died' as many as seven times."

Gibson adds, "We found forty-one names of men who seemed to have achieved the impossible. This raises a stark question. With each failed attempt to assassinate a man on the kill list, who filled the body bag in his place?" In fact, Reprieve discovered that, in going after those forty-one "targets" numerous times, an estimated 1,147 people were killed in Pakistan by drones. Typical was the present leader of al-Qaeda, Ayman al-Zawahiri. In two strikes against "him" over the years, according to Reprieve, seventy-six children and twenty-nine adults have died, but not al-Zawahiri.

Deserting the Cubicle

Back in the United States, a combination of lower-class status in the military, overwork, and psychological trauma appears to be taking its mental toll on drone pilots. During the Vietnam War, soldiers would desert, flee to Canada, or even "frag"—kill

—their officers. But what do you do when you've had it with your war, but your battle station is a cubicle in Nevada and your weapon is a keyboard?

Is it possible that, like their victims in Pakistan and Yemen who say that they are going mad from the constant buzz of drones overhead and the fear of sudden death without warning, drone pilots, too, are fleeing into the night as soon as they can? Since the Civil War in the U.S., war of every modern sort has produced mental disturbances that have been given a variety of labels, including what we today call PTSD. In a way, it would be surprising if a completely new form of warfare didn't produce a new form of disturbance.

We don't yet know just what this might turn out to be, but it bodes ill for the form of battle that the White House and Washington are most proud of—the well-advertised, sleek, new, robotic, no-casualty, precision conflict that now dominates the war on terror. Indeed if the pilots themselves are dropping out of desktop killing, can this new way of war survive?

Editor's Note
* On account of low staffing, Defense Secretary Ashton Carter approved a plan to drop the number of daily patrols from 65 to 60 by October 2015.

Bibliography

"About Digital Collections and Services." *LOC*. Library of Congress. 2015. Web. Jul 12 2015.

"About the Foreign Intelligence Surveillance Court." *USCourts*. United States Foreign Intelligence Surveillance Courts. 2015. Web. Jul 1 2015.

Aditi, Paul. "Cyberpsychology, Behavior, and Social Networking." *Cyber*. Vol 17, No 10, 664-667. Oct 2014.

Allen, I Elaine and Jeff Seaman. "Grade Change: Tracking Online Education in the United States." *Online Learning Survey*. Babson Survey Research Group and Quahog Research Group, LLC. 2014. Pdf. Jul 5 2015.

"The Arab Spring: A Year of Revolution." *NPR*. National Public Radio. Dec 17 2011. Web. Jul 13 2015.

Auerbach, David. "The Sony Hackers Are Terrorists." Slate. The Slate Group. Dec 17 2104. Web. Jul 4 2015.

Ault, Susanne. "Survey: YouTube Stare More Popular Than Mainstream Celebs Among U.S. Teens." *Variety*. Variety Media LLC. Aug 5 2014. Web. Jul 2 2015.

Bailyn, Evan. "The Difference Between Slacktivism And Activism: How 'Kony 2012' Is Narrowing the Gap." *Huffington Post*. Huffington Post. May 19 2012. Web. Jul 5 2015.

Balko, Radley. "Model Legislation for Police Body Cameras." *Washington Post*. Nash Holdings. May 21 2015. Web. Jul 6 2015.

Ball, James. "Twitter: From Free Speech Champion to Selective Censor?" *The Guardian*. Guardian News and Media. Aug 21 2014. Web. Jul 1 2015.

Bankston, Kevin. "Breaking News on EFF Victory: Appeals Court Holds that Email Privacy Protected by Fourth Amendment." *Electronic Frontier Foundation*. Dec. 14 2010. Web. Jul 1 2015.

Bercovici, Jeff. "YouTube's Policies Are Clear: Beheading Is Not An Act of Free Speech." *Forbes*. Forbes Inc. Sep 3 2014. Web Jul 1 2015.

Berend, Ivan. *An Economic History of Nineteenth Century Europe: Diversity and Industrialization*. New York: Cambridge University Press, 2013. Print.

Berman, Mark. "Justice Dept. Will Spend $20 Million on Police Body Cameras Nationwide." *Washington Post*. Nash Holdings. May 1 2015. Web. Jul 17 2015.

Boone, Jon. "US Drone Strikes Could be Classed as War Crimes, Says Amnesty International." *The Guardian. Guardian News and Media*. Oct 22 2013. Web. Jul 17 2015.

Casserly, Martyn. "What is Hacktivism? A Short History of Anonymous, Lulzsec and the Arab Spring." *PC Advisor*. IDG United Kingdom.

Caumont, Andrea. "12 Trends Shaping Digital News." *Pew Research Center*. Pew Research. Oct 16 2013. Web. Jul 2 2015.

Citron, Danielle Keats. *Hate Crimes in Cyberspace*. Cambridge, MA: *Harvard University Press*. 2014. Print.

Coyle, Jake. "Is Twitter the 21ˢᵗ Century News Source?" *Huffington Post*. The Huffington Post Inc. May 25 2011. Web. Jul 2 2015.

Crawford, Susan P. "The New Digital Divide." *New York Times*. New York Times Company. Dec 3 2011. Web. Jul 3 2015.

"Data Policy." *Facbook*. Facebook Inc. Jan 30 2015. Web. Jul 1 2015.

Davidson, Jacob. "Uber Has Pretty Much Destroyed Regular Taxis in San Francisco." *Time*. Money. Time, Inc. Sep 18 2014. Web. Jul 4 2015.

Davis, Joshua. "The Crypto-Currency." *New Yorker*. Conde Nast. Oct 10 2011. Web. Jul 6 2015.

"Digital Divide." *Stanford*. Stanford University. 2014. Web. Jul 13 2015.

Drucker, Peter F. *The Age of Discontinuity: Guidelines to Our Changing Society*. London: William Heinemann Ltd. 1969. Print.

Duffy, Owen. "Board Games' Golden Age: Sociable, Brilliant and Driven by the Internet." *The Guardian*. Guardian News and Media. Nov 25 2014. Web. Jul 2 2015.

Eggers, William D., Hamill, Rob, and Abed Ali. "Data as the New Currency." *Dupress*. Deloitte University Press. Jul 24 2013. Web. Jul 4 2015.

"Factsheet on the 'Right to be Forgotten' Ruling." *Europa*. European Commission. 2014. Web. Jul 6 2015.

Finley, Klint. "Inventor of the Web is Right: We Need an Internet Bill of Rights." *Wired*. Conde Nast. Mar 12 2014. Web. Jul 6 2015.

Fisher, Daniel. "The Big Question With Uber, Airbnb And the Rest of the 'Sharing Economy': Who to Sue." *Forbes*. Forbes, Inc. Mar 25 2015. Web. Jul 4 2015.

Fitzpatrick, Michael. "Classroom Lectures Go Digital." *New York Times*. New York Times Company. Jun 24 2012. Web. Jul 3 2015.

Foroohar, Rana. "The Digital Economy is Profoundly Unequal." *Time*. Time, Inc. Apr 11 2014. Web. Jul 5 2014.

Fraser, Kym. *The future of Learning and Teaching in Next Generation Learning Spaces*. Bingley, UK: Emerald Group, 2014. Print.

Frey, Carl Benedikt, and Michael Osborne. "Technology At Work: The Future of Innovation and Employment." *Oxford Martin*. University of Oxford. Feb 2015. Pdf. Jul 5 2015.

Frizell, Sam. "Experts Doubt ISIS Could Launch Major Cyberattack Against the U.S." *Time*. Time Inc. Sep 19 2014. Web. Jul 4 2015.

Gellman, Barton. "NSA Collects Millions of E-Mail Address Books Globally." *Washington Post*. Nash Holdings. Oct 14 2013. Web. Jul 1 2015.

Gleick, James. "The Information Palace," *NYBooks*. New York Review. Dec 8 2010. Web. Jul 12 2015.

Goldfarb, Ronald. *After Snowden: Privacy, Secrecy, and Security in the Information Age*. New York: Thomas Dunne Books, 2015.

Goodman, David J. "N.Y. Officer Won't Be Indicted for Fatal Choking." *Boston Globe*. Boston Globe Media Partners. Dec 4 2014. Web. Jul 4 2015.

Gray, Kelly, Esmail, Asraf, and Lisa Eargle, "Cyberbullying from Schoolyard to Cyberspace: An Evolution," in Esmail, Ashraf, ed. *Alleviating Bullying: Conquering the Challenge of Violent Crimes.* Lanham, MD: University Press of America, 2014. Print.

Greenwald, Glenn. "NSA Collecting Phone Records of Millions of Verizon Customers Daily." *The Guardian.* Guardian News and Media. Jun. 6 2013. Web. Apr. 30 2015.

Gross, Doug, "Why Can't Americans Vote Online?" *CNN.* Cable News Network. Nov. 8 2011. Web. Jul 9 2015.

Gupta, Tanya. "Addressing the Digital Divide." *World Bank.* The World Bank Group. Apr 24 2012. Web. Jul 2 2015.

Harress, Christopher. "Obama Says Cyberterrorism Is Country's Biggest Threat, U.S. Government Assembles, 'Cyber Warriors'." *IBTimes.* International Business Times. IBT Media. Feb 18 2014. Web. Jul 4 2015.

Hess, Amanda. "Why Women Aren't Welcome on the Internet." *PSMag.* Pacific Standard. The Miller-McCune Center for Research, Media and Public Policy. Jan 6 2014. Web. Jul 4 2015.

"Internet Users (Per 100 People)." *World Bank.* World Bank Group. 2015. Web. Jul 6 2015.

Howard, Philip N. and Muzammil M. Hussain. *Democracy's Fourth Wave.* New York: Oxford University Press, 2013. Print.

"H.R. 4681 – Intelligence Authorization Act for Fiscal Year 2015." *Congress.* United States Congress. 2015. Web. May 1 2015.

"H.R. 6304 – FISA Amendments Act of 2008." *Congress.* United States Library of Congress. 2015. Web. Jul 1 2015.

Jabr, Ferris. "The Reading Brain in the Digital Age: The Science of Paper versus Screens." *Scientific American.* Nature America, Inc. Apr 11 2013. Web. Jul 3 2015.

James, Randy. "A Brief History of Cybercrime." *Time.* Time Inc. Jun 1 2009. Web. Jul 4 2105.

Jeffries, Stuart. "How the Web Lost its Way—And its Founding Principles." *The Guardian.* Guardian News and Media. Aug 24 2014. Web. Jul 13 2015.

Johnson, Eric Michael. "Misogyny Is Not Human Nature." *Slate.* Slate Group. Sep 24 2014. Web. Jul 4 2015.

Jurkowitz, Mark. "The Growth in Digital Reporting." *Pew Research Center.* Pew Research. Mar 26 2014. Web. Jul 2 2015.

Jurkowitz, Mark. "What the Digital News Boom Means for Consumers." *Pew Research Journalism Project.* Pew Research Foundation. Mar 26 2011. Web. Jul 2 2015.

Kang, Jay Caspian. "Our Demand Is Simple: Stop Killing Us." *New York Times.* New York Times Company. May 4 2014. Web. Jul 10 2015.

Kaplan, Sarah. "#HashtagActivismMatters: Some experts see online-to-IRL change in police protests." *Washington Post.* Nash Holdings. Dec 14 2014. Web. Jul 7 2015.

Kelley, Peter. "Study Shines Light on What Makes Digital Activism Effective." *Washington*. UW Today. University of Washington. Nov 20 2013. Web. Jul 6 2015.

Konnikova, Maria. "The Limits of Friendship." *The New Yorker*. Conde Nast. Oct 7 2014. Web. Jul 2 2015.

Kurtzleben, Danielle. "Volunteering Hits Lowest Rate in More than 10 Years." *U.S. News*. U.S. News and World Report. Feb. 26 2014. Web. Jul 5 2015.

Kurwa, NIshat. "'Black Lives Matter Slogan Becomes a Bigger Movement." *NPR*. National Public Radio, Youth Radio. Dec 4 2014. Web. Jul 6 2015.

Landler, Mark. "A Filipino Linked to 'Love Bug' Talks About His License to Hack." *New York Times*. New York Times Company. Oct 21 2000. Web. Jul 4 2015.

Lang, Brent. "As Theaters Boycott Netflix, Collapsed Windows Seen as Inevitable." *Variety*. Variety Media, LLC. Sep 30 2014. Web. Jul 6 2015.

Lanier, Jaron. "Fixing the Digital Economy." **New York Times**. New York Times Company. Jun 8 2013. Web. Jul 5 2015.

Lee, Timothy B. "Here's Everythign We Know About PRISM To Date." Jun 12 2013. Web. Jul 1 2015.

Lewin, Tamar. "Instruction for Masses Knocks Down Campus Walls." *New York Times*. New York Times Company. Education. Mar 4 2012. Web. Jul 3 2015.

Lin, Helen Lee. "How Your Cell Phone Hurts Your Relationships." *Scientific American*. Nature America, Inc. Sep. 4 2012. Web. Jul 3 2014.

Linder, Doug. "The Right to Privacy." *UMKC*. University of Missouri, Kansas City Law. Exploring Constitutional Conflicts. 2011. Web. Jul 1 2015.

Liu, Edward C., Nolan, Andrew and Richard M. Thompson II. "Overview of Constitutional Challenges to NSA Collection Activities and Recent Developments." *CRS*. Congressional Research Service. Apr. 1 2014. Web. Jul 1 2015.

MacDougall, Ian. "The Fourth Amendment Goes Digital." *Slate*. The Slate Group. Jun 26 2014. Web. Jul 4 2015.

Magid, Larry. "Households Abandoning Cable and Satellite for Streaming." *Forbes*. Dow Jones & Company. Mar 19 2013. Web. Jul 4 2015.

Mazzetti, Mark and Michael R. Gordon. "ISIS Is Winning the Social Media War, U.S. Concludes." *New York Times*. New York Times Company. Jun 12 2015. Web. Jul 5 2015.

McPhail, Irving Pressley. "The 'New' American Dilemma: STEM and Minorities." *USNews*. U.S. News and World Report. Oct 11 2011. Web. Jul 7 2015.

Michaels, Jim. "NSA Data Mining Can Help Stop Cybercrime, Analysts Say." *USA Today*. Gannet Company. Jun 6 2013. Web. Jul 4 2015.

Mitchell, Gail. "Usher Introduces Teen Singer Justin Bieber." *Billboard*. Billboard Inc. Apr 28 2009. Web. Jul 2 2015.

Morgan, Jacob. "What LinkedIn's Acquisition of Lynda Means for Talent Management." *Forbes*. Forbes Inc. Apr 28 2015. Web. Jul 6 2015.

Nagel, David. "One-Third of U.S. Students Use School-Issued Mobile Devices." *The Journal*. Public Sector Media Group. Apr 8 2014. Web. Jul 6 2015.

Novack, Janet. "Should College Students Be Forced To Buy E-Books?" *Forbes*. Forbes, Inc. May 18 2012. Web. Jul 3 2015.

Pagliery, Jose. "The Evolution of Hacking." *CNN*. Cable News Network. Jun 4 2015. Web. Jul 4 2015.

Poole, Gary Andrew. "A New Gulf in American Education, the Digital Divide." *New York Times*. New York Times Co. Business Day. Jan 29 1996. Web. Jul 3 2015.

Poulsen, Kevin. "Visit the Wrong Website, And the FBI Could End Up In Your Computer." *Wired*. Conde Nast. Aug 5 2014. Web. Jul 4 2015.

Prensky, Marc. "Digital Natives, Digital Immigrants." *Marcprensky*. On the Horizon. 2001. Pdf. Jul 3 2015.

Press Association. "Timeline: Isis Hostage Killings." *The Guardian*. Guardian News and Media. Nov 16 2014. Web Jul 6 2015.

Purcell, Kristen, Buchanan, Judy and Linda Friedrich. "The Impact of Digital Tools on Student Writing and How Writing is Taught in Schools." *Pew Internet*. Pew Research Center. Jul 16 2013. Web. Jul 3 2015.

Rainie, Lee. "The State of Digital Divides." *Pew Internet*. Pew Research Center. Nov 5 2013. Web. Jul 3 2015.

Rhodes, Jerry. "National Agenda 2014." *UDel*. UDaily. University of Deleware. Oct 2 2014. Web. Jul 5 2015.

"Riley v. California." *Supreme Court*. Supreme Court of the United States. Jun 25 2014. Pdf. Jul 4 2015.

Risen, James and Laura Poitras. "N.S.A. Collecting Millions of Faces from Web Images." *New York Times*. New York Times Company. May 31 2014. Web. Jul 1 2015.

Ronson, Jon. *So You've Been Publically Shamed*. New York: Riverhead Books, 2015. Print.

Ross, Terrance. "When Students Can't Go Online." *The Atlantic*. Atlantic Monthly Group. Mar 13 2015. Web. Jul 6 2015.

Satell, Greg. "The Future Of TV Is Here. Can Cable Survive?" *Forbes*. Forbes Inc. Jun 6 2015. Web. Jul 2 2015.

Savage, Charlie. "Judge Questions Legality of N.S.A. Phone Records." *New York Times*. New York Times Co. Dec. 16 2013. Web. Jul 1 2015.

Schell, Bernadette H. and Clemens Martin. *Cybercrime: A Reference Handbook*. Santa Barbara, CA: ABC-CLIO, Inc. 2004.

Schwartzel, Erich and Ben Fritz." "Fewer Americans Go to the Movies." *Wall Street Journal*. Dow Jones & Company. Mar 25 2014. Web. Jul 2 2015.

Seabrook, John. "Streaming Dreams." **The New Yorker**. Conde Nast. Jan 16 2012. Web. Jul 2 2015.

Seay, Laura. "Does Slacktivism Work?" *Washington Post*. Nash Holdings. Mar 12 2014. Web. Jul 5 2015.

Simmons, Andrew. "Facebook Has Transformed My Students' Writing—For the Better." *The Atlantic*. The Atlantic Monthly Group. Nov 18 2013. Web. Jul 3 2015.

Smith, Aaron. "Civic Engagement in the Digital Age." *Pew Internet*. Pew Research Center. Apr 25 2013. Web. Jul 5 2015.

Snyder, Tom. "The Benefits of Online Learning." *Huffington Post*. The Blog. Huffington Post.Com. Apr 1 2013. Web. Jul 3 2015.

Sohn, Emily. "Does Online Dating Work? Yes and No." *Discovery*. Discovery Communications LLC. Feb 8 2012. Web. Jul 2 2015.

"Student Reports of Bullying and Cyber-Bullying: Results from the 2011 School Crime Supplement to the National Crime Victimization Survey." *ED*. U.S. Department of Education. 2014. Pdf. Jul 6 2015.

Thill, Scott. "March 17, 1948: William Gibson, Father of Cyberspace." *Wired*. Conde Nast. Mar 17 2009. Web. Jul 12 2015.

Thornton, Bill, Faires, Alyson, Robbins, Maija, and Eric Rollins. "The Mere Presence of a Cell Phone May be Distracting." *Social Psychology*. Vol. 45, Iss 6. May 2014. Web. Jul 3 2015.

Timberg, Craig. "New Surveillance Technology Can Track Everyone in an Area for Several Hours at a Time." *Washington Post*. Nash Holdings. Feb 5 2014. Web. Jul 6 2015.

Tucker, Jeffrey A. "The Inventor of the Digital Age." *Mises*. Mises Institute. Sep 14 2011. Web. Jul 14 2015.

Verini, James. "The Great Cyberheist." *New York Times*. New York Times Company. Nov 10 2010. Web. Jul 4 2015.

Wakefield, Jane. "World Wakes Up To Digital Divide." *BBC News*. BBC. Mar 19 2010. Web. Jul 5 2015.

Waldrop, Mitchell. "Claude Shannon: Reluctant Father of the Digital Age." *MIT Technology Review*. Jul 1 2001. Web. Jul 13 2015.

Wall, Thompson, "How to Reign Over the New 'Digital Economy'." *Inc*. Mansueto Ventures. Jan 22 2015. Web. Jul 4 2015.

Wallop, Harry. "The Kindle is Dead, The Book is Back. Or is it?" *The Telegraph*. Telegraph Media Group Limited. Jan 9 2015. Web. Jul 2 2015.

Walters, Joanna. "Tablets and Smartphones May Affect Social and Emotional Development, Scientists Speculate." *The Guardian*. Guardian News and Media. Feb 2 2015. Web. Jul 2 2015.

Wang, Yunqian. "In China, Digital Activists Are Starting to Meet Up in Person." *The Atlantic*. Atlantic Monthly Group. Mar 21 2013. Web. Jul 5 2015.

Wartzman, Rick. "What Peter Drucker Knew About 2020." *HBR*. Harvard Business Review. Oct 16 2014. Web. Jul 5 2015.

Webley, Kayla. "A Brief History of Online Shopping." *Time*. Time, Inc. Jul 16 2010. Web. Jul 4 2015.

Williams, Rhiannon. "Web Browsers: A Brief History." *Telegraph*. Telegraph Media Group Limited. May 2 2015. Web. Jul 6 2015.

Winkler, Rolfe. "YouTube: 1 Billion Viewers, No Profit." *Wall Street Journal*. Dow Jones & Company. Feb 25 2015. Web. Jul 2 2015.

Wladawsky-Berger, Irving. "Some Puzzling Questions About Innovation in the Digital Economy." *Wall Street Journal*. Dow Jones & Co. Feb 28 2014. Web. Jul 4 2015.

Wohlsen, Marcus. "Amazon Could Finally Grow Its Profits—By Selling Other People's Stuff." *Wired*. Conde Nast. Jan 5 2015. Web. Jul 4 2015.

Wolpert, Stuard. "In Our Digital World, Are Young People Losing the Ability to Read Emotions." *UCLA Newsroom*. University of California Los Angeles. Aug 21 2014. Web. Jul 2 2015.

Woodruff, Judy. "Can the Music Industry Survive the Streaming Revolution." *PBS*. NewsHour Productions LLC. Feb 4 2015. Web. Jul 6 2015.

"Working Paper: Digital Economy – Facts & Figures." *Europa*. European Commission Expert Group on Taxation of the Digital Economy. Mar 4 2014. Pdf. Jul 4 2015.

"Youth Engagement Falls: Registration Also Declines." *People-Press*. Pew Research Center. Sep 28 2012. Web. Jul 5 2015.

Zetter, Kim. "An Unprecedented Look at Stuxnet, The World's First Digital Weapon." *Wired*. Conde Nast. Nov 3 2014. Web. Jul 4 2015.

Zetter, Kim. "Tor Torches Online Tracking." *Wired*. Conde Nast. May.17 2005. Web. May 1 2015.

Websites

Avaaz
https://www.avaaz.org

Avaaz is a civic organization that promotes online activism and enables people to take action on pressing global, regional, and national issues, from corruption and poverty to climate change. The website facilitates distributing petitions and getting involved in other ways such as emailing, calling, and lobbying government officials and organizing "offline" protests and events.

Center for Democracy and Technology
https://cdt.org/

This nonprofit organization supports laws, corporate policies, and technology tools that protect the privacy of Internet users and advocates for stronger legal controls on government surveillance.

Change.org
https://www.change.org/

Change.org serves as a platform where organizations and people, from unaffiliated individuals to representatives of the government, business, and the media, can start campaigns, raise awareness, and mobilize supporters for important issues and movements.

Class Central
https://www.class-central.com/

An aggregator of massive open online courses (MOOCS), Class Central allows users to browse available options from various institutions.

Codecademy
https://www.codecademy.com/

An interactive educational platform, Codecademy teaches coding for beginners and provides classes in several different programming languages.

Electronic Frontier Foundation

https://www.eff.org/

The Electronic Frontier Foundation is a leading nonprofit organization devoted to defending civil liberties in the digital world through litigation, policy analysis, grassroots activism, and technology development.

Khan Academy

https://www.khanacademy.org/

Khan Academy is a nonprofit educational organization that provides practice exercises, instructional videos, and other resources to help learners study at their own pace in and outside of the classroom. Subjects covered on its website include math, science, computer programming, history, art history, and economics.

Open Technology Institute

https://www.newamerica.org/oti/

The Open Technology Institute at New America is committed to freedom and social justice in the digital age. The organization conducts data-driven research, intervenes in traditional policy debates, and builds technology designed for privacy and security. It studies the impacts of technology and policy on people, commerce, and communities.

Reddit

https://www.reddit.com/

Reddit is an entertainment, social networking, and news site where registered members can submit content—such as text or linked material—and vote posted content up or down in order to determine its ranking and order of appearance. Subcategories called "subreddits" focus on particular issues from politics, movies, and books to fitness and food.

TakingITGlobal.com

http://www.tigweb.org

TakingITGlobal.org is an online community that works to foster intercultural dialogue and encourage active citizenship in youth by providing users tools to get involved in their local and global communities.

TED

https://www.ted.com/

TED is nonprofit organization devoted to disseminating ideas, usually in the form of short, powerful talks (18 minutes or less) given by leading thinkers in almost all fields—including science, business, and global issues— and in more than 100 languages.

Udacity

https://www.udacity.com/

A leading platform of massive open online courses (MOOCs) where users can take higher education classes, with some material available free of charge and some available for purchase.

WordPress.com

https://wordpress.com/

WordPress.com is platform where people, businesses, or other organizations can create websites or blogs.

Index